Appendices

TRAINING

First Edition 2016

Real Alien Worlds: A Brief Encyclopaedia
A unique book documenting the result of 2 years research using controlled out of body exploration by specialist investigators.

McCready Publishing
Bridge House
52 Twelvetrees Crescent
London E3 3GT
United Kingdom

www.GreatSimulator.com

info@GreatSimulator.com

Ref: CS160204
ISBN: 9780955713811

Printed by CreatSpace an Amazon company

First Edition Typos

Due to the sheer volume of complex material in this first edition of the book, it was not possible to purge it of all typos within a reasonable timeframe. So a pragmatic decision was made to release the first edition with some yet-to-be-identified typos. If you should find a typo, then please send us an email at the above email address with "Typo(s)" quoted in the heading. Note that "Earht Plane" is not a typo. Please identify the location of any lingering typos by:
Page, Paragraph, Line, ERROR
Eg: 107, 3, 7, where = were

Thank you for your assistance.

Real Alien Worlds
A Brief Encyclopaedia
by
David McCready

First Edition

THE BOOK'S PURPOSE

Until the 21st century, advanced alien civilisations that visited the Earth revealed very little about themselves. Accordingly, human beings were largely isolated from all the other residents in this and other universes.

In order to assist human beings develop, the 21st century was chosen as the point in which human beings would be given a careful introduction to their many neighbours.

The primary purpose of increasing contact is to enable human society to have access to the social models more advanced cultures have already successfully developed. Similarly, that souls who are currently experiencing living as human beings, benefit from access to helpful reminders upon the practicalities of reawakening their higher consciousness.

Without this reawakening, humankind will remain in a relatively primitive warlike state.

This book is a tool which enables the reader to rediscover more advanced worlds, and import the fundamental advances you will be shown.

You could say this book is a new form of intergalactic Internet.

Contents

PREFACE

ENCYCLOPAEDIA

CREDITS

Lead Researcher and Compiler:

David McCready

Research Team:

Antony Othona
Charlie Farleigh
Chris BB
Dan Abbott
David P
Elvis Garnham
Michelle Allen
Serge Schoenmakers
Wenda Ramsamy

And many thanks to everyone else not wishing to be identified

Principle Editor:

Cathleen McGuire

Copy Editors:

Gillian Jay
Mags Lowe

Cover Image:

Derived from NASA material

ABOUT THE AUTHOR

David McCready was born in the United Kingdom in 1963 as the first son of two homeopathic doctors. Both parents displayed good intuitive skills, and his maternal grandfather was ahead of his time in this regard.

Young David displayed no obvious clairvoyant skills, and his interests mainly lay with mechanical things. David ultimately qualified as a professional structural engineer and project manager. He went on to principally work as a building and maintenance contractor dealing with a comprehensive range of mechanical and electrical systems.

David always had an interest in otherwise invisible or unreachable worlds. In 1995 David achieved reliable access to the Astral World and an array of non-physical beings who were able to take over his adult education. David was then able to set aside his engineering profession and instead specialise in training people in astral science and projection.

In 2014 David was upgraded with special consciousness abilities which would enable him to lead pioneering research into extraterrestrial worlds using astral projection.

David (2016) is married with a wonderful wife and two sensitive children.

ENCYCLOPAEDIA STRUCTURE

PREFACE

The full preface of the encyclopaedia explains the system behind which it is possible to explore distant alien worlds.

The initial preface alerts you to some of the difficulties you may encounter when reading this encyclopaedia. For example, because the main body of the encyclopaedia is designed to connect your consciousness to alien worlds located in different dimensions, there is often a limit to how much you can read at any one time.

The full preface where possible details insights and research which are common to all the chapters in the main body of the encyclopaedia.

ENCYCLOPAEDIA

The main body of the encyclopaedia is designed to give you both insights into, and contact with, distant alien worlds. Each encyclopaedia chapter links you to alien researchers and friends who can assist your human consciousness to explore that location and civilisation.

The encyclopaedia catalogues examples of helpful representative alien species, who by various means are interacting with humankind. By connecting with any one group, you have the potential to get introductions to other groups not yet catalogued by this encyclopaedia.

Reading a chapter increases your potential to astrally visit that world. Similarly it generates a two-way link between that world and the Earth you are currently experiencing. In effect, reading a chapter is designed to open a sort of portal between worlds, through which the respective inhabitants are able to share important insights and experiences.

APPENDICES

The appendices of the encyclopaedia deal with matters that are of great relevance to the reader, and are easier to document in a separate section.

The ultimate Creator of the world the reader is experiencing is documented, along with insights into how you can contribute to this important research into the Creator.

The Earth's moon is explored at different dimensions, and thriving communities of inhabitants documented. Similarly, one of the wonders of the universe, the "Large Greys 1 Domes", is explored. In these engineered habitats you will find a unique collection of humanoid and other species who live together in harmonious communities.

Finally, a summary of the some of the insights and advances identified in this encyclopaedia is given. It is worth studying this summary because ways of making practical improvements to the life you are experiencing are all too often forgotten.

TRAINING

Details of where you can get expert training in advanced astral projection techniques are provided.

PREFACE

P1 Up-Front Statements

RESEARCH TECHNIQUE

Nearly everything written in this encyclopaedia is the result of research conducted via the medium of Astral Projection or Out of Body Consciousness. Similarly, at the time of pre-publication released in late 2015, the only way to verify most of the information and observations recorded was by employing Astral Projection.

This first draft of the encyclopaedia may contain errors. A helpful analogy is an early map of the world drafted from the initially crude observations made by the first intrepid explorers. Such maps inevitably contain errors. But nevertheless, it makes it possible for other explorers to retrace the navigation. Hence validate, or where appropriate correct, the map.

Europeans did not bother trying to sail to the Americas until Christopher Columbus brought its existence to their attention. This is an invitation to the reader, to personally explore everything that is described. If you do not already know how, then you, the reader, can learn the requisite Astral Projection techniques which enable such exploration.

READING THIS BOOK

When You Are Allowed

This book is designed to create an energetic connection, or portal, between the reader and other worlds the reader can explore.

If you speed read this book, you will miss out on much of the access to other worlds you, the reader, might wish to gain personal insights into.

P1 Up-Front Statement

If you gently read this book, you will receive unique insights that will assist your human mind's development. But this comes at the expense of being able to read dozens of pages at a time.

When You Are Not Allowed

Human minds are often prevented from making new and interesting discoveries. Should this obstruction come to affect your human mind, you will find it almost impossible to read this book. Even if you appear to overcome the difficulty, you can end up reading in a dreamy state after which it will be difficult to remember what you read.

The solution is to try reading it later when you are in a happy alert state, and read only as far as is comfortable.

General Warning

This book was compiled through contact with numerous extraterrestrial species. Souls manifesting as advanced extraterrestrial beings often reside in worlds that vibrate at higher speeds compared to what the reader is accustomed to on Earth. Reading this text will connect the reader's consciousness to other dimensions and higher vibrations. Until you become acclimatised, this can have a disturbing effect (e.g. Headaches, Dizziness, etc). If this occurs, let both your body and the book rest until you have regained a healthy happy alert state. DO NOT push yourself to read this book.

P2 A New Age Of Discovery

INTRODUCTION

For humans to physically travel to alien worlds in order to meet and interact with their inhabitants has, at least up to the early part of the 21st century, been technologically beyond humankind's capability. There are, of course, close encounters with alien beings and their UFOs, but these are inevitably brief and very little about their worlds and cultures has so far emerged.

Humankind has found itself effectively imprisoned like some caged animal in a zoo. Where other beings can visit us, we cannot physically escape Earth and visit them. The result of this confinement is that humans know very little about extraterrestrials, whilst they know a great deal about us. Unsurprisingly, the alien beings who do visit us are of the opinion that humans are currently still in a primitive state.

Fortunately, there are plenty of alien beings who are enthusiastic about assisting Earthlings to discover more about other advanced beings in the universe. Metaphorically speaking, the human species is being offered a chance to improve itself and join an inter-galactic club of highly advanced species.

This encyclopaedia is an example of the type of assistance being offered. With the support of advanced beings, it has been possible to compile a groundbreaking set of observations detailing who some of our galactic "friends and neighbours" are.

Reading this encyclopaedia has the effect of connecting your consciousness to these advanced beings. You are being given a "contact list" of alien beings who want to help you, the reader, evolve.

Exploration of the Unknown

All advanced alien races are aware of simple techniques which can enable any moderately advanced conscious animal to escape the confines of its body, and project its awareness to almost any location in the universe. On Earth, this is most commonly known as Astral Projection, or inducing controlled out-of-body experiences (OBEs), or remote viewing.

Using Astral Projection to visit alien worlds has already been accomplished by many individuals. But the scale of such activity has hitherto been so limited that it has only provided brief and very incomplete insights into who and what is out there.

This encyclopaedia is the first significant exploration of alien civilisations that are interacting with humans, and identifies many of the significant races you can visit using Astral Projection. Whilst it only scratches the surface of the multitude of intelligent beings in the universe that can be potentially visited, it nevertheless provides an important series of insights on the races which it examined.

Due to the very nature of Astral Projection, it is inevitable that these initial findings will contain some errors and misunderstandings. However, they provide a benchmark for others to validate, expand upon, and where necessary, correct.

Think of this encyclopaedia as being akin to a very early map of the world. Whilst inevitably some of the continents might not have been accurately drawn, their existence and approximate location are thus established. By using this early map and improving upon it, it will become increasingly more accurate and detailed.

Stuck In the Cage

This encyclopaedia was initially previewed in late 2015, a point in time in which the average human being was unaware of the possibility of being able to explore the universe beyond planet Earth using Astral Projection.

Returning to the analogy that humans are comparable to animals stuck in cages being visited by more advanced species, but whom to date have largely been unable to reciprocate such visits, an extraordinary fact has emerged. The minds of human beings are under the influence of a force that makes them decide to mostly stay put. It's as if the animals in the zoo's cages have somehow been hypnotised so that they want to stay where they are, and have yet to demonstrate the necessary free will to escape.

So despite most human beings having the capability to learn the necessary Astral Projection skills to visit the rest of the universe, they have to date, barely used them. Furthermore, even for those humans who have developed this ability and discovered the existence of alien worlds, they have persistently neglected to return. It's not that they couldn't return, it's just that they needed to be alerted to the fact that you have to unlock the mind on an on-going basis in order to enable astral travel. It's akin to owning a top-of-the-range new phone with amazing features, only to keep forgetting to use them.

A rational human being might well suggest that this proposition is absurd, and any individual determined to undertake such astral exploration would face no such obstacle. However, this encyclopaedia is not a debate on what is or is not available, but simply the recording of a set of observations based on using astral projection to explore alien worlds. Because of obstructing apathy, any reader wishing to verify these observations will find it to be an exceedingly difficult task.

Nearly all human minds have had their ability to astrally explore the universe substantially disabled by their higher selves. The result of such programming is that you, the reader, are initially more likely to fantasise about such explorations than to engage in them. Getting out of the "cage" requires bypassing this mental programming designed to make you fantasise as opposed to proactively explore. With appropriate training, ordinary Astral Projection is relatively easy, but for the reason just identified, exploring alien worlds is much more demanding to accomplish.

Galactic Access

Advanced alien races consider human beings to be only now finally emerging from a relatively primitive existence. Furthermore, advanced aliens are of the view that this is an appropriate point at which to assist human beings to start exploring the universe around them. To this end, they are tentatively assisting appropriate human minds to gradually escape the invisible boundaries that otherwise confine them.

Human beings can be likened to a child that has hitherto had its Internet access restricted by a parental lock which requires access codes to disable. This "parental lock" is applied by your higher self, who has given advanced alien beings the permission to disengage it.

The price of such access turns out to be nothing more onerous than demonstrating more mature, self-aware behaviour.

Whilst researching this encyclopaedia, it was found that most of the alien worlds explored were otherwise unreachable without assistance from their inhabitants, along with better access to your self-awareness. Hence, the "parental lock" analogy. Once humans achieve self-awareness, access to other worlds becomes easily possible.

Are You a Human Being?

Everyday life tends to reinforce a perception that you are a human being. However, you are only experiencing life as a human being. You are in fact actually something else. From a spiritual or soul perspective, you are merely a visitor to Earth.

The relevance of this fact is two-fold: F*irstly*, many of the readers interested in this encyclopaedia experience some difficulties fitting in with human life on Earth since they themselves have strong alien connections. S*econdly*, your higher self wishes to assist you in discovering how to hack or otherwise undo the parental lock it has placed upon the human mind you are experiencing, thus enabling you to see the greater reality of what you are for yourself.

Whilst it might be exciting and comforting to fantasise that you might be more than a human being, such imaginative thoughts are in practice counter-productive. If you do want to discover the truth for yourself, then you need to train the mind how to perceive without imagining. That means using your mind to observe reality, without instantly creating an imagined memory of the thought you just observed. Making this advance enormously improves your astral access to the rest of the universe.

PATTERNS OF DEVELOPMENT

Many Similarities

Had life on Earth spontaneously evolved from nothing, all on its own, then there would either be no other life forms in the universe, or they would be completely different. Researching this encyclopaedia revealed that most of the alien physical life forms you might encounter have a great deal in common with elements that already exist on Earth.

By far the vast majority of alien visitors to Earth are bipeds (walk upright on two legs) and generally of humanoid appearance. Researching these alien species reveals that the majority of them were evolved from species similar to those already found on Earth.

Genetic Seeding

The similarities between life forms on Earth and those found elsewhere provide strong evidence that organic life had both been introduced to Earth and manipulated so as to produce premeditated results. Meeting alien beings soon reveals that many of them claim to have been involved in the development and manipulation of life on Earth.

Furthermore, many samples of life forms that have been evolved on Earth have in turn been taken by alien beings, and the said life forms have then reproduced elsewhere. A good example of this is human beings who have been recreated in other worlds using human DNA samples taken on Earth.

Self-Aware Species

In very simplistic terms, a self-aware species is one who knows what created it and why. Humans by comparison, for the most part, have not reached this milestone. Belief and speculation are no substitute for actual knowledge and hard information. Personal validation is crucial.

Earth was designed to produce a number of self-aware species. It is therefore useful for humankind to have the opportunity to examine other worlds where similar experiments have been undertaken and thus observe useful parallels. For example, how do other species with self-awareness actually behave?

All self-aware species are inclined to support and assist humans striving for this milestone of development. It follows that they are for the most part inclined to share their insights along with how to take advantage of them.

Ending the Isolation

Prior to this encyclopaedia, whilst there have been endless alien encounters, only very limited technological or cultural exchanges have occurred. However, the isolation is now ending.

One of the most relevant advances many species go through is the moment when they begin making meaningful contact with other species that are more advanced and alien to them. This is a very challenging phase because with greater access to the universe comes greater responsibility. So increased access can only be phased-in depending on how well new thinking and behaviour patterns are adopted.

Furthermore, too much access to advanced species has the potential to destabilise the previously isolated species' own unique development. The plan is not to make a species a clone of other advanced species, but rather uniquely self-aware in their own right. All advanced life is an experiment pointed towards each species being able to arrive at its own independent observation. So a balance has to be struck between assisting a species develop, and pre-determining what the outcome of that development will be.

Historically on Earth there have been multiple examples of one human culture trampling upon another. For example, the effect of Europeans on the indigenous population of the Americas. By comparison, advanced aliens are mindful not to do the same to human beings, as this would dilute their unique observational ability.

Technological Advancement

In general terms, all species need to make similar technological advances. It follows that Earthlings are now being given access to numerous technological breakthroughs which have already been acquired by alien races.

However, it would be inaccurate to think that humankind has always invented things for itself. Instead, it would be more accurate to observe that the ideas behind technological advances have been downloaded into the minds of human beings by aliens or non-physical beings.

So readers alive on Earth today are about to witness a progressive shift, from people perceiving that new ideas apparently drop into their brains out of nowhere, to learning that such advances were specifically revealed to them by other beings.

ASTRAL ACCESS

Little Physical Alternative

At the start of the 21st century, it is unlikely the average person has encountered a UFO, and even less likely to have actually met an alien. So for most people, the likelihood of having an intelligent conversation with an alien would appear to be fantasy. This perception has the effect of making human minds tend to discount the reality that astral communications are easily achievable.

Aliens have shown up here and there, but have historically appeared to have mostly taken a somewhat hands-off approach and generally tried not to obviously interfere in earthly events. They have made contact with government officials, but there has been no significant interaction, even through that medium.

So people who want to initiate interaction with alien beings have traditionally been limited to activities such as hanging around places where previous alien encounters occurred. In such a situation wearing a placard saying "We believe in you, please visit" or the proverbial "Take me to your leader" would at least identify your intentions to other human beings curious as to why you might be loitering expectantly in the middle of nowhere.

For some people the alien encounters have occurred in the form of "abductions," which generally are not pleasant experiences.

In summary, the history of alien encounters remains just that: encounters. Human beings know almost nothing about them. Similarly, at the point of first publication in 2015, there was no physical means of reaching their worlds.

Advancing an Existing Technology

Almost every human being has encountered some minor form of out-of-body experience. A very simple example would be the weightless feeling that occurs when your physical body falls asleep and your spirit partially disengages. If your mind is still just about awake, the resulting weightless sensation is generally perceived as falling or tripping, which can thus wake up the body with a jolt.

Most individual's experiences of out-of-body projection are associated with falling to sleep or even taking hallucinogenic drugs. The breakthrough that has occurred is that techniques to reliably Astrally Project whilst fully awake have now been revealed to humans. Thus, what was previously very difficult for most people is now an easy, dependable technology even a child can learn.

Human beings have achieved alien contact now and again using Astral Projection. But for most people replicating such achievement has been beyond them as crucial aspects about the techniques have not been publicly revealed. The difference is that now, through the disclosure of critical information, it is becoming possible for almost any interested person to achieve contact, as opposed to just an obscure few.

An analogy would be the well-established technology of fire. Fire on its own just burns things and turns them to ash. But if you harness fire within an internal combustion engine, such as is found in automobiles or aircraft, it will propel you around the world. It's easy to forget that whilst our early ancestors had access to fire for several million years, it is only in the last 200 years or so that the human species discovered how to use it for propulsion.

Quality of New Access

Astral Projection has been around since the beginning of history. But Astral Projection training of the calibre required has hitherto been practically nonexistent in the Western world. Similarly, in modern times, the calibre of training required was barely available even in Eastern countries.

P2 A New Age Of Discovery

With proper training, nearly anyone interested in Astral Projection can learn how to project their consciousness to almost any alien world, and see and experience those worlds directly through interactions with alien hosts. Similarly, aliens use human minds to access insights into life on Earth. You are in effect accessing a two-way portal when you connect with aliens.

Communication is largely telepathic, and whilst the training techniques are straightforward, there is a physical component which needs to be practised. Human beings at this point in our evolution are generally poorly versed in telepathic communication, so aliens initially keep it quite simple. This may be irritating for fast intellectual human minds who forget that they are in effect learning a new language.

Telepathy harnesses parts of the mind often used for imagination, which causes beginners considerable initial confusion. If the human mind is compared to a computer screen, then imagination is the equivalent of spending all day watching fictional movies or a screen saver. By comparison, telepathy would be using that same screen for a more interactive experience such as video conferencing. The same parts of the brain are required, but the experience is very different.

Similar to video conferencing, two or more people can simultaneously project to the same alien world and compare their perceptions. Whilst there will always be a minor variation in perception, it will normally be substantially similar. In practice, two or more people Astrally Projecting to the same location can discuss their visit and interactions whilst projecting. This has made it relatively straightforward to validate the observations made as well as significantly adding to them.

All the substantial information in this encyclopaedia has been validated by at least two or more people making simultaneous projections.

Technique and Training

Human spirits disconnect from their bodies every time they fall asleep. Unsurprisingly, traditional Astral Projection has taken advantage of this fact and uses a technique which could be described as staying awake whilst your body falls asleep. This approach produces a very "heavy" Astral Projection, which rarely produces access to alien worlds.

Reliably reaching alien worlds normally requires using a "lighter" Astral Projection technique in which you remain as awake as possible. In practice you "download" a higher awareness which gives your consciousness a very high flight "power-to-weight ratio." In such a state you are also clairvoyant (e.g. able to see auras) and mediumistic (e.g. able to perceive deceased relatives).

How the technique works can be explained in relatively few words: Basically a practitioner physically sits straight, smiles and breathes properly. To actually learn how to apply the technique on your own, however, usually results in a lot of muddling through. If you go through the author's 1–2–1 training, though, you can get near-immediate results. An interested person in their 20s will typically be meeting and interacting with aliens within 10 hours of regular practice. Older people generally take longer, as they find it more challenging to relearn how to think.

Access Portal

Science fiction has often entertained fantasies that it might be possible to create some sort of portal that could transmit you from A to B. Such fantasies involve a lot of unspecified high-technology equipment as in "Beam me up, Scotty." With Astral Projection, no such equipment is physically visible, but you will often notice your consciousness is being drawn through some kind of portal.

The concept of portals is one way of understanding how astral access is achieved. It also transpires that the human mind is subjected to initially mysterious forces which can effectively wipe your memory as to how access to such portals is achieved. To say your memory gets wiped by something is a phenomena that will still surprise you when it happens. So until you get proficient at Astral Projection, you will all too often progressively lose access to a portal within a matter of days of having been taken through one.

Pairing

Attempting to visit distant alien worlds unaided is impossible for an ordinary human mind. The programming of the early 21st century typical human mind by and large prevents most people from accessing alien worlds. As you relearn to access the astral world from which all alien planets can be reached, it becomes obvious that this is only possible because of assistance from beings that are invisible in what we perceive as the "normal" physical world.

These previously invisible beings will assist you to meet aliens in their worlds, at which point it will become obvious that such visits are prearranged. You will frequently find that alien beings are assigned to work with you, as your visits often form part of their own research projects. Thus, you will often frequently find yourself paired with alien beings intent upon working with you. Such partnerships are essential.

Too Good To Be True?

Even people experienced in traditional "heavy" astral projection might consider reports of what can be achieved using the advanced "light projection" techniques, to appear far-fetched. When the earthly author of this book reported his findings at one of Earth's largest Astral Projection forums, he was met with considerable derision. When one of the forum's readers experimented with the author's 1–2–1 training, the reader found the claims to be wholly validated. However, when that reader posted his own personal experience of what was possible on the forum, the author was banned from the site for "Attempting to undermine the forum's membership."

In summary, the first reporting of this information appeared far-fetched to many experienced astral travellers, as well as the uninitiated. If you have previously focused upon attempting "heavy" Astral Projection, the alternative "light" approach is quite different. If you have never consciously experienced useful Astral Projection, then this is a wake-up call.

EXPANDING HUMAN AWARENESS

Human beings know surprisingly little about the advanced alien races which regularly visit the Earth. So whilst there have been many instances of limited alien contact with human beings, those alien beings had divulged very little as to where they came from and what their worlds are like. Nevertheless, bit by bit, various authors and researchers are achieving alien contact of sufficient quality to progressively redress the substantial lack of information about alien worlds and their inhabitants.

This encyclopaedia is a ground-breaking invitation by a host of alien races to get to know them better. Ground-breaking because this book is designed to energetically connect the reader to a catalogue of alien races and their worlds.

In principle, it could have been possible to examine over 100 alien worlds in considerable detail for this first edition of the encyclopaedia. However, in practice it took a year and a half to cover a mere 20 alien cultures and in brief detail at that. Thus, it must be acknowledged that whilst in principle a great deal more content could theoretically have been compiled, that would have been at the expense of delaying publication for many years. As such, this first edition of the encyclopaedia is just a very brief snapshot of what is out there.

Primitive Humans

As explained earlier, advanced aliens find human beings to still be a relatively primitive race. However, advanced aliens consider that humanity has now reached a point where a significant step forward has become reasonably achievable.

Human beings were evolved for good practical reasons; "evolved" in the sense that the natural evolutionary process has also been steered to some extent by a wide-ranging series of experiments. Such experimental manipulation, or directed evolution, of the human species continues to this day. The reasons are complex, in large part because you must personally grasp the greater reality of the universe in order to be able to understand those reasons. Nevertheless, the main reason humans are being manipulated is so that a human mind can understand from a new perspective what has actually created it.

What should be obvious is that human beings are undergoing an accelerating pace of change. Not to their physiology, but rather to their behaviour and abilities.

In simplistic terms, human beings are learning how to understand radical new concepts. Such knowledge fundamentally upgrades a human being's abilities. Hence, humankind is being elevated from its relatively primitive condition.

All to say, this encyclopaedia is designed to make you, the reader, more capable by expanding your awareness.

Examples of Primitiveness

By giving human beings the opportunity to study how more advanced civilisations live, immediate comparisons can therefore be made. Human beings are adept at copying each other's advances, and it is anticipated that this will extend to advances made by alien species as well.

Stages of moving beyond primitiveness are:

1. F*irstly*; moving from a state of low self-awareness. The principle criticism that can justifiably be levied is that experiencing a human mind currently makes it very challenging to remember who and what you really are. Whilst you inhabit a human body, it's challenging to recognise that your adopted body is just a vehicle, and not who you really are. Though on the other hand, this is a good challenge to undertake.

2. S*econdly*; advancing away from murderous tendencies. The human mind tends to perceive that the ultimate answer to most difficulties comes down to killing each other. Any species which is handicapped by such an attitude is a danger to all other life forms. Little by little, humans are progressing beyond this.

3. T*hirdly*; no longer staying put. Despite human beings entertaining endless fantasies about accessing the whole universe, this is part of the system to keep them where they are. The fact that most human minds have difficulty noticing the aforementioned "parental lock" restricting their movements is a clear indicator of a residual primitive condition. If you have not yet encountered such restrictions, it simply means you have not progressed enough to validate this fact. Or you are already an amazing alien visitor with unrestricted astral access.

Learn How to Astrally Project to Other Home Planets

Many human beings' consciousnesses have been seeded with what could be described as alien spirits. Experiencing the relatively barbaric human mind is somewhat of an adventure. However, such visitors to Earth can ultimately find the place disturbing, depressing and even isolating. It often takes considerable practice before a visitor truly enjoys the beauty of Earth.

Amongst the first wave of readers who read this encyclopaedia and relearn the necessary Astral Projection techniques, there is a 100% chance that you will find original friends and family on other planets in alien form if you genuinely try. You could say that this book is part of the kit which enables you to go somewhere that feels like a different yet familiar "home." You are fundamentally neither human nor alien, but use the physical body as an experiential device. On examination, you may even find certain alien species more comforting and familiar company than our own human species.

Discover New Materials and Technologies

Alien beings have been dropping clever ideas into human heads for as long as humans have existed. However, this is a slow developmental approach. The new experiment is to give participating human minds more direct intuition and insights.

The principle language of all advanced species is a combination of higher awareness and telepathy. Up until now, human beings have not scored highly relative to what is possible even for human beings. However, with minimal practice, a human mind can comprehend enough basic telepathy in order to download new ideas and insights.

Try This For Yourself

Christopher Columbus revealed the existence of the Americas to the Europeans. He was able to achieve this using relatively crude but available technology. Similarly, you now have access in principle to a universe of alien species. Go forth and explore.

Feel free to communicate your findings back to the author so that new discoveries can be incorporated into future editions.

YOU HAVE BEEN HERE BEFORE

Have you ever thought of all the things that could have been done differently and better in your adopted human life had a smarter approach been taken ? If so, then pay attention now.

Similar Patterns Across the Universe

From a developmental perspective, a human being can be likened to a tempestuous teenager starting to show some sensible maturity. This leaves open the twin possibilities of incredible and rapid advancement, or the alternative—a return to self-obsessed chaos. But this is hardly the first time we have been at this fork in the road.

Other species, with a great deal in common with humankind's developmental path, are scattered across the universe. Advanced alien civilisations have themselves faced a great many of the challenges that now confront the human species. So whilst humans have interesting new possibilities to explore, in many ways you have been here before.

The Collective Consciousness

You, your consciousness, are an extension of the super-consciousness. You are part of a system of multiple, interconnected extensions that are interlinked and form into a vast collective consciousness able to interact with and assist each other. At this higher level, all these extensions are joined as a oneness. It follows that when embracing the scope of all the different lives you have created, you have amassed considerable wisdom and experience.

In many worlds there are aspects of the greater you that live in civilisations that have already been through most of the challenges humans now face. In most respects, you have been through the same developmental advances being experienced on Earth many times before in other worlds.

Why not draw from the wealth of your past experience ?

P3 Astral Dimensions

ASTRAL SCIENCE

This chapter covers an overview of the astral science that enables exploration of alien worlds. If you have not experienced advanced astral projection, you will probably find yourself attempting to imagine a very different reality, with somewhat inaccurate results. Without proper astral experience, the challenge you face is similar to a caveman trying to understand how a computer or smartphone works, which would be difficult and inclined to produce inaccurate assumptions. Alternatively, with minimal proper training, first-hand experience will enlighten anyone quickly; i.e. If you gave a caveman experience of using a smartphone, he would start to understand it much faster.

Making Better Use of the Brain

It is often suggested that human beings are only using a small proportion of their brains. The extent to which this may be true is debatable. However, what any proficient astral projector will confirm is that it places demands upon your mind that significantly exceed that of typical day-to-day activity.

Astral projection harnesses the parts of the brain otherwise devoted to imagination, along with the parts devoted to more physical brain functions. Switching your brain to perceiving alien worlds places a considerable, and arguably healthy, strain upon both your brain and whole body. So if you want to make better use of your brain, astral projection is an excellent stimulus.

Imagination is like an automobile engine revving when no forward gear has been selected. Whereas, astral projection is what occurs when the engine engages and drives the automobile's wheels so as to take you somewhere interesting.

Astral Basics

Astral projection gives you access to a vast Astral World. What can be categorised as physical alien worlds only take up a small portion of the Astral World. Furthermore, these physical worlds mostly manifest at relatively low dimensions. Achieving access to alien worlds is made much easier if you receive training that gives you access to the entire Astral World. The greater an explorer's overall ability, the easier it becomes to access advanced alien species and their physical worlds.

The objective of this chapter is to explain the basic astral science enabling the creation of this encyclopaedia. If Christopher Columbus had written an encyclopaedia of the Americas (the parts he had encountered), then an equivalent chapter would probably have been titled "Sailing Technology".

If the science seems too confusing, you can skip it.

Alternatively, if you wish to personally verify the information in this encyclopaedia, then you will most probably require specialised training in advanced astral projection. Such training will give you a practical understanding of all the science summarised in this chapter. Once trained in advanced astral projection, you can then personally verify and expand upon everything written here. You will find that astral projection is a physically tangible activity and easy to distinguish from mere contemplation or imagination.

MULTIPLE DIMENSIONS

It may come as a surprise to many people that there are alien cities and populations already well-established on Earth. This is because alternative dimensions can co-exist in the same place. Thus, at higher dimensions, there is an abundance of future humans and aliens already living upon the Earth.

Simple Dimensions

A helpful way to categorise dimensions is to define the current dimension you, the reader, are principally experiencing as the "Earht Plane" dimension (The deliberate miss-spelling is intended to stimulate awareness).

The Earht Plane is the physical world you perceive, which is connected to an imagined world you probably spend much of the day in. The imagined world is a very low and limited astral dimension or plane. All your Earht Plane experiences are perceived via this adjacent imagined world.

Everything you can physically perceive constitutes one dimension. Dimensions roughly correspond to the speed at which matter vibrates. When matter vibrates significantly faster or slower than your observation vibration, it is classified by physics as "invisible" or "dark matter" So whilst there is plenty of other physical matter, it is not readily detectable from the Earht Plane. It's similar to how changing frequencies on an old radio tunes you into different radio stations and their programmes. Thus, many different frequencies can co-exist and be detectable, but you can only listen to one radio frequency at a time.

In the Astral World, you don't really see physical matter at all because you lack physical eyes. On the other hand, you can perceive the energetic forces which create the illusion of physical matter. In other words, you see the Astral World using your consciousness or higher awareness.

Whilst physically it is difficult to change frequency or dimension, by comparison in the Astral World it is absurdly easy for your consciousness to do so. Hence, you can easily experience what may appear as higher or lower dimensions relative to the Earht Plane.

Overlapping Time

On the Earht Plane time appears to be linear; i.e. One moment appears to chronologically follow the next. The greater reality is that all moments co-exist. This is initially very difficult for the untrained human mind to comprehend. It is fair to say that a human mind will never properly understand this until it experiences examples of it.

Using the astral projection approach to exploration, you soon find that you can visit what appears to be the past or the future. This allows you to have meaningful communications with some of the human beings in the past or future. Similarly, when encountering aliens whilst using astral projection, it is helpful to be alert to potentially different "time zones".

A common feature of interacting with advanced aliens is that time for them will often be running slower when compared to Earth time. You will also tend to find this effect when interacting with future human beings.

Astral projection is always best carried out in the company of some sort of guiding spirits of one sort or another. Between it being possible to transcend time, and interact with beings experiencing a different speed of time, or occasionally no time at all, this is all very challenging for anyone to properly comprehend on their own.

Layers Upon Layers or Overlapping Dimensions

Anyone who has become proficient with astral projection can confirm that there appear to be multiple dimensions layered one on top of another, also described as different planes. By adjusting your energetic level, you can move up and down through these layers, encountering different entities. Thus to meet a particular species obviously requires finding it at the correct layer.

A simple example of the effect of layers or planes is that human astronauts and people using a heavy astral projection approach will find the Earth's moon to be a barren and lifeless rock. Go up a layer and you start finding a variety of alien species residing there.

Any search for alien life that is only conducted at the Earht Plane dimension will result in a very limited set of findings. In the case of the Earth's moon, you would miss 100% of the life forms.

Furthermore, most advanced aliens who visit Earth, cannot easily live here as they come from higher dimensions. When removed from their normal plane and transposed into the relatively lower Earht Plane, their bodies run too slowly and ultimately decompose. Whereas a human body on their world would instead burn up as a result of the body's cells running too fast and being literally shaken to bits. The effect on a human body can be similar to that of gamma radiation or X-rays.

There is generally little in the way of obvious boundaries between one layer or dimension and the next. So when any reference is made to such distinctions, remember that how they are calibrated and defined is generally a matter of convenience. Typically when moving between dimensions, it is not as if you suddenly go from, say, something similar to water into air. Rather, the changes are more subtle.

Parallel Dimensions

Using the analogy of a chess board, higher or lower dimensions are the equivalent of moving up and down the board. Similarly, parallel dimensions are the equivalent of moving laterally, or from side to side. If for example, the Earht Plane is near the bottom middle of the chess board, then there are parallel dimensions either side.

Parallel dimensions allow multiple possibilities to be explored. For example, in the lifetime you are currently experiencing, no doubt you may have wondered what would occur had you made different choices. Parallel dimensions allow for the different possibilities to be experimented with and experienced.

Researching this encyclopaedia often uncovered that experiments, or developments, in parallel dimensions have been fed back into the Earht Plane. Furthermore, aliens from other parallel universes have gained access to the Earht Plane. There is a surprisingly integrated system at work.

Moving Through Space and Time Via the Singularity

The conventionally known Earht Plane and the universe you are experiencing appears to be many billions of light years across. If you explore this universe astrally, you will find that the whole thing appears to be emitted from some sort of vortex, at the centre of which is a singularity containing the source of all known space and time.

It appears that the universe is an expanded projection of that singularity. So in practice, all earthly space and time exists at one point in that vortex, at the co-existent singularity. You, the reader, are experiencing a projection from that singularity.

An analogy which helps explain the singularity is comparing it to a movie. The movie's celluloid film is put through a projector which creates an illusory projection upon a screen in front of you. Yet the actual film itself is normally out of sight behind you.

Whilst the conventionally known universe appears to be a vast expanse, from the Astral World, this appears to be an illusion. Hence, because everything is already co-existent at one point, you do not have to go anywhere in order to experience any other part of the universe.

Once you have gained access to the singularity at the centre of the vortex, you have access to everything that appears to be emitted from it. So you can explore any time, location or dimension you wish, within the human capability to do so. Distance and time are therefore no longer obstacles.

The Vortex

The vortex is so named because that is what it looks like. If you are good at heavy astral projection techniques, you might occasionally see the underside of it. If you are using the lighter astral projection approach you can find what lies above it, and similarly see it from above. It is also possible to convert a heavy astral projection into a light one mid-flight, thus any original distinction between the two projection methods fades away.

Above the vortex you find a bright super-consciousness, or God the ultimate Creator. Below the vortex you find the energetic source of "The Big Bang", which it should be noted appears to be on-going as opposed to a past event. Similarly, you find various planes or dimensions being emitted from the vortex.

As you examine the vortex in more detail, it becomes apparent that all these planes or dimensions are, as a point of fact, not actually emitted from the vortex. Instead they merely appear to be emitted or projected from it. This is why the world you experience is often referred to as an illusion; i.e. Everything you are experiencing on Earth actually exists as a singularity, at the singularity. Similarly, the vastness of everything physically around you is just part of this illusion.

The alien worlds the encyclopaedia focuses upon are sub-vortex and therefore manifest varying degrees of physical form. It should be readily apparent that there are plenty of worlds to potentially explore. However, for the time being we are mostly exploring planes or dimensions where the "traditional" alien beings are to be found and interacted with.

In conclusion, if you were looking for all the "dark" or traditionally undetectable matter thought to comprise the total (humans + aliens) universes, you can find it all below the vortex.

Summary

Advanced astral projection allows a human mind to investigate the far reaches of the known and suspected universe. In practice it is possible to literally drop into these worlds and explore them.

When this encyclopaedia was first published in 2015, most people attempting astral projection were using a "heavy" approach that rarely gave them the necessary access to far away worlds. Hence, the majority of people who had at least some concept of how it might be done, had not yet succeeded in accessing a multitude of alien worlds.

HOW DIMENSIONS OVERLAP

When this encyclopaedia was first published in 2015 there was no conventional scientific means of detecting "dark matter". This was principally due to the fact that most of the human scientists hunting for it did not appreciate the degree to which it was literally under their noses. So a good starting place is to better understand what the existing (detectable) matter actually is.

The Good News For Creationists

Creationists, the people who believe God created everything, will receive some comfort from the next few paragraphs.

When astrally projecting above the vortex, you can observe a big bright thing. You can observe that this bright thing is powering your existence as you are in fact a part of it. This bright thing is typically referred to as a super-consciousness, or God, or the ultimate Creator. There is no question as to whether or not it exists, because it is there for anyone and everyone to observe.

The super-consciousness emits a wonderful unconditional love full of unformed intent; i.e. The intention is there, but the form it might take is not fully specified, hence it is ultimately unconditional. By analogy, an intention in human terms might be to create a cake of some sort, without specifying whether it should ultimately be a sponge or fruit cake.

Let us label this intent as being what ultimately creates an "intention template", which can often be seen as an "aura".

Below the vortex, the intention template causes all matter to appear out of raw energy. Recall Einstein's equation $E = mc^2$. Setting aside where the "E" or universal energy came from, it can be observed that the universe is full of energy. Matter "m" is energy apparently slowed down by the speed of light "c" x "c". So the illusion of physical matter is created by making raw energy "E" appear to be slowed down.

The form of physical matter is defined by the intention template. So, for example, the intention template causes atoms and molecules to appear to exist. If you examine them closely, they have no actual substance, and for that reason they are actually an illusion.

The intention template similarly has the effect of creating life, and what that life might potentially do. Hence the notion that the super-consciousness or God created Earth and human kind is valid, albeit there is some practical engineering required to make it all occur.

Multiple Dimensions Overlap

The raw energy from which the physical matter you experience on Earth is created, can also manifest other physical forms at other vibrations. A simple example is the human aura, or the energy field which helps create a human being. A clairvoyant person both feels and sees human auras. The aura and human being can be observed to exist in different dimensions, yet both the body and aura can be detectable at the same time overlapping the same space.

In the Astral World you can move between different dimensions or levels. However, as mentioned earlier, on further inspection everything will appear to be located in the same place. This is because everything sub-vortex is actually located at a single point of the singularity. But you will generally experience the illusion that this single point has been expanded into an incredibly large universe.

This phenomenon makes it valid to state that everything is all in one spot, and equally valid to recognise that all physical forms exist in an illusion of vast time and distance. When dealing with multiple dimensions, how then do you identify where everything is, particularly if it all appears to be confusingly lumped together ? The solution most people adopt is not to perceive everything as a real singularity, but an illusory expanded universe.

Dimensional Compatibility

When astrally projecting, a typical human consciousness is configured to operate happily in the dimensions immediately above the Earht Plane. This up and down transition feels natural and compatible. Conversely, when heading (sideways) into parallel dimensions, it physically feels difficult unless you adapt to the local energetic environment. The distress does not amount to pain, more a discomfort. An analogy to dimensional incompatibility would be like trying to put on a shoe that is too small for your foot. You can try and squeeze your foot in, but it will not fit unless you change your physical size.

The practical issue this raises is that in the Astral World you can ascend out of the Earht Plane. But to then visit an alien world you typically need to descend into a different location in order to make useful observations. A human consciousness can find the descent into an alien world too distressing and therefore access is effectively barred.

A good practical solution is to borrow an alien body or host. Sharing or pairing up with an alien body creates a far more stable body from which to explore that world. To some extent an alien body acts as some sort of spacesuit for your consciousness. Thus instead of changing your human astral body to suit an alien world, you borrow an alien's astral body.

It correspondingly becomes obvious that aliens have a similar difficulty and therefore like to share or adopt human bodies when visiting Earth. So you can explore their world, whilst they get to explore yours. Hence the compatibility issue is easily resolved by interspecies cooperation or pairing.

CATEGORIES OF DIMENSIONS

There are three fundamental dimensions a human consciousness can readily observe, along with further points or regions of interest.

1. Creator Dimension

Above the singularity is the Creator's World. From here you can easily observe a convenient projection of the super-consciousness or God, which of course is part of the human consciousness you are experiencing.

This is a timeless place, and timelessness is something your human consciousness may find very challenging because it is designed to interpret everything in linear time.

At this level you can find the experiential moments or the momentary intentions which create everything that therefore comes into existence. Moments appear as repeating or looped actions. A simple example would be an experiential moment where someone would experience sneezing. Thus that moment would appear to be one sneeze endlessly repeating itself.

The Singularity

The singularity is the ultimate home of everything, and gateway to everything. Everything is projected from it. It's not really a dimension because it is infinitely small, to the point of appearing to be nothing. Hence you can pass through it and not even notice having passed through "apparently nothing".

Below the vortex is the Astral World you will mostly be (or become) familiar with. However, it is worth pausing here to recognise that from the singularity you can enter different versions of the Astral World and thus altogether different universes.

2. Most Relevant Astral World Dimension

"Most Relevant" referring to the fact that this is the main region a human consciousness will experience below the vortex.

The Astral World is really constructed from intention templates, or energies for things to occur, and the experiential moments which contribute to them. Human minds will mostly be interested in how this created personalities, and the lower you go, the greater the extent and complexity of those personalities.

Near the vortex the Astral World becomes progressively more and more timeless. Whilst the lower you go, the more you encounter linear time (one moment apparently following another).

Lower down in the Astral World is where all the physical worlds appear to exist. So for example, you will find a low region we can describe as the Earht Plane, which incorporates the intention template which forms the illusion of the Earth itself. You will similarly find other planes which create alternative dimensions including parallel or alternative Earths.

3. Physical Dimensions

This is where the Earth and most of the alien worlds dealt with in this encyclopaedia will appear to exist. An important fact to always bear in mind is that the physical matter and the energy which manifests all these worlds or universes is created out of nothing. The intention template causes matter in the form of particles, atoms, and molecules, etc, to appear to exist.

The atoms and molecules of the physical dimension are themselves drawn together by further intention templates to form planets, and physical beings such as humans. If for example, that intention is removed from a human being, the body would die and decompose.

The templates by their very nature span all the physical dimensions. This allows templates to create similar manifestations in different dimensions.

Physical Sub-Dimensions

When exploring the majority of relevant alien worlds, the "physical sub-dimension" (often referred to as just higher or lower [physical] dimensions) are what will mostly concern a human mind.

Experienced astral explorers will find themselves able to move between these sub-dimensions with considerable ease. The existence of these sub-dimensions is the principle source of all the "dark matter" in the universe. Matter from one dimension does not readily interact with matter from another dimension, which makes it exasperatingly difficult for early 21st century human scientists to detect the matter in the other dimensions. Though with respect to the formation of space-time, there are detectable interactions which are progressively being uncovered.

Astral explorers can detect the otherwise dark matter because they can simply scan across all the dimensions. Thus when astrally exploring, it is possible to examine any location and then compare changes at different dimensions.

Alternative Universes

The Astral Worlds and the many physical sub-dimensions the reader can explore are all clustered together and appear to contain a great many similarities. However, with the right guidance, projecting via the singularity at the centre of the vortex, it is possible to access completely different universes.

In the physical sub-dimensions of the universe the reader currently experiences, the laws of physics are broadly similar, and the main differences concern the density of matter and the speed of light. In alternative universes such parallels are fewer, and in many instances there are fewer physical forms.

Since the dark matter of parallel dimensions affects the visible universe the reader is experiencing, then by definition an alternative universe is one which does not physically affect this universe. However, what occurs in any one universe still affects all the other ones in other ways. So for example, people's behaviour is influenced by what occurs in alternative universes.

HOW ASTRAL PROJECTION WORKS

It is possible for a reader, in fact any consciousness, to sense and experience things outside the boundaries of their physical body. The strange thing about experiencing being alive in a physical body, is that you are not really there in the first place. Fuller technicalities behind this are detailed in "The Great Simulator" series of books (www.GreatSimulator.com). In the meantime, here is a helpful summary of how astral projection works.

The simple fundamental fact which explains why astral projection works is that; you actually exist at the singularity. All the vastness of space-time, other worlds and universes, etc, all exist at the singularity. Everything you are currently experiencing is an illusory projection from the singularity. Because you fundamentally only exist at the singularity, you have access to any conceivable illusory projection from it.

Normality

The super-consciousness can be observed in a projected form in the Creator's World above the singularity in the centre of the vortex. However, super-consciousness actually exists at the singularity.

You, the reader, are an extension of the super-consciousness, and are in no way separated from it. So in principle you have access to everything created by the super-consciousness. Experiencing life as a human being is only a temporary condition. You are experiencing a special mechanical system which makes you perceive you are a human being.

In simple terms, when your physical body dies, the effect of that mechanical system is vastly reduced and you begin to notice what you actually are. To reiterate the vital point; you are not a human being, rather you are experiencing being one.

Focusing Machine

You are experiencing a mechanical system which compresses your consciousness into a very small entity. The last stage of this mechanical system gives you the impression of being in a human body in a physical world.

If the physical body dies, you are still subjected to this system, but not to the same extent. In simplistic terms, the Astral World, as a whole, is this compressing machine. As you go lower in the Astral World the compression gets greater and you perceive yourself to be an individual.

You Are Actually Everywhere

When seen from above, it is clear that the physical world you are experiencing is actually all compressed into the infinitely small singularity. That is why astral projection can instantly take you anywhere in the universe, because in reality that universe is tiny, and you occupy all of it.

In principle there is no reason why you cannot be focused anywhere in the Astral World. What prevents you from exploring at this instant, is that your consciousness is being focused in what will appear to be a human body. So by simply reducing the extent to which you appear to be focused in a human body, you can instead become focused anywhere else in the Astral World, (and in principle) including any alien world.

You the reader, can experience being anywhere, because you are already there.

Heavy Astral Projection

A "heavy" astral projection occurs when the body falls to sleep and your spirit body floats free. However, as that spirit body is also a focusing machine designed to make you think you are a human being, it restricts you from travelling too far in the Astral World. This is why most people using this form of projection will generally be earthbound and not get much further than their bedrooms, or compelling lucid dream worlds.

Light Projection

If you keep the mind more awake, it is much easier to leave that heavy spirit body behind with the physical body. You could say you park the two of them and venture forth using your consciousness. This produces an interesting duality in which, you remain aware of the physical body, but also become able to perceive other parts of the Astral World.

Alien Worlds

Physical alien worlds are low down in the Astral World. Thus, to physically perceive them you need a heavier spirit body to act as your focusing machine.

If you are using light astral projection, your human spirit body is best left with your physical body. However, the lack of a focusing machine makes it difficult to perceive the world you are visiting. What you really need is an alien focusing machine, because it is designed to perceive the alien location and dimension you want to visit.

This is why visiting alien worlds is really only achievable by invitation. The aliens who reside there can supply you with an alien spirit body (focusing machine), which will enable you to perceive their world. When visiting, you will generally find that you get best results by aligning your energy system with a host alien body. The result is that you will find you will to a certain extent, perceive that alien world as an alien would.

Training

When this encyclopaedia was previewed in 2015, and first published at the beginning of 2016, the relevant science behind astral projection was, by and large poorly understood. A simple consequence of that was if a reader wished to procure the necessary quality of training to visit alien worlds, it could easily have taken a very long time to find it.

Yet the basic scientific understandings which enable astral projection are not very complicated to grasp.

With proper training, most readers can tangibly experience the Astral World within an hour. So with minimal practice it is possible for most readers to visit alien worlds within a few training sessions and start verifying everything for themselves. You simply have to train the human mind how to function differently, which is achieved using very straightforward exercises.

The age of astral projection to alien worlds appearing to be mysterious and difficult is ending, whilst a new age of exploration and discovery is commencing. In humankind's future, astral projection and telepathy are some of the core subjects taught to youngsters.

P4 Categories of Alien

EARTH PARALLELS

Science fiction often imagines alien races living on planets not entirely dissimilar to Earth. When exploring dimensionally nearby alien worlds, you will find this assumption has reasonable foundations. Conversely, when exploring dimensions significantly distant from the Earht Plane, the parallels are fewer.

Primitive Races

On Earth, human beings are the dominant species, and this encyclopaedia focuses upon equivalent dominant species. Whilst the majority of alien life forms are less advanced than human beings, the focus of this encyclopaedia's first edition is to catalogue a selection of the more advanced species with whom it is educational to interact.

By comparison, advanced alien races consider human beings of the early 21st century to still be somewhat primitive. Similarly, they consider human beings have hitherto not been ready to engage in meaningful cultural exchanges with more advanced species. One of the prerequisites for such exchanges is that human beings should establish some preliminary contact using advanced astral projection.

Advanced aliens also point out that early 21st century humankind is still a potentially hostile species inclined to warfare. This constitutes further evidence of a primitive culture and overall low self-awareness.

Across the universe it is possible to find plenty of other alien races who, like humankind, are technologically advancing, but handicapped by a general failure to acquire a more self-aware culture. This has left many aliens with similar residual warlike tendencies to the ones influencing humankind.

The insights such primitive alien races have to offer are always interesting, but are largely lacking in useful advancements humankind can readily adopt. If early 21st century humankind or primitive alien races had the physical means to visit each other's worlds, there would tend to be strong cultural clashes and probably war. Mindful of this, advanced alien races are not disposed towards disclosing the technological means of long-distance, inter-planetary travel to primitive races. So the majority of primitive races tend to develop in relative isolation from their similar warlike neighbours.

Most primitive alien races have very little, if any, awareness of humankind's current existence on Earth. If they have any encounters, it is mostly with more advanced future human beings. Those primitive aliens who have developed advanced astral projection abilities have a better awareness of what exists in the universe, and some of them are therefore attempting to make a more formal contact.

A reader might imagine that all races would be keen to explore the universe. But similar to early 21st century human beings, less advanced aliens with the astral projection skills are mostly constrained by emotions that inhibit them from such exploration.

Eco Disaster Planets

For environmentally interested readers, there are some planets where ecological misfortune has struck. In fact, some alien races no longer have a home planet.

By and large, aliens who have found themselves homeless due to ecological disasters are not at fault. In the majority of cases such ecological disasters were planned by the creators of these worlds so as to make room for another species to evolve on that planet.

Completely poisoning a planet through general incompetence and industrial processes appears very difficult to achieve in practice. Scarring a planet with atomic, fission or fusion weapons is not uncommon, but usually leaves a planet habitable once the radiation subsides.

The biggest single sudden problem appears to be planetary collisions; in particular, asteroids. These can truly be devastating, and in later versions of this encyclopaedia the research will be extended to incorporate more detail about such disasters.

The major long-term issue is when an atmosphere becomes unbreathable which, for example, can occur due to volcanic activity. Similarly, Earth itself has undergone such a typical disaster when early micro-organisms poisoned the atmosphere with oxygen and wiped out 90% of the species.

DNA Organisms

All physical life on Earth is DNA-based and originated from primitive bacteria and viruses, mostly seeded approximately 3.5 billion years ago. The encyclopaedia includes an introduction to the beings principally responsible for such seeding and subsequent genetic modifications and improvements.

It turns out that these aliens had been busy elsewhere in the universe humans experience, having seeded many other planets in this and similar dimensions. The whole subject of exactly who did what is further complicated by time travel and races contributing to their own early development.

Overall, whilst all organic life will tend to evolve of its own accord, researching the encyclopaedia repeatedly points towards advanced aliens clearly having had a hand in nudging the evolutionary process in some specific directions. It's also fair to say that some species have been evolved in particular directions for specific purposes. For example, creating challenging predators can help a dominant species to evolve faster.

Researching this encyclopaedia also revealed that the type of DNA seen on Earth is common to many other worlds, and is in many ways interchangeable.

Evolutionary Parallels

On Earth there is a pattern of evolutionary development in which various niches and trends have occurred such as the trend towards specialised species. For example, flying animals such as birds and bats. Alien worlds all show similar parallels. However, it transpires that ape-like mammals do not have a monopoly on reaching the top of the evolutionary ladder. Nor are they the highest form of development.

Even before specifically researching this encyclopaedia, it had become apparent that of all the species, advanced insect evolutions appeared surprisingly common. But that is not to say that further research will prove otherwise in regard to species that have yet to be encountered.

Development Loop

If you astrally travel forward in time on Earth, you will see the practical effects of meaningful alien interaction with the human race. In many ways there would appear to be some sort of developmental loop whereby a universe of species are creating and re-creating each other.

In this arrangement, advanced species create primitive ones and then assist their creations' advancement. The souls which occupy and animate the advanced species' bodies then have the opportunity to experiment with being the more primitive species just created. The "game" is then to advance the primitive species and explore new possibilities.

In this context, all the research so far conducted for this encyclopaedia points to humankind being just such an experiment in advancing a species. Advanced alien species have been actively contributing to the process of achieving humankind's evolution from a forest-dwelling ape to a (future) technologically-advanced, highly self-aware species.

In the light of these facts, it should come as no great surprise that humankind has a great deal in common with the great majority of advanced alien species so far discovered.

CATEGORIES OF ALIENS

Dimensions

For simplicity, aliens can be found in three categories of physical dimensions, plus the greater non-physical reality of the Astral World:

1. E*arht Plane* and the current physical universe: This is the physical dimension you, the reader, principally experience.

2. O*ther physical planes* or dimensions in the complete universe: Most of the physical universe falls within the category of dark matter; i.e. Matter that early 21st century earthly science cannot physically detect, but is nevertheless recognised to exist. Aliens living within these dimensions are responsible for the majority of UFO sightings when they enter the Earht Plane dimension.

3. O*ther universes*: Other physical universes which are separate from the current universe including its otherwise invisible dark matter. Whilst there is interaction between different universes, physical matter cannot be transported from one to another, only recreated afresh at the new location.

4. A*stral World*: This is the non-physical reality in which everything physical is created. All physical life forms are illusory projections from this non-physical dimension. This is where, for example, human heavens are found.

For completeness, there is also a sub-Earht Plane dimension below Earth. However, explorations have yet to find anything particularly advanced to report. If you do explore it, you will find a lot of partially-formed and forming matter. Beings at that level are somewhat elemental. Accordingly, human beings appear to reside at the bottom level of what one could reasonably categorise as the first well-formed worlds, which are located above the part formed sub-level(s).

With respect to astral projection to higher dimensions such as human heaven and the world above the vortex, this version of the encyclopaedia does not explore them to any great extent. It is mainly concerned with beings that exhibit a reasonable degree of physicality. Human heaven and the world above the vortex is currently better dealt with in The Great Simulator books.

Simplified Species Categories

This alien categorisation draws on earthly parallels for ease of understanding.

B*acteria*

Common to all worlds as a single-form organism, but by and large not ranking as anything with which one could have insightful interactions.

V*iruses*

Common to most worlds, and all lower ones. Viruses can become advanced enough to be intelligent life-forms in their own right, albeit peculiar to communicate with.

P*lants*

Aliens that, whilst evolved, are technically actually plants.

A*quatic*

Aliens that live in water. There are many sub-species within this group, although very few of them have physical interactions with 21st century human beings.

Molluscs
These beings are with or without shells. To draw on a science fiction analogy, think of Jabba the Hut from Star Wars.

Insects
Aliens that still exhibit their insectoid origins.

Reptilian
Similar to earthly reptiles.

Mammalian
Similar to earthly mammals.

Hybrid
These beings take characteristics from the list above. An example of a hybrid is the "Star Child" species.

Mechanoid
Organic beings integrated into machinery. To draw on a science fiction analogy, think of the Daleks from Doctor Who.

Robots
Science fiction regularly suggests Earth is in danger of invasion from machines that constitute a race of their own. However, all robots so far discovered appear to have organic masters and so are not really a species in their own right.

Manufactured
20th century humankind recognised that it is in principle possible to grow an embryo into a fully-grown baby using an artificial womb. Extending this principle, it is possible to grow that embryo into a complete adult before it is born. Some alien species have adopted this process to the point of no longer needing to reproduce naturally and thus abandoning that ability.

Hostile Aliens

There are plenty of hostile life forms to be found if you go looking for them. However, none of those unearthed by the research for the encyclopaedia's first edition were particularly advanced, hence were mostly left out. Gaining access to advanced astral projection technology entails greater use of unconditional love. Accordingly, aliens who have advanced up to and beyond that milestone lose most of their primitive hostility.

In general, hostile aliens are not given physical access to the rest of the universe. Even though they can theoretically discover the necessary technology to transcend space-time, it appears to be surprisingly easy to restrict such advances. If you, the reader, think this suggestion is far-fetched, then notice how humankind has similarly been restricted. Humans have had access to astral projection technology for around 2 million years. So in theory humans have had the ability to thoroughly map the universe. Yet in practice, humans have mostly been apathetic and disinterested in doing so.

Language

On Earth, societies all tend to have an appointed leader of some description (as evidenced by the expression "take me to your leader"). Early 21st century humans, however, have not reached a point where it is possible to appoint a single leader for the whole planet. Whilst such a development is likely in the long-term, it is dependent upon there being a single common language, which in Earth's case is heading towards being English.

All advanced aliens likewise rely on a common language. In all cases researched to date, that language is or includes telepathy. Learning telepathy enables the human race to interact with all advanced beings.

Since telepathy is a universal language, the main divergence that arises is the extent to which advanced alien races also rely upon other systems of communication such as:

- Sound and speech
- Visual signals (gestures and colour changes)

- Chemical or odour (smells)
- Body parts (releasing or gathering parts of a body; i.e. Body parts can detach and reattach from the main body, as part of a communication protocol)

For the human astral explorer, telepathy is all that is required as all other communication systems translate into it.

Leadership

Returning to the theme of who is in charge; a principle that has run throughout humankind's development since the last ice age 8,000 years ago, is divine rule. Humankind has flirted on and off with the possibility that rulers could, or even should, be God's representatives on Earth.

Meanwhile, advanced alien societies have consistently been able to implement the divine rule system. Alien divine rule, however, has tended towards the Judaic (Jewish) version in which everyone has access to divine will, not just a specially-trained elite (which is often the Christian interpretation).

Researching this encyclopaedia revealed that advanced species end up creating their own sub-God, which is in many ways a product of their collective group consciousness. The super-consciousness creates the seed of a potential sub-God, and a species wishing to experience divine rule energises it into a fully-fledged consciousness. In some instances advanced aliens also have a member(s) of their society channel this divine group consciousness so that they have a living God(s) to lead them.

In summary, across the diversity of many alien races, all possible governmental permutations exist. However, as these alien societies advance, they all incorporate some form of divine rule. Most human beings will only have experienced poorly-functioning versions of such leadership, and hence need to observe fully-functioning versions so as to understand how it really works.

COMMON ADVANCES

Standard Advances

From a technological and psychological standpoint, it is fair to observe that most species need to grasp a common set of advances or developments. These common advances broadly fall into two categories; technological and self-awareness. For example, a species might have a very high self-awareness, but technologically be relatively backward. In the early 21st century, human beings were technologically advancing whilst mostly having a relatively low self-awareness.

The following advances briefly highlight those made by most advanced species:

Technological Advances

Stone Age
Wooden tools and stone blades.

Heavy Industry
Iron, steel, steam engines.

Electricity
Electrical power, computers, communications.

Genetics
Create and modify life-forms.

Matter Transfer
Collapsing atomic structures and reconstituting them elsewhere.

Time Travel
Matter reconstitution across time.

Self-Awareness

Ability To Contemplate
Imagine and think about ideas relating to the past, present and future.

Astral or Psychic Awareness
Ability to sense and see the Astral World. Most life-forms possess this, but it is often lost as a result of increasing intellectual functions.

Telepathy
The universal communication language. It involves sensing the energies which make or will make events occur.

Astral Projection
The ability to consciously navigate the Astral World. Whilst most animals possess rudimentary psychic and telepathic skills, translating them to navigate the Astral World is a significant advance.

Awareness of the Super-Consciousness
First-hand, personal experience of how you are truly an extension of the super-consciousness causes a vital advance in your body's capability.

Creation
Accessing Free Will enables life-forms to become part of the team who create universes and their contents.

Categorisation By Advance Difficulties

Since advanced alien races are intent on assisting humankind, the reader is likely to encounter groups with such an intention. It is possible to find less advanced alien species, but since they are generally not proactively attempting to connect with human beings, such encounters tend to be seldom. Therefore, a reader beginning their own exploration of the Astral World will mostly tend to encounter alien species which are relatively more advanced than humankind.

It can initially be difficult for the reader to establish how much more advanced a particular alien species is. When compared to mankind, most of the initial encounters simply reveal that the majority of alien species appear to be significantly more advanced. An analogy would be a poor person earning $1 a day having difficulty distinguishing between wealthy people who earn $1,000 a day versus those who earn $10,000 a day.

So whilst it is possible to categorise aliens by the advances they have made, this will mostly be of little practical use to the reader, and therefore not focused on in the early versions of the encyclopaedia.

TIME ZONES

Understanding the point in time from which an alien being exists relative to the reader can be very perplexing. Nonetheless, from a categorisation perspective, where possible, it is helpful to understand everything's relative position in space-time.

Alternative Location

If you are being invited by alien hosts to a particular location, you will be instructed as to where to go. Alternatively, if you proceed without such guidance, your astral projection may take you to a similar location, but not necessarily quite the one you originally intended.

Another practical effect of not having sufficient guidance is that an astral projection may bring you to, for example, the correct location, but not your intended point in time. Since a beginner's mind has a habit of filtering out or otherwise discarding things it may not understand, it is easy to apparently experience "getting nothing." Not because there was nothing to perceive, but because the mind was discarding what it did perceive.

Should you find yourself astrally projecting to an unexpectedly different point in space-time, allow the mind to perceive where you actually are as this unexpected location may also be worth visiting.

Similar Time Zone or Not

When visiting alien beings, it is sensible to try to ascertain their relative position in space-time compared to 21st century Earth. Generally they will know and therefore be in a position to enlighten you on this point.

An astral projector who is not alert to, or wary of, this point will not be hindered from enjoying the connection, but may fail to grasp key facts. A simple example is exploring the alien races who live on Earth at higher dimensions. If you are not alert to where they might be located, your description of where to find the aliens may not be clear enough for anyone else trying to project there and validate your discoveries.

Record Analogy

Everything physical or astral really exists in the form of a singularity, or one infinitely small point. However, you the reader will mostly be experiencing a projection from this point into a vast universe. In this case we will liken the universe to an old vinyl record which has the normal single groove wound into a spiral which terminates near the centre.

The space-time you experience is located within that groove, so each moment is another point along the groove. To reach another point in the groove you can either travel along your groove until you reach it, or simply hop into the groove's adjacent parallel location, should that be a shorter route. In simplistic terms, if you hop from one parallel part of the groove into another and towards the centre, you can go up a dimension, and yet still remain in the same geographical location.

In terms of categorising aliens, it is helpful to recognise that a lot of them are, in many ways, adjacent to you in terms of parallel grooves on a record, although a huge distance away if you were to travel the length of the groove to reach them. As such, it is helpful to stay alert to which dimension and time zone they are in.

ALTERNATIVE HUMANS

Composing the first edition of this encyclopaedia took around a year and a half. The first edition is designed to give a snapshot of advanced alien species with whom it can be educational to interact. However, during this period it became apparent that the experiment of creating human beings was not an isolated incident at all.

Many Alternative Human Races

Preliminary research indicates that there a great many humanoid species with considerable similarities to human beings. The human body you experience inhabiting is a well-used design that has been deployed in many other worlds.

Caution

Twenty-first century human beings tend to have greater interest in the more humanoid alien species. From an educational perspective, however, it is important to at least be aware of a broader horizon of advanced aliens.

P5 Time Distortions and Shifts

ASTRAL ACCESS TO DIFFERENT TIME ZONES

"The distinction between past, present, and future is only a stubbornly persistent illusion" - Albert Einstein, 1955

On the Earht Plane the time distortions and shifts you consciously experience are minimal. Most people are barely aware that their satellite GPS (Global Positioning System) in their automobile depends on being able to accurately correct minor time distortions. However, once you start astrally projecting beyond the Earht Plane it soon becomes obvious that you can access altogether different moments in time. Furthermore, the relative rate at which time passes can be different (and usually is) for the aliens you may visit.

Linear Time

Time as you will normally relate to it is made from moments. If you scan your memories, you will find they are stored as moments. These moments do not have to be arranged in chronological order. On further inspection, it transpires that the arrangement of any moments into chronological order is engineered and a constructed illusion.

Physically experiencing moments on the Earht Plane is engineered into an apparently chronological order which is, for practical purposes, a function of distance. A helpful analogy is the example of an old movie where each moment is defined by a frame on the film. As you move along the film, you experience a linear succession of moments or time passing. Alternatively, as the film is moved through a projector, you will get the impression of linear time in action. Hence, time is measured by the distance you have moved along the film.

On the Earht Plane you will experience being locked into a system where you are always apparently moving from one moment to the next. Your human form is locked into this system and cannot revert to a previous moment nor jump to a future one. Also, whilst your human mind may perceive itself as stationary, it is equally valid to suggest that you are instead moving along a stream or film of moments, and that each moment occurs at a separate location.

Note the important point: each moment you experience occurs at a different physical location.

No Time

If you astrally project at a low level of the Earht Plane, you will find you are subjected to the normal linear passage of moments. Alternatively, if you ascend into the higher Astral World the moments all become apparently closer together and ultimately no longer separated by distance. The effect of removing the distance between moments is to eliminate time; i.e. If there is no distance between moments, there is no longer any time.

Once you have astrally ascended to a level where all the moments are clustered together, you are no longer locked into which one you are experiencing. You can move between them. You therefore have access to time travel because you can now drop into these moments at any point and join a stream.

Repeating Moments

For completeness, if you examine raw moments you will find that they repeat. It's a bit like an old vinyl record where the needle keeps jumping back into the same part of a groove. Hence, the music keeps repeating itself without progressing.

Experiencing such raw moments assists you in recognising them for what they actually are.

Time Travel

Time travel of sorts is not only possible during astral projection, but when using advanced astral techniques it becomes normal. A typical example is that you can have a conversation with another being who would otherwise be elsewhere in linear time, provided of course that such a being manages to interact with you.

This means that in principle you can interact with other beings wherever you might find them in their linear time. However, if the being you are visiting does not have the ability to notice your presence, interaction of any sort obviously would be difficult or impossible.

Time Distortions

Astral projection involves being focused outside of your physical form. However, you are still connected to your original physical form which retains a connection to your local linear time. When interacting with advanced aliens, you will often notice that time for you is running faster than it is for them. For example, ten minutes for you might equate to five minutes for them.

As the aliens beings you interact with become more advanced, you will often find that the distortions become more extreme. For example, a minute for them can equate to a year of a human life. Noticing such distortions assists your ability to recognise what sort of beings you are encountering.

Altering Moments

The reader might wonder if astral projection might alter the course of events. However, this would not be possible for a less advanced consciousness, because it would not have the ability to alter moments. So for practical purposes, whilst the reader can experience interactions in the apparent past, in practice that interaction has probably already occurred. So everything is as it was; i.e. For people in the apparent past, you would already have visited them, and you are now simply acting out this event in your present time or moment.

However, if you the reader have access to Free Will, then you will be able to alter moments. Since moments are all interconnected, if you alter one, you affect everything around it. Thus, using Free Will to alter any moment affects other moments, not only in the future, but also in the past.

The effect of truly altering moments brings the scope of the first edition of this encyclopaedia tantalisingly close to the mechanics of parallel dimensions. However, too much digression now would divert the principle direction of the present book.

ACHIEVING WIDE RANGING ACCESS

Advanced astral projection allows you, the observer, to move backwards and forwards in space and time. This might incline you, the reader, to imagine that you could become the time traveller of your dreams. Unfortunately this will probably not be the case as the reality of the matter is likely to be different, and you will probably need to significantly advance your human form's ability.

Limiting Ego

You might think the personality you are experiencing is you, but it is not. You are experiencing a human form that is not actually you. The normal human ego often prevents exciting bouts of time travel from occurring.

The limitation your normal human ego applies might appear to be a tedious mistake. In fact, you choose to experience that ego, which is why you will now not readily escape it. This limitation is likely to persist until the act of you continuing to choose that ego is both understood and is consciously experienced by your adopted human mind; i.e. To change what you are experiencing, it is normally essential to observe what you are already actively choosing.

Access Egos

If a human mind is taken over by an alternative ego or personality that is programmed to engage in advanced astral projection, that is what the human mind will then experience. Think of it as computer software or an app. If your human mind runs that advanced astral projection APP, then it will manifest new abilities.

A quick witted inexperienced human mind will then contemplate, "How can I download that app ?"

However, it turns out that such an Access Ego is actually more alive than a human mind. A human body can be likened to a computer, and it is the software or the app that turns out to be more alive because it is accompanied by its own operator.

Practical Effect

This means that for such an Access Ego to download itself into a human mind and permit astral time travel, the original human ego has to take a back seat. You could say the Access Ego is choosing the human mind it will work with, and is for practical purposes in charge of what occurs.

The implication, the possibly irritating implication, is therefore that the typical human ego you, the reader, might be experiencing has a very restricted say in what occurs; i.e. It cannot choose what will be downloaded next. However, all the human egos you are experiencing have the ability to cooperate and allow more advanced apps to take over if they so choose.

ADVANTAGE OF SPACE-TIME SHIFTING

For anyone learning astral projection, it soon becomes apparent that beings from your apparent future are working to assist you. For example, sometimes a future version of you might work to educate and train you, its primitive predecessor. Alternatively, a future version of you might be researching the past, and therefore require access to a relatively earlier point in time.

Alien Assistance

When first studying astral science, it soon becomes apparent that alien beings have consistently been assisting humankind's development. In fact, you are entering an exciting new era where aliens can provide even more assistance. Previously, they were dropping ideas into human minds without the said humans noticing. Now human minds can notice what is occurring and take greater advantage of the process.

Before this encyclopaedia was published, there was considerable suspicion that some aliens might in fact be human beings from the future. In this encyclopaedia we will explore this occurrence.

Self-Help For Humankind

Mankind can, and will, advance a lot faster by accessing the minds of future human beings. You could say mankind of the future is facilitating its own evolution.

Researching this encyclopaedia revealed repeated evidence that human beings from the future were actively assisting human beings from their relative past. It's as if the future human beings were working to ensure their own destiny.

For you, the reader, this means that there is an abundance of help on tap, and you are being encouraged to access it.

Historical Enquiry

In principle, astral projection allows an investigator to research any location in space-time. Though in practice it soon becomes apparent that invitations of various sorts are necessary to achieve this, as some kind of higher assistance is needed. Nevertheless, in principle it can be and often is done. Accordingly, readers, through these words, are being encouraged to undertake their own investigations. So be alert for potential invitations to do so, which may, for example, come in the form of a sudden sense to research a subject or location.

The historical enquiries you might make fall into two categories: interactive and observational. Sometime you can interact with beings in the past or future, whilst on other occasions you can only really observe them. In the case of research conducted for this encyclopaedia, most of it was interactive. Similarly, should the reader attempt to validate any of that research, this too should normally be an interactive experience with the advanced beings who are assisting you.

P6 Interactions With Human Beings

INTRODUCTION

Covering Their Tracks

The average person might wonder why, despite numerous UFO sightings and alien encounters, it's extremely difficult to find any official record of one that has not been attributed to yet another rogue weather balloon or something similar. For the typical person, unless they lived next to a weather balloon launching point, the chance of actually seeing one is very remote. So a typical person is probably more likely to encounter a UFO as opposed to an actual weather balloon.

The question then is, why do governments persistently cover up UFO sightings and actual encounters ?

F*act 1.* No official greetings yet.

If an advanced alien race wanted to say hello to the human race, it would have no difficulty doing so. It follows then that alien races are probably reluctant to be seen landing on the front lawn of the White House in Washington and asking if the U.S. President is available for a quick photo opportunity. Thus, it can be inferred that alien races are currently shy of publicity. At least up to the point of first publication of this encyclopaedia. However, an alternative invitation to meet advanced aliens is in place through, for example, books such as this.

F*act 2.* You are just visiting in human form.

You, the human reader, are not always in control of your adopted human mind. Every life form is operated by something greater than its mere physical manifestation. The personality you experience being is not actually you. The real you adopts a human personality and then experiences being it; i.e. You have chosen to experience being something very different to what you really are. At a higher level you are in control and direct the life you are now experiencing. The human mind and your adopted personality or ego you are experience being is not actually in control. You are a visitor to the Earth.

F*act 3.* Human minds are easily influenced.

Your adopted human mind is constantly influenced by external forces which determine its thoughts and actions. People who believe they cannot be influenced, are the easiest to influence because they do not question where thoughts and desires come from. Alien beings, or really the greater entities which animate them, have no difficulty influencing human minds. It follows that by targeting and influencing a relatively small number of human beings in positions of authority, this is sufficient to make a global cover-up system appear to function. Thus, the majority of people employed in cover-ups would never be conscious of what actually influenced their thoughts and behaviour.

In summary, governments get the blame for covering-up UFO activity, but this is a wholly unfair apportionment of blame. The pliable human mind is easily influenced, particularly by advanced beings who are familiar with influencing primitive species. By this means aliens cover their tracks.

A Cautious Hello

This encyclopaedia is part of a cautious hello from a "club" of advanced beings who are tentatively inviting members of the human race to join. Obviously human beings have had alien encounters since the evolution of modern humans, though such encounters are largely sporadic and hardly upon equal terms. This invitation is an experiment to explore the extent to which some human being capabilities have evolved.

Human beings do not currently have the mechanical technologies to physically visit alien worlds. Whereas, advanced aliens both have access to such technology along with the ability to download an understanding of it into human minds. However, enabling human beings to physically visit alien worlds is considered to be altogether risky by their inhabitants. Instead a more measured and safer approach is to allow human beings non-physical or astral access. Rather in the same way a child might be allowed to see something delicate, but restrained from actually touching it.

Advanced aliens consider human beings to still be all too close in temperament to wild animals. By analogy, you might allow a pet dog or cat in your home. But on the other hand you would not invite a wild grizzly bear to visit, or any other wild animal for that matter. It would neither be practical nor safe. So educating, and in many ways taming, human beings via non-physical or astral access to alien worlds, is a sensible preliminary step before allowing unfettered physical access.

Giving human beings, or any other evolving race, improved Astral Projection technology is a safe and sensible method of introducing them to the many alien worlds. Human access can thereby be restricted and easily controlled. Similarly, it is easy for advanced aliens to educate and for practical purposes, tame visiting human beings, so that greater access becomes a viable proposition.

Experts in Unconditional Love

To enable human beings to astrally project to alien worlds requires improving their access to unconditional love. It follows that some of the aliens you, the reader, have the potential to interact with, such as Grasshoppers 1, will assist you. Hence, practicing astral projection in collaboration with such alien beings significantly improves your human form's connection to this vital energetic force.

When visiting worlds where advanced aliens have succeeded in channelling far greater amounts of unconditional love, it is easy for you to observe how they accomplish this. Similarly, it is fascinating to examine the effect unconditional love has on their societies and ways of life.

Human beings are familiar with the fact that healthy societies rely on good organisation, and to a lesser extent upon technical advances. What is less well understood is the importance of the emotional energies needed to drive them. So it is refreshing to observe the effect of greater unconditional love upon alien societies and the considerable degree to which this advances them.

UNCONDITIONAL LOVE

Most human minds reading this encyclopaedia have encountered unconditional love. The source of this emotional energy is the super-consciousness or God which is the origin of all life, and in fact everything.

Acknowledge Your Part

You, the reader, are a manifestation of this unconditional love, but at the time this encyclopaedia was first published, it was very difficult for most humans to notice this on an on-going basis. Typically, most human beings will only notice unconditional love from time to time, instead of experiencing it on an on-going basis. In fact, for a human being to achieve this observation at least once a day was exceptional. Note that imagining unconditional love ten times a day is better than nothing, but just imagining something is, of course, not a substitute for actually experiencing it.

Connecting to the wonderful unconditional love, which has created the universe you are experiencing, affects your abilities and behaviour. This improvement affects your influence on everything around you. The more human beings acknowledge and channel this energy, the more it affects the environment around them.

Play your part.

Alien Unconditional Love

When connecting with advanced alien consciousnesses, their unconditional love may initially be difficult to sense, but it will normally be present. An indicator of a poor connection is that you may perceive such advanced beings to lack compassion. Connecting with their sub-god normally remedies this deficiency.

Astral Projection Fuel

The quality of advanced Astral Projection you need to reliably visit alien worlds is a skill you are being encouraged to develop. The human form you are experiencing living through is designed and programmed to give you the compelling impression that you are a human being, and to a large extent earthbound. A vital part of transcending this human condition involves experiencing unconditional love to a significantly greater extent.

Advanced Astral Projection (fairly basic Astral Projection as far as most advanced alien races are concerned, but never mind) relies on running different programming through the human mind. As you probably know, if a computer is running too much software or programs at the same time, the system often freezes up. A reboot is in order if you want to get that computer running properly again. Similarly, an unconditional love reboot, followed by principally running some better "mental software" is the easiest way to keep the human operating system clear.

To summarise: Unconditional love is the emotional energy which enables you to easily de-clutter your mind and run the necessary "mental software" which makes Astral Projection possible. You could describe unconditional love as a fuel which makes advanced Astral Projection possible.

Use Unconditional Love Playfully

Many people enjoy blending with unconditional love as a retreat from the anxieties and pressures of the world around them. They find being unconditionally loving in the midst of life's daily challenges too demanding. This is a self-evident shortcoming.

The answer is to learn how to access this energy playfully. By practicing the playful approach you significantly improve your ability to do Astral Projection.

UNPLEASANT INTERACTIONS

If you are taking an astral projection approach to visiting alien worlds, then the likelihood of coming to harm is very low. The reason is that your hosts are inviting you into their realms, and only tend to invite in their friends or potential friends. Note that without an invitation, you will find projecting to such worlds very difficult in a way that will make you tend to rapidly desist. Either way, no actual harm is likely.

Whereas, if you are involved in an earthly physical meeting with aliens, the chances of having an unpleasant interaction are far higher. The vast majority of close interactions (meeting them up close as opposed to seeing a distant object) seem to fall within the category of scientific research by aliens. Furthermore, you will tend to have had very little conscious choice in the matter, even though your consent invariably exists at a higher level.

Not Lab Rats

The reader may wonder if more technologically advanced species sometimes regard human beings to be little more than lab rats ?

The response was that the various soul groups from which earthly rats, humans, and aliens are all ultimately drawn from, all have the same source. Therefore aliens conducting experiments treat humans rather better than humans treat earthly rats. Any affected humans should realise that they are merely assisting scientific advancement, and have chosen this noble path.

Scientific Research

In the same way that scientists research the lives of different animals on Earth, so do alien scientists perform research on human beings. Whilst it is rare for a human being to be permanently abducted, temporary abductions for scientific research purposes are all too common.

In terms of the sorts of research carried out, comparing it to that done by human scientists on animals makes a helpful comparison. Human beings' development is of interest to aliens and unsurprisingly they often examine human specimens to monitor progress.

Considering the diversity of life on Earth, it is noteworthy that aliens seem to generally be more interested in human development than all other species on the planet put together. There are three reasons for this interest:

1. Aliens were responsible for all the physical steps involving the development of all life on Earth and had a hand in most of the significant evolutionary advances. So the subsequent monitoring of human progress is therefore hardly surprising.

2. The spirit beings which manifest as aliens can also often manifest as human beings, so monitoring adaptations which improve human manifestation is also unsurprising.

3. Whilst the "victims" of alien abduction might disagree, most of them have soul links to the aliens who abducted and interfered with them. The said aliens would consider that in many ways they were looking in upon one of their soul friends who is manifesting as a human being.

Monitoring

No doubt you are familiar with the concept of attaching a radio collar to an animal and then monitoring its movements. However, you are extremely unlikely to find someone wandering around wearing a radio collar of alien origin. Such an attachment would run contrary to aliens' standard policy of keeping a low profile.

Meanwhile, clairvoyants occasionally report that people have been fitted with non-physical attachments. An alternative way of understanding it is that some people have been fitted with physical attachments that are not physically visible at the Earht Plane dimension.

The bulk of monitoring devices tend to affect the human energy system, and it is quite common for someone thus tagged to experience mental health issues. Luckily for the rest of the tagged people, they are either not aware or do not feel a kinship with alien races. So for them there will not be an issue.

With respect to being "checked up upon," many people have experienced being drawn out of their bedrooms and into alien spacecraft, often on a regular basis. In many such instances the people in question have not been physically abducted, but had their Astral Bodies pulled out. Many people who have experienced Astral Projection will have at some stage had the experience of someone pulling them from their physical body. If you did not consciously wish for such an experience, it can be very disturbing and frightening.

DNA Experiments

Fundamentally, any physical body, be it human or alien, is a vehicle through which a soul being can experience physical form. The more advanced the physical body, the more interesting and useful the physical experience becomes. It follows that aliens are very interested in making on-going improvements to human beings. Similarly, the key to such improvements involves optimising human DNA so as to allow better self-awareness.

Thus, the dominant category of physical alien experiments involves improvements to human DNA and reproduction. In an obvious way, this mostly occurs in the form of taking samples of DNA and reproductive cells such as human sperm and eggs. Less obviously, many experiments involve modifying human DNA by, for example, using virus technology.

Whilst these sorts of experiments may appear unduly invasive and potentially harmful, they have nevertheless contributed to humankind's advancement. Humans associate viruses with unpleasant illnesses such as colds. However the vast majority of viruses we are exposed to cause no obvious harm and are thus largely ignored. Using otherwise harmless viruses, it is possible to "infect" just a few individuals who will in turn spread a virus to most of a population.

Research indicates that human beings have been repeatedly "infected" with otherwise harmless viruses which can modify human DNA. So whilst abduction and "infection" tend to be somewhat unpleasant, these sorts of experiments have led to considerable advances in human intelligence.

Reproduction Experiments

For human males, experiments frequently involve the taking of sperm samples, often by encouraging them to copulate with what will appear to be highly attractive females. However, as female sperm recipients tend to be modified aliens from higher dimensions, a human male involved in such an experiment will be exposed to the equivalent of X-rays and may damage his subsequent fertility.

For human females, having their eggs and sometimes whole ovaries removed is even more unpleasant as the procedures tend to be highly invasive. It is also not unknown for female humans to find that they have been inseminated with modified sperm or embryos in order to make them pregnant.

ADVICE AND ADVANCES

Any form of significant advance on the Earht Plane requires considerable human input. Whilst fiction often portrays the image of a single (sometimes mad) scientist making technological leaps and building amazing new machines or weapons, the reality is that major advances are normally a team effort. For example, the

1940s Manhattan Project required the majority of the world's top nuclear physicists, plus the efforts of 130,000 people to build the atomic bomb. Hence, major advances are generally going to require a lot of people.

Telepathic Communication

Advanced alien races are all very telepathically capable, and human beings are only gradually catching up. At the beginning of the 21st century, human beings were mostly close to "illiterate" with respect to telepathic ability. With a very modest amount of training, rudimentary ability can be achieved. The relevance of this is that whilst, for example, English has become the Earthly international communications language, the rest of the universe uses telepathy.

Without getting caught up in the technicalities of how telepathy works, most humans are telepathically illiterate, and that makes it challenging for aliens to interactively communicate with them.

Telepathy operates from a starting point of what you already know. If you are familiar with engineering, then receiving telepathic advances based upon your existing knowledge of engineering is possible. But technically-advanced experts must also be telepathic experts in order to communicate with advanced aliens. To demonstrate this inherent difficulty, take the possibility of making improvements to mobile phone technology using insights from an alien race. For this to be achieved, it would require telepathically passing the awareness of potential advances into the minds of mobile phone technology experts. How many mobile phone experts do you know who are also telepathically literate ?

Accelerating Advances

Visionaries such as Leonardo Da Vinci conceived of building tanks and helicopters. But without the supporting technology, these inventions remained fanciful ideas for another

400 years. So any significant advance will require a great many people making many progressive advances across a variety of fields.

Aliens have been downloading awareness of technical advances into human minds since human beings came into existence. However, human beings have largely thought new ideas were the result of their own genius and gave little thought to the possibility that they were being given considerable help. Going forward, this lack of awareness is changing as you read these words.

Human beings are now becoming aware of advanced alien races and gaining access to them through Astral Projection and telepathic communication. As this becomes widespread, there will be large numbers of technically-advanced human beings becoming sufficiently proficient with basic telepathy to start further accelerating the rate of human progress.

Apathy

This exciting possibility of human beings making rapid advances is hindered by one major practicality: The effect of apathy. Whilst human beings can easily be trained how to astrally project to other planets and meet alien races, the majority are subjected to apathetic thoughts which considerably hinder their enthusiasm for putting this opportunity into practice.

Often the apathy takes the form of fantasising about communicating with advanced aliens, as opposed to actually doing so.

Duality Awareness

Duality means being aware of two states at once. For example, duality can be the physical world around you, along with an alien world you are connecting to.

If you spend most of your day with typical early 21st century urban human beings, you find this easily keeps you in a relatively low state of awareness. Alternatively, if you instead were mostly in the company of more advanced future human beings or aliens, you would find that you had a significantly higher state of awareness. In conclusion, your overall state of awareness would be influenced by the company you kept.

What is meant by awareness ?

A simple example is the extent to which your adopted mind notices you are just experiencing human form as opposed to actually being a human. This sort of awareness depends upon your adopted mind being conscious of; an alternate reality where you are actually somewhere else, and by comparison the human life on Earth is clearly an interesting illusion you are actively choosing to experience. Being simultaneously aware of both realities is described here as "duality awareness."

In practice, duality is achieved by your consciousness rapidly oscillating between the reality of what and where you are versus enjoying the illusion of living a human life.

When this encyclopaedia was first published in 2015, there were minimal opportunities for readers to spend significant periods of time with human companions who were happily functioning with duality awareness. This lack of such company will hinder a reader's development.

The important assistance offered by advanced aliens or future human beings (there being little practical difference between the two) is that you, the reader, can be paired with at least one of them. Your partner in this exercise will keep reminding you to be aware and generally assist in the development of your human consciousness.

In summary, the reader is being offered access to good company through the available astral connection or portal. This represents a potentially very significant advance in the quality of one's life.

Unconditional Love

The 21st century Earht Plane can be a difficult environment in which to experience unconditional love. By comparison, whenever you experience living in more advanced alien worlds, this becomes a great deal easier.

This encyclopaedia has been drafted in a very matter of fact way, with the intention that the reader should, as far as possible, validate everything for themselves.

The reason for any perceivable "lack of compassion" is to avoid artificially lifting the reader into a blissful state. An analogy is that; helping a child learn to walk involves eventually letting go of the infant so as to allow it to develop its own independent balance.

Human beings' development relies on learning how to manifest unconditional love in the challenging environments they inhabit.

If the reader perceives a lack of unconditional love whilst reading these chapters, this is typically because of implicit exercises that have been implanted into the text.

During your human experience, you can allow unconditional love to manifest in any situation. It's often a case of just letting this to occur. Allow the higher beings who understand the process and assist your adopted human form, unconditional access to that body.

When reading the text of this encyclopaedia, it should be obvious if you are permitting higher beings the necessary access to your adopted human form. When successful, you will experience a mutually unconditionally loving connection with advanced alien beings.

It may be the case that whilst reading the encyclopaedia, you experience some physical discomfort as this process of attuning your human body occurs. Know that this process can and will only take place with the full permission of your higher aspects. Do not push yourself to read. Instead, simply lay the book down as necessary, and spend some time in nature, enjoying the serenity which will re-stabilise you.

More specific directions upon manifesting unconditional love are explained in The Great Simulator part 3.

ENCYCLOPAEDIA

E01 Grasshoppers 1

INTRODUCTION

Grasshoppers I are far from the first alien species to have been encountered by humans. A brief study of sightings (or lack of them) do not reveal any physical visitations to the Earht Plane. However, species such as this are very relevant to humankind as members of its population are actively seeking to assist human development.

This species is loosely described as Grasshoppers 1 because they are probably the nearest type of earthly animal one would compare them to. They appear to have evolved from an insect and now typically grow to around 2 m (7 ft) tall in their typical upright stance.

Assistance

For mankind to easily use astral projection in order to visit alien civilisations, unconditional love is the vital energetic lubricant which makes this most possible. Grasshoppers 1 are experts in assisting human minds to access this vital emotional energy.

Furthermore, successfully astrally visiting alien worlds and interacting with advanced species often requires an invitation and supervision. Many of the Grasshopper 1 species are enthusiastic about helping human consciousnesses meet these visitation requirements. The only real proviso is that the human mind must practice cooperating.

LOCATION

Physical Location

Not yet describable in relation to the known Earth's universe.

Dimension

Grasshoppers 1 reside at a significantly higher dimension than the Earht Plane. At this dimension, their physical world has many similarities to Earth, yet some notable differences. In particular, even though the planet rotates like Earth, there is no proper night time. This appears to be due to the fact that at higher dimensions space is no longer as dark as it would be at lower dimensions.

Grasshoppers 1 higher dimension is a universe where everything is closer together; i.e. Relatively less space-time. So whilst planets are similar to those in lower dimensions, the distances between them tend to be less.

The Grasshoppers 1 planet is not ordinarily detectable from the Earht Plane dimension. Nor do Grasshoppers 1 normally physically visit the Earht Plane as their bodies are unsuited to such a low level. However, they can adopt an alternative humanoid physical form which overcomes the difficulties of operating in lower dimensions.

Time

When interacting with Grasshoppers 1 and their world there is an immediate time distortion to be mindful of. Time in their world appears to be passing far more slowly than it does on the Earht Plane. However, this does not have the effect of causing Grasshoppers 1 to appear to be operating in some sort of slow motion.

When astrally interacting with Grasshoppers 1 and their world, time may initially appear to be passing at roughly the same speed that it would on the Earht Plane. The fact that there is some difference is evident when you become aware of their perception of their interaction with you. In their world they might have a conversation with you that appears to last the equivalent of an hour. Instead, your experience of that interaction, for example, could appear to have occurred in fragments of over 100 instances spread across a year.

In summary, when astrally interacting with Grasshoppers 1, time may at first appear to be passing at the same speed. If this interaction continues in a fragmented way over any length of earthly time, the time distortion becomes more obvious. Thus, Grasshoppers 1 can experience all the fragmented moments of your mutual interaction as if they were one event. For them, however, you would have repeatedly drifted in and out during the astral interaction.

SPECIES

Insectoid

Anatomically, Grasshoppers 1 have many similarities to earthly insects. The key physical differences are that they have much bigger brains, are overall much larger than any insect currently alive on Earth, and have a different digestive tract.

Grasshoppers 1 have an external skeletal shell, though mostly covered with a layer of skin which has the capability to change colour. Typically they appear brown or green with many other possible shades. With a sense of amusement, they wish to convey to us that they can appear in red, purple and even pink shades.

Relative Size

They are slightly bigger than a human being, with a typical male being approximately 2 m (7 ft) tall. Females tend to have smaller bodies, but similar-sized brains. Continuing the comparison to a human being, legs are of similar proportionate length, but arms are relatively longer as they are fundamentally legs.

Anatomy

Grasshoppers 1 have a large lower abdomen, large side-breathing lungs, and a very large heart. Their abdomen serves as a "fuel tank" for a fatty fluid which supplies the flight muscles. The fatty fluid can amount to up to half their overall body weight. Females have egg-laying organs at the bottom of their abdomen. Males have a spiral extendable penis arrangement tucked into their lower abdomen.

There is no obvious sign of a thorax. (Many Earth insects are built in three distinct sections, whereas this species only exhibits two.)

They have wings on their back which are powered by a muscle group that is located at the top of the abdomen. Their local atmosphere appears to be around 50% oxygen which makes flight for such a heavy animal both possible and easy.

They have a symmetrical arrangement of legs and arms. There appear to be six principle abdominal limbs, with the middle pair often redundant. Legs are very spindly and not suitable for leaping (as an earthly grasshopper does), but adequate for walking or running. Grasshoppers 1 mostly walk on their hind legs with a birdlike arrangement of two forward toes and one rear one. The two upper limbs act as arms like a human being, but with three opposing fingers at the end. Their finger tips are enlarged and each finger ends in a small array of tiny claws.

They have a large head containing a large brain which is bigger than a human being's. Two large lateral compound eyes have the ability to focus, but not swivel. They have very good night and day vision, but lack the hunting perspective of (human) forward-set eyes. Antennae are on their head.

The stomach is located just behind the mouth and does not lead into an abdominal digestive tract. Food waste products are excreted through the mouth. There are additional small limbs around the mouth to aid eating. They have no ears or nose, but their bodies are nevertheless sensitive to chemicals in the air and sound vibrations.

Communication

Their lungs are not connected to the mouth so that means there is nothing similar to human speech. Sound communication is often in the form of drumming or scratching their bodies. Such sounds are often used for mutual comfort as opposed to complex communication.

Telepathy is the dominant form of communication. By comparison, a typical human's telepathy, if any, is incredibly primitive. This species also appears to have some means of recording telepathic communication.

Entertainment

To set the perspective, human beings entertain themselves with imagined things such as movies, novels, gossip, daydreaming, etc. This species does not imagine much, but instead senses the reality of everything, which they find both stimulating and entertaining.

Sex is not for pleasure, but a bodily function. As such, they find observing human sex for pleasure along with its abundant fantasising very entertaining.

Great pleasure is derived from assisting human beings along with other developing species.

Reproduction

On Earth you find family units. In the Grasshoppers 1 world, there are loose similarities, but less of a strict pairing arrangement between males and females. Communities collaborate to breed and tend their young.

Males inject females with sperm, producing roughly 100 mm (4 inch) sized eggs. These are placed into incubators and hatch out into caterpillar-type animals. These caterpillars feed on a combination of vegetation and insects until approximately 2 m (7 ft) long. They then cocoon for what in Earth-terms would be around two-to-three months before emerging as a nearly fully-grown adult.

Adults copulate in order to allow specific soul beings to have physical existence. The population is therefore well-managed and stable.

PLANET

Overview

The home planet of Grasshoppers 1 is a little larger than Earth and has many similarities. However, there are no large oceans, and what would otherwise be sea has been overgrown by floating vegetation. The result is that the planet is mostly landmass plus extensive swampy areas. Populated areas are mostly located on land, very green and similar to jungle, possibly rainforest. The planet appears too warm for arctic regions. There are some desert and arid areas, most of which are highlands, and seemingly very little in the way of mountains.

From space the planet looks persistently obscured by a thin hazy cloud several kilometres (miles) thick.

The planet rotates slowly producing long days and nights. Because it is of a higher dimension, the nights are not that dark so space is not as pitch black as it would otherwise be observed in the Earht Plane dimension. Night-time is pleasantly warm.

Other Species

A helpful parallel is to compare the planet with the evolution of species on Earth, in circumstances where the development level of reptiles or mammals was never attained. The lower atmosphere appears to be around 50% oxygen and a very high carbon dioxide level of 10% to 20%. The effect of this is to make it ideal for insects who form all the top species. Fortunately, there is not much in the way of big stinging insects; e.g. No monster-sized wasps.

Similar to Earth, there have been a number of extinctions due to natural disasters such as severe volcanic eruptions. For example, much in the same way that Earth had the woolly mammoth, there were also some very large beetle like creatures that presently appear extinct.

Plenty of animal species live in the mostly floating swamps. But since there is not much in the way of open water, there is little substantial aquatic life deep below the floating swamps.

Food

Adult Grasshoppers 1 mostly live off other insect grubs, which they farm. Grasshoppers 1 prefer their food fresh, so when visiting their homes and buildings, you will often find these insect grubs living in foliage, which sometimes lines internal walls. A swift decapitation of these farmed grubs enables their internal contents to be squeezed out. An analogy would be squeezing out a large toothpaste tube of food directly into your mouth.

Technology

Electricity, computers, and most things mechanical a human might imagine have all been accomplished. Beyond that, Grasshoppers 1 have developed very advanced genetics technology and have an abundance of non-fossil fuel energy.

They have learnt from other advanced species how to travel the universe by collapsing space-time and transporting themselves to wherever they wish. However, it transpired that their normal insect bodies were not well adapted to the rigours of such transportation technology. In response, they developed an alternative, somewhat humanoid, alternative body form that is better suited to dematerialisation and rematerialisation. Thus, their astronauts are quite different to the rest of the population, if not a separate species altogether. The soul groups who occupy Grasshoppers 1 and their astronauts, however, are the same. Grasshoppers 1 astronauts are described in more detail in the chapter "Big Eyed Humanoids 1."

Housing

A defining feature of their home planet is their live-work communal homes. At first impression they resemble an architectural style based on tall slender pyramids typically around 500 m (1,600 ft) tall. However, the architectural embellishments preclude the clean lines that define a normal pyramid.

An alternative way to describe this housing is that they are a modern equivalent of huge imposing termite mounds, constructed using both traditional and modern materials. These tend to be separated by kilometres (or miles) and are dotted across the landscape.

Inside, their communal homes are modern and loosely comparable with human architecture. Most internal areas are fundamentally public spaces. Sleeping and work areas are intermingled. Doors and windows are rarely used, or not present at all. Instead there are plenty of openings to outside and the internal areas. Modern lighting is clearly evident. The internal spaces lead to many outside terraces which double as convenient landing and take-off points for Grasshoppers 1 to fly to and from. A human ear would be struck by the humming noises made by airborne arrivals and departures.

There are a few cities where tall buildings are in close proximity without belts of forest and jungle between them. The population, though, mostly lives in the countryside. There are very few roads linking the country population because air transport is much more advanced.

Capsule (Space) Ports

These constructions affect the atmosphere itself. They are industrial-looking complexes where capsules in particular are shot into space in dematerialising darts of light. Similarly, returning capsules flash back towards receivers.

The local atmosphere is affected and no longer radiates diffused light. The effect is to give the impression that you are looking out into space on a clear night. Yet a few kilometres (miles) away you would be back into the normal diffused daylight. Thus, your first impression of visiting these space ports is that you are doing so at night, observing an artificially-lit complex.

CULTURE

Overview

This race long ago gave up warfare and is very mutually cooperative. There is a strong recognition that they are all part of the super-consciousness. Wanton murder of each other is frowned upon by all. However, farming and consumption of other insect grubs is considered necessary and done in a very loving way.

However, their unconditional love and respect for living creatures they consume does not render them docile. They can be very adventurous and are curious about adventures experienced by other species. With respect to their interaction with less-advanced warlike civilisations, they willingly educate them regarding better alternatives.

Finance

This is a world that operates without money. The population is happy to contribute to the greater community, which in turn meets all their material needs.

The simple insight is that once your happiness is no longer based on possessions, everyone gets along better. Most things you could reasonably want are available to you.

Education

This is dealt with in two phases, and appears to bypass the traditional classroom education process human beings are familiar with. Note that Grasshoppers 1 do not have childlike offspring to educate.

Grasshoppers 1 start their lives as grubs, which for the most part spend all day eating and getting larger. This equates to a human foetus developing in its mother's womb. By and large, the grub stage can be accomplished in an automated way. When the grub eventually converts itself to an adult, that adult emerges in a well-educated state. Learning experiences from other lifetimes can be incorporated into the present, largely dispensing with the education process needed by human beings.

Grasshoppers 1 are able to carry clear memories and skills from one lifetime to another, mostly because they avoid the distressing emotions that humans, by comparison, regularly indulge in. A human mind can be likened to an overloaded computer which needs to regularly be rebooted through death in order to clear clutter and errors out of the computation process. By avoiding most of the clutter in the first place, Grasshoppers 1 are able to process the energy, which gives access to skills and memories from other existences.

INTERACTION WITH HUMAN BEINGS

Alien beings have been improving human DNA and minds for millions of years and have made important contributions throughout humankind's evolutionary process.

Whilst there is evidence of some aliens "playfully" manipulating human minds in a corrupting way, the majority of interventions are beneficial. Conspiracy theories about alien interference are exaggerated interpretations for what should really be categorised as "practical jokes."

Grasshoppers 1 fall comfortably within the groups of aliens that specialise in assisting humans, as opposed to teasing them. Furthermore, their activities are concerned with important educational advances.

Up until the start of the early 21st century, there were very few proper interactions between human beings and alien races. Aliens frequently physically visited Earth, but at the point of this book's first publication, rarely entered into any sort of physical educational process. Nor have they had much opportunity to connect astrally to provide educational input.

Grasshoppers 1 Objective

For humankind to achieve reliable astral access to the rest of the advanced species in the many dimensions and universes, there are a number of essential upgrades that need to occur. There is no monopoly upon who can deliver these upgrades, but Grasshoppers 1 are enthusiastic about making their own important contributions.

Unconditional Love

Grasshoppers 1 are very skilled at the practicalities of accessing the energies of unconditional love. They can help retrain a human mind to have a much better connection to this essential fuel or lubricant, which makes access to all forms of higher awareness easier and more far-reaching. Being able to channel this crucial force requires considerable reprogramming as to how the human mind perceives where it is and what is occurring. By replacing fantasies with an awareness of truth, the human mind becomes a far more dynamic partner in a process it is beginning to learn about.

Higher awareness implicitly involves connecting to higher energies, all of which are intertwined with unconditional love energies. It is impossible to access one without the other. Grasshoppers 1 will readily give human minds practical training as to how to better accomplish this enhanced state.

Practical Training

From the Astral World, it is easy enough for any advanced being to identify which human bodies are better attuned to unconditional love and higher awareness. Grasshoppers 1 will therefore tend to seek out the more advanced minds that are in a position to respond to them. By working with the more capable human minds, Grasshoppers 1 get to participate in the fascinating adventure of experiencing human life.

From a higher perspective there is no significant distinction between an alien body and a human one. They are all experiential vehicles. So the souls which animate Grasshopper 1 bodies can simultaneously influence and animate human bodies.

Before many modern human beings were born, part of the intention that delivered them onto the Earht Plane was that they would at some stage gain access to a network linking human and advanced alien minds. The practical effect is that most readers can experience (in a limited way) being advanced aliens, and those aliens can reciprocally experience human minds.

Making such a smooth link normally requires training the human mind to operate in new and more efficient ways. Hence, Grasshoppers 1 are contributing to the physical training necessary to link human minds to a variety of other higher intelligences.

For you, the reader, rediscovering your soul friends, in this case manifesting as members of the Grasshoppers 1 species, will be of enormous benefit. This chapter forms part of an invitation to rekindle that relationship.

Prospective Advance

Gaining a better access to unconditional love energies gives human minds access to an entire universe of other beings. Enormous social and technological advances not only become possible, but organically occur simply by gaining access to more advanced societies.

Some very sensitive artistic human beings find they are most at home with a flavour of unconditional love that is the speciality of angelic beings. However, this very refined emotion is easily disrupted by day-to-day human life. Realistically, a more robust connection to unconditional love is required for day-to-day activities.

Advanced alien beings, and in particular Grasshoppers 1, are experts in accessing a practical day-to-day version of unconditional love. By accessing more unconditional love, humankind will achieve greater communications with advanced intelligent beings across the universe.

By simple analogy, notice the effect the Internet and computerised communication systems have had on society. Take a moment to recognise the effect of enabling humankind to communicate with the rest of the universes.

E02 Big Eyed Humanoids 1

INTRODUCTION

Big-Eyed Humanoids 1 are specially-evolved astronauts designed with adaptations to enable them to withstand the controlled disintegration and reassembly involved with space-time flight.

Whilst Big-Eyed Humanoids 1 outwardly appear close to the general shape of human beings, they are actually an alternative manifestation for the insect-based Grasshoppers 1 species. Souls or higher beings which energise and give life to the bodies of humans and aliens beings are not restricted to one type of body. For example, a soul that could manifest as a human being can also (with some adjustments) in principle manifest in the body of a Grasshopper 1.

All advanced alien races assist other races. As the Grasshopper 1 race became more advanced, it was given access to '"black hole technology" (or BHT, see the section in the Appendices on how the universe works). Black holes remove matter from one part of the universe and deposit it elsewhere. If you wish to physically transport something from one part of the universe to another, the limitation of the speed of light is problematic due to the incredible distances. So to achieve long-distance physical travel, it is more practical to dematerialise yourself at your departure point and then reconstitute yourself at your arrival point.

When dematerialising and reconstituting organic life-forms from one location to another, it helps to place them in some form of capsule. The reason is because capsules have stable exterior dimensions which are easier to define at the arrival location. The organic life-forms carried within capsules are more complex entities which are also in motion; e.g. Fluids pumping through physical bodies. So the interior of a transportation capsule provides a more stable environment in which the life-form's motion can be protected, whilst the exterior presents easier-to-define transmission parameters.

Any organic life-form is inherently complex, and thus fundamentally not readily suited to being dematerialised and then reconstituted elsewhere. The best solution is to adapt organic life-forms to deal with the process better. Good examples of such adaptations are the many species of Greys that human beings have physically encountered. These various Grey astronaut species have been specially adapted to withstand the rigours of advanced space-time travel.

The bodies of Grasshoppers 1 were not that well-suited to being dematerialised and reconstituted using BHT. So when the Grasshopper 1 race was introduced to this technical innovation, it was difficult for them to make practical use of it. This is part of the reason why, for example, Grasshopper 1 aliens have not ordinarily been seen stepping out of a UFO visiting Earth.

To enable Grasshoppers 1 to make use of the BHT innovation, they were subsequently given access to a new body design, which is better suited for dematerialisation and reconstitution. The souls that would otherwise have been manifesting in the bodies of Grasshoppers 1 similarly started manifesting in the engineered astronaut bodies of Big-Eyed Humanoids 1.

It is important to recognise that because this body design is available to other races, there are further variations of it when operated by other soul groups.

Dematerialisation and Reconstitutions

The BHT available to Big-Eyed Humanoids 1 is not the most complex version available. Nevertheless, it is challenging to make use of.

E02 Big Eyed Humanoids 1

By comparison to Big-Eyed Humanoids 1, ordinary early 21st century earthly human bodies are not well suited to dematerialisation and reconstitution. Whilst the process is not impossible to withstand, it will always result in some degree of disruption or damage to any organic life-form.

The ultimate modification necessary for any physical form to withstand repeated dematerialisation and reconstitution is a good "in the moment" awareness of what you really are. The current crop of early 21st century humans struggle to understand who they really are, and therefore lack the ability to dematerialise and reconstitute with the requisite stability. For example, almost every reader awakens from sleep each day wrongly perceiving that they are just a human being. Imagining you are not a human being does not constitute the requisite ability.

Dematerialisation can be likened to being given a general anaesthetic. The physical mind will cease to function because there will no longer be a physical mind after dematerialisation.

What you experience after dematerialisation and before rematerialisation is similar to the consciousness you have between lifetimes. Some alien astronauts will physically remember, whilst yet others may not. Anything similar to an early 21st century human being will not remember much, and will normally only regain consciousness as if rapidly awakening from an anaesthetic; i.e. Will typically have no conscious memory of the intermediate state, with possibly even a denial of its existence.

If the process of dematerialisation and rematerialisation goes well, you would physically feel very alive and energised. Alternatively, there is the possibility that a very different version of the greater you would awaken in the rematerialized body. It is not unknown for the entire crew of a transportation capsule to accidentally awaken as different "people" who do not know each other.

Common challenges include new personality traits entering a rematerializing body, or existing traits failing to reattach. Hence, space-time astronauts often need some degree of personality maintenance to repair the disruptions. For example, a human married couple could dematerialise as lovers and rematerialize as strangers.

Typically, if all goes well, the dematerialisation and rematerialisation process is similar to a rapid death and rebirth. It can even be pleasant and entertaining. The intermediate phase can be drawn out if desired to, for example, incorporate a "holiday" with your deceased relatives or other soul friends in the heavens.

Some species need organs, such as hearts, restarted upon rematerialisation (if they possess them). Hence, rematerialisation occurs with a jolt.

SPECIES

Similar To Reptiles

In general appearance, Big-Eyed Humanoids 1 will appear to have many similarities to human beings. But since they have some shape-shifting ability, they can adjust themselves to display alternative appearances. When this research was conducted, they repeatedly wore dark flight suits with exposed hands, feet, and faces. It can be difficult to initially distinguish males from females.

These astronaut bodies are designed to feel similar to a Grasshopper 1, but minus the wings. Their anatomy incorporates features that can be seen in insects, reptiles and mammals.

Anatomy

Big-Eyed Humanoids 1 are slightly bigger than human beings, with a typical male's height of approximately 2 m (7 ft) tall. Females tend to be smaller. The species basically looks like an elongated human being with an enlarged head. Many of its features have multiple capabilities.

They have a nose and mouth with lungs located in the main part of the body below. Limbs have internal bones with muscles on the outside. Hands and fingers are relatively large compared to a human's. Hands and feet are webbed, though on land the webbing normally is retracted.

The eyes are large, dark and compound with good lateral vision. Within the compound eyes are different specialist eyes enabling vision across a range of different light conditions. So it is possible for them to see well in both low-light and bright-light conditions. The eyelids are configured to shield the outer more light-sensitive parts of the compound eye in bright-light conditions. Ultra-violet and infrared light can also be seen. Finally, some of the eyes within the compound have luminous cells, acting as faint torches to make it easy to see in dark caves and underground passageways.

There is a small pocket behind the mouth which serves as a stomach for highly nutritious foods similar to egg yolk or nectar. There is also a digestive tract for foods that require greater digestion such as vegetables. If the digestive tract is not in use, it collapses down to a small size thereby making more room for expansion of the lungs.

The lungs are particularly large and able to function well in relatively low pressure atmospheres. This species is capable of running up Mount Everest. If necessary, the lungs can be closed off with the neck expanding to open up a set of gills. Thus, it is possible for this species to live underwater, if required.

The skin is relatively leathery and would not ordinarily lose much moisture. There is also a system for drying exhaled air in the throat, similar to a camel.

In summary, this species can live above or below water, in wet or dry climates, in high or low pressure atmospheres, and in high or low light levels. It is also relatively robust with respect to radiation exposure.

Reproduction

Big-Eyed Humanoids 1 are the result of very extensive, creative genetic manipulation. Their reproductive process is designed to make new modifications easy to incorporate. They are also designed to have a variety of options for gestating their offspring.

Copulation is functional and only takes place when necessary. Males deliver a packet of sperm into females. The sperm within the packet are mostly dormant and designed to hibernate within these packets for as long as required. The sperm also seem to need minimal swimming ability. The result is that relatively few males are required and most Big-Eyed Humanoids 1 are female.

It is very easy to implant females with modified embryos when a new experimental genetic design is being introduced. In principle, fertilisation could occur externally in a laboratory. Fertilisation in females is preferred, however, since it helps regulate which souls get access to a particular body. Females are usually given a lifetime fertilisation shortly after birth by one or more males. If necessary, further sperm packets can be added later. Similarly, genetically-modified sperm packets can be implanted and selectively drawn from.

Under the circumstances, a human mind might wonder if there was perhaps some advantage in dispensing with males altogether. The response is twofold. F*irstly*; retaining males creates better genetic diversity. S*econdly*; being relatively expendable, males have their uses.

Females can produce small eggs of around 60-to-80 mm (approximately 3 in). The eggs are soft-shelled and able to absorb nutrients, but need to develop in nutrient baths because the yolks are very small. This makes the eggs ideal for artificial gestation since they can be left in automated nutrient baths. Alternatively, tubing can be inserted through the shell and nutrients supplied by that means. The eggs have soft expandable shells which allow the offspring to grow to adult size and become fully developed before hatching.

If artificial gestation is not available, then a single egg gestates within a female until it is about the size of a human toddler. The disadvantage of producing a child-sized being is that it has to complete its growth before becoming useful.

Lifespan

Most advanced alien species appear to live relatively long lives; e.g. Grasshoppers 1 can live as long as a future human being. By comparison, Big-Eyed Humanoids 1 often have lifespans comparable to mice and dogs with bodies likewise considered disposable.

It is possible to create a fully-grown adult hatched from an egg, and it's easy for its soul to switch from one body to the next. If an observant outsider met an individual Big Eyed Humanoid 1 over a long period of time, it would be apparent this being was in fact a succession of adults inhabited by the same soul.

The body switching is not to appear permanently young. Rather, it is because their bodies, and in particular their minds, can become badly damaged by their astronaut activities. Accordingly, it is prudent for a soul to have a good supply of replacement physical forms. With strenuous use, a change of body may be required after the equivalent of only six earthly months.

Consistent with this species' remarkable versatility, they are also well-suited for suspended animation, almost indefinitely.

A useful insight concerns human beings' fear of death. Early 21st century human beings strive to prolong physical life. Perhaps a more practical approach is, when needed, to simply adopt a new fresh physical body.

Communication

Unlike Grasshoppers 1, Big-Eyed Humanoids 1 also have speech ability due to the lungs exiting through the mouth. This feature helps when communicating by speech with less advanced species.

Amongst themselves, telepathy remains the dominant form of communication as this is the universal communication language.

Astronauts

The souls that give life to all animals can reincarnate into a variety of different bodies. So if a Grasshopper 1 soul wants to be an astronaut in any particular lifetime, the Big-Eyed Humanoids 1 body is a perfect body to use. The reasons are twofold:

- F*irstly*; travelling to other planets to visit other races often involves having to breathe their atmosphere. So having a body that can breathe a variety of different atmospheres is a huge advantage. The ability to operate under water is possible as well.

- S*econdly*; as described earlier, dematerialising and reconstituting a body is very disturbing. For many species it renders them dysfunctional, if not dead. So it makes perfect sense to engineer a body which copes well with the many difficulties that can arise. Should an astronaut body become severely compromised, typically due to excessive contamination of its cognitive process, it is easy to swap into a new body.

PLANET

In General

This species has no obviously identifiable home planet in its current form apart from the home of Grasshoppers 1. It is truly a hybrid, incorporating DNA coding supplied by a number of alien races. Hence, it is difficult to identify to which planet Big-Eyed Humanoids 1 are truly native. Some of their fundamental anatomy seems to have been derived from a forest-and-swamp-dwelling reptile with an intelligence equivalent to an early human being.

INTERACTION WITH HUMAN BEINGS

As mentioned earlier, due to dimensional differences, Grasshoppers 1 cannot easily visit the Earht Plane. Instead their souls have adopted the Big Eyed Humanoid 1 bodies and have thus been able to make visits.

How Earth Compares to Other Planets with Respect to Human Awareness

Researching alien perception of Earth made it immediately apparent that Earth was just one of many worlds they visit. Therefore recording some of their observations would be potentially informative.

The human race's failure to notice parallel dimensions layered upon Earth is, at this time, a cause of some amusement. Human beings could en masse make such an observation, but a blanket of protective energies discourages them from doing so. A few humans skilled in astral projection have at least recognised parallel worlds that are immediately adjacent, but their number and influence at the time of the first publication of this encyclopaedia was insignificant. So whilst the relatively distant Grasshopper 1 race (including the Big-Eyed Humanoids 1) have a well-established relationship with the inhabitants of these parallel worlds, the more adjacent human beings do not.

This failure to notice immediately adjacent parallel dimensions is a function of the human race's well developed false ego. Higher beings experiencing human form find this degree of illusory ego particularly challenging. Human beings tend to believe they are a dominant race and could ultimately conquer any aggressor. This sense of dominance makes them oblivious to what or who has created them. Even humans who engage in religious observance mostly confine their view of how they were created to a very restricted interpretation. In summary, human minds are prone to ignore higher beings. Hence, noticing adjacent more advanced races is beyond them.

With respect to humans' self-centred ego, most advanced alien races achieve contact with other alien races when the latter are at a less technologically-advanced state. A hypothetical analogy would be if the Greeks or Romans had developed relationships with alien races. Human beings are so inherently warlike, that it has been considered better to leave them substantially alone until this tendency is purged, or at least shows imminent signs of being purged. For example, whilst the Mayans (America 2000 BC until AD 250) had the benefit of alien visitations, very little technological sharing occurred.

Living as a human being is a very interesting experience. Their minds are actually quite receptive, but cluttered with fantasies and petty concerns. On a developing planet, one group of souls will typically dominate the most advanced species. With the human race, however, multiple different categories of soul groups have taken up residence in human form. It can seem as if sometimes "no one is in charge," although ultimately that proves to be an entertaining illusion.

How Earth Compares to Other Planets with Respect to Habitability

The gravity on Earth is below average compared to typical inhabitable planets with organic life-forms. Intriguingly, if you have a larger planet producing a greater amount of geothermal energy, the additional heat enables it to be further away from its sun. A larger planet situation also facilitates much warmer oceans which are excellent habitats for organic life-forms.

Earth has both a pleasant and interesting rotation (day and night). Most other inhabitable planets rotate slower, which renders half of them inhospitable. Or in the case of very slow rotation, can cause the population to be in a state of permanent migration. As mitigation, this leads to the development of plants that walk. However, slow rotation is less of an issue at higher dimensions where space is brighter.

Earth's seasons, whilst not unique, are relatively uncommon.

Similar to many other habitats that are used for experimentation in genetic seeding, the biodiversity of Earth's life-forms is a common type of environment.

Scientific Experiments

In light of what may appear to be a free-for-all of competing groups influencing the behaviour of human minds, a great many alien races have indeed followed through on the opportunity to carry out their own experiments.

Humans are familiar with alien visitors carrying out the occasional scientific visit, taking a few samples, etc. Hence, human beings are mainly concerned with abduction scenarios. However, (this is difficult to accurately gauge) approximately 1,000 times more mind experiments are run on humans compared to physical experiments. These mind experiments rarely involve abduction or physically-observable close encounters, and as such can occur without human detection. The activities of Icke's Lizards (see their own chapter) is a very good example of mind experiments.

Lumping the activities of Grasshoppers 1 and Big-Eyed Humanoids 1 together (since they are the same group), the question becomes: What have they all been up to ? Like so many other visiting races, they have done their fair share of sample-taking. In addition, they are very interested in being one of the first groups to succeed in making substantial contact.

Since the new millennium (year 2000 and on), the protective energies blanketing Earth have become much lighter, and it is relatively easy to make alien contact using astral projection.

One of the more interesting current experiments being run by Grasshoppers 1 and Big-Eyed Humanoids 1 is to see if human minds will finally start to notice astral presence of these beings. These beings can see and are aware of people reading this book, but do you, the reader, notice these beings ?

If you read this book, they are observing you. If you think about them, they will pick up the signals. The human mind will often perceive itself to be the source of such thoughts. In fact, the reverse is normally true. If your human mind wants to read this book, the question to be asked is: Who put that thought or desire in your adopted human mind ?

Most importantly, advanced aliens are refining methods for helping human beings to more readily access unconditional love. Should the reader sense an astral visitation, be alert to this wonderful loving emotional energy.

E03 Icke's Lizards 1

INTRODUCTION

David Icke is a controversial British writer, public speaker, former professional footballer and sports broadcaster. He has had disturbing visions of alien lizard or reptilian beings influencing human minds in malevolent ways. David Icke has further stated that the existence and activities of these particular aliens was revealed to him by angelic beings.

These observations provided a useful inspiration to conduct fresh research into the alien lizards or reptilians in question.

Upon investigation, the angelic beings turned out to be a higher manifestation of the alien reptiles themselves. So whilst this species does indeed influence human beings to "misbehave," far from seeking to disguise their actions, they instead revealed them to Icke, as well as to others.

Amusing Joke

It is not being suggested that David Icke has made inherently incorrect observations. Merely that further observation of, and interaction with, these aliens strongly suggests their inspiration for influencing human minds is amusement rather than malevolence.

Taking all the available facts into account, a researcher is likely to conclude that Icke's Lizards 1 are engaged in a grand practical joke. Playing with human minds is a common activity in which plenty of other alien species also happily engage in.

LOCATION

Multiple Dimensions

Icke's Lizards 1 manifest across a range of dimensions in a way that human minds will often initially have difficulty comprehending.

Human beings consider themselves focused upon one physical Earht Plane dimension, yet there are plenty of other versions of humans in parallel or higher dimensions. At the time of the first publication of this encyclopaedia, most human beings did not relate to themselves as being similarly multi-dimensional. At best, most human beings understood themselves to be in one of two places: alive on Earth, or dead (yet somehow preserved in the heavens).

Icke's Lizards 1 on the other hand, are well aware that they are operating through a "spirit form", which can be anchored in physical form. In other words, their dominant perception is not a physical form (which is the human experience), but rather their spirit form. Their astral projection skills are so advanced that they experience a near seamless transition between the physical and astral planes.

Icke's Lizards 1 are also aware of other versions of their species. Similarly, this species has the ability to roam the universe, easily accessing different worlds.

With respect to Icke's Lizards' 1 original home planet, it appears to be very close to the Earht Plane with further dimensions of it layered on top.

By comparison, the physical bodies of aliens such as Grasshoppers 1 are to a large extent located in a higher dimension, so they have a closer relationship to the unconditional loving energies of the super-consciousness

Physical Location

Located at a lower dimension close to the Earht Plane, Icke's Lizards 1 have a home planet within the Milky Way galaxy. The planet appears to be approximately one-third the galaxy's diameter away. This places it beyond humankind's current ability to physically observe it, though the planet's sun is probably detectable.

SPECIES

Anatomy

Their fundamental anatomy is reptilian, and the immediate difference you notice with this race compared to earthly reptiles is their upright stance. Researching this encyclopaedia has repeatedly revealed that a biped stance assists a species' technological development. Having forearms free to work with tools in turn stimulates the evolution of the mind.

Their height when standing is anywhere between 1 to 2 m (3 to 7 ft) with an overall length including their tails of roughly double that. Hands appear claw-like with a minimal-opposing digit (similar to earthly chimpanzees). They have triangular-pointed faces or heads, and two complex eyes that are slightly forward-facing, predator style. Slits (similar-looking to gills) are located at the back of the head or top of the neck, but do not operate as gills. There are also minor projections extending from the back along the spine and down to the tail.

Research suggests an anatomical skeleton that has a lot in common with earthly birds and dinosaurs.

Communication

Icke's Lizards 1 appear quite skilled at speech and have well-developed vocal chords. For a simple insight into how they sound, try speaking using plenty of breath whilst pulling your lips back as far as your rear molar teeth.

Unsurprisingly, they are very skilled at telepathic conversation, but when communicating with physical forms, they appear to enjoy using verbal and posturing communication.

This species enjoys misleading people should the opportunity present itself. So when researching them, it is helpful to deal with Icke's Lizards 1 much in the same way that you might deal with lower spirit forms: Use plenty of unconditional love.

Reproduction

Suggesting Icke's Lizards 1 have a lot in common with human beings is a helpful analogy because then it is easy to gain an understanding of them by highlighting differences. They enjoy copulation, but only do so rapidly and for the express purposes of bringing new offspring into the world. Unlike early 21st century human beings, they have a good working relationship with the souls to whom they are about to give life.

Offspring require education, but to a lesser extent than that of early 21st century human children. The obvious difference is that the offspring of Icke's Lizards 1 learn faster. Unlike some slightly more advanced species, however, their offspring do not experience a strong sense of previous incarnations. Thus, they have a lot to re-learn.

Species Variations

Some species such as ants and termites specifically create new numbers of their population according to their society's needs. Icke's Lizards 1 adopt a similar approach and create offspring with specialities such as high intelligence, creativity, good drone workers, etc. The populace frowns upon any divergence from the creation of a well-engineered society. Observation suggests that this social model functions well.

Icke's Lizards 1 drone workers are mostly disinterested in anything a more intelligent being might find curious. The more intelligent of Icke's Lizards 1 facilitating this research took the view that if you placed a human drone worker and a lizard drone worker in a room together they would be very disinterested in each other. It was also commented that both liked fantasising and being entertained for pleasure.

With respect to leadership, the Icke's Lizards' 1 leader is a non-physical being. Its directives and insights are enacted by physical sub-leaders. Thus, Icke's Lizards 1 have achieved the milestone of being ruled by their collective consciousnesses' sub-god.

PLANET

In General

The terrain is mostly land mass and relatively arid. There are oceans, but in reverse proportion to those of Earth, hence a lot less water. There are also congested tectonic plates that don't have enough room to more freely move around. This results in many earthquakes, so their buildings have to be very robust.

The size of the planet appears to be between that of Earth and Mars. The atmosphere is relatively clear and less cloudy than Earth's. There is rainfall, but precipitation is more likely to come in the form of mist.

It can often get very cold and drop below freezing. Since the conditions are mostly arid, there is not much ice, and in turn not much frost. To deal with very low temperatures, Icke's Lizards 1 wear clothes. This gives them a tremendous evolutionary advantage against other species on their planet, making it possible to move faster in cold weather than other animals. Since there are no furry animals, there are no fur coats.

From space the surface appears to be a mostly light-brown colour with patches of green and blue. On the ground the impression is that the whole place is a little dusty.

Other Species

This is a planet where large dinosaur-type species have evolved and many variants are still alive, although anything hazardous to Icke's Lizards 1 was wiped out by them long ago. However, said hazardous dinosaur-type species were not lost for good. Other alien races had studied their DNA and taken copies of the codes. It is therefore possible to re-engineer samples of otherwise extinct species and place them in protective environments. The re-engineered species are animated by different soul-groups to the originals, often resulting in a much higher intelligence than was originally the case.

There are no feathered birds, but there are plenty of flying reptiles who tend to resemble earthly bats or pterodactyls. Since oxygen levels are similar to 21st century Earth, none of these flying animals or even insects are able to grow much bigger than would be observed on Earth.

Other reptiles are farmed for food, and a relatively small number are kept for pets.

CULTURE

Playful

This is a culture in which having fun is important. These lizards get bored rather easily. The intelligent ones get bored the fastest, whilst less intelligent workers are happy to be kept busy.

The less emotionally mature members of the community are principally responsible for what human beings would consider to be "difficulties" on Earth.

Building Architecture

The architecture varies considerably as there are a variety of cultural groups on the planet. So whilst there is a central leadership, there are considerable cultural variations with associated divergent opinions upon how they should all live. This level of freedom is unusual because as cultures become more advanced, there tends to be a homogenising, levelling effect.

The population is spread out across the planet, as opposed to the tendency towards megacities seen on Earth. There is a general desire to avoid cities and overpopulation.

Some of the population live in extremely modern homes with very complex architecture. Whilst at the other extreme, given how very dry the planet is, some prefer to live in burrows which take advantage of the dryness and as a result are comfortable dwellings.

Overall, they favour wooden buildings. Interestingly, whilst on Earth humans favour dead wood as a building material, Icke's Lizards 1 prefer living wood. Thus, many homes are woven from living material and have very pleasant internal energetic atmospheres.

Caste System

A lizard is bred for its role in society and stays at that station in life. Unlike Earth, where such systems are ultimately based on social-class modelling, theirs is based on genetic modelling.

An example would be their warlike previous history during which large numbers of male soldier lizards were bred. Through technological advances, though, this approach to world domination was superseded. After a brief flirtation with nuclear war, they learnt to get on better and adopted a sole-leader system. Having observed how more advanced alien civilisations are ruled, they upgraded to a non-physical sub-god leadership. A non-physical leader approach also has the advantage of rendering political assassinations pointless.

INTERACTION WITH HUMAN BEINGS

Bored

Since Icke's Lizards 1 have developed a very civilised society, the more intelligent lizards quickly get bored. Since their society is well-regulated, behaviours such as severe violence must be experienced elsewhere. As such, their relationship with human beings has been substantially inspired by boredom.

Icke Got It Half Right

Icke's Lizards 1 are no longer inclined to actually war with each other back home, but Earth provides them with a rich playground where they can engage in a variety of games. An unaware human mind will at first perceive this as some sort of malevolent invasion. However, at a higher level the Creators happily permit this interjection.

David Icke speculated that there is a certain class of human leaders who are readily possessed by these beings. The Icke's Lizards 1, however, do not consider that to be the case. As far as they are concerned, there are enough human beings who prove to be susceptible to their influence that they rarely need to encourage the selective breeding of humans, and even then only briefly.

Furthermore, Icke's Lizards 1 see little point in sacrificing human children and drinking their blood. When researching their views for this encyclopaedia, they wanted to make it clear that they viewed such practices as pointless, although they find the human need to foster such fantasies very amusing.

Assisting With Conflicts

Where humans are aligned to war with each other, Icke's Lizards 1 have helped in that effort, but not to the point of being instrumental in fermenting conflict. Their rationale is that they merely help events along.

Much in the way groups of humans take and support sides in any social competitions from football matches to wars, Icke's Lizards 1 are predisposed to taking different sides in human confrontations. They take the view that this is all entertaining fun and ultimately no real harm is done. In their opinion they do no more than assist.

Yet, when conflict is over and peace and reconciliation is needed, Icke's Lizards 1 assist with that as well. An analogy would be children putting a game away once it has been played for the day.

Sexual Perversion

The vast majority of human sexual pleasure is related to exciting fantasies. So in this respect, most human beings, even most children, can be considered perverted. However, the majority of fantasies and desires are deemed normal by most humans, yet due to the inevitability of extremes, they expect abnormality.

The encouraging of paedophilia by Icke's Lizards 1 is a repeated accusation, and on the observable facts is a fair charge. But the lizards see this a bit differently. In their view, sexual perversion is fun, and they are far from the only ones encouraging this aspect of human imagination and behaviour.

Icke's Lizards 1 are typical of many beings who influence human behaviour. They find it amusing to take a relatively pure and energised human mind, and corrupt it with self-pleasing lower influences. For example, enticing a young virgin girl to desire a rough "gang-bang." Similarly, goading an innocent child to have sex with an adult is also great fun for them, as is getting someone to desire sexual torture and humiliation.

Icke's Lizards 1 indeed feed off the energies these sexual perversions produce, and to be fair, all too many humans similarly feed off such emotional energies.

Paranoia

One of the best methods Icke's Lizards 1 have of increasing their influence is using their activities to induce paranoia. Once you realise that many human minds are their "play things," you become more alert to evidence of their intervention. Icke's Lizards 1 make no effort to cover their tracks. In fact, they make sure that as many people as possible know about them.

As far as Icke's Lizards 1 are concerned, they are encouraging people like David Icke. They expressed the view this was not that difficult for them to achieve. Their idea of fun is being a corrupting influence.

Occasionally Angelic

Icke's Lizards 1 also have higher manifestations, some of which can appear to be angelic. These sort of beings are safe to communicate with as they are unlikely to harm a visitor's perceptions of reality.

Addendum

The lizards assisting with this research were amused by being designated as "David Icke's Lizards." They requested this chapter finish with their view that such labelling is akin to naming an earthly dog owner after the dog.

E04 Grey Goblins 1

INTRODUCTION

Grey Goblins 1 look like typical small "Grey" aliens, albeit their skin colour is more often greenish as opposed to grey. They are one of the most likely category of aliens the inexperienced astral traveller will unwittingly encounter. Conversely, readers are physically unlikely to encounter this species because Grey Goblins 1 do not normally physically manifest.

Curious and Opportunistic

Grey Goblins 1 are likely to become aware of you, the reader, simply because you are reading about them. If you possess even modest clairvoyance you will probably be able to immediately detect a cluster of them observing you. They happily feed off human emotional energy. If you are fearful, that increases their influence.

Low-level astral projection often carries you into their planes of operation. If you are wandering around these planes or dimensions, your curiosity is inclined to attract them. What happens next has the randomness of bumping into strangers on a city street. Some Grey Goblins 1 will be friendly, whilst others are likely to interfere. Anyone using a drug-induced astral projection approach is particularly open to interference. It's similar to how getting drunk at night in a city centre can expose you to assault and robbery.

Astral projection beginners who may be experimenting with the "heavy" half-asleep approach are quite likely to encounter this species at least once. Since the heavy astral projection technique normally operates with the human intellect in a suppressed state, it is easy to be confused and misled by the Grey Goblins 1.

Conversely, if you are using a stable, fully conscious "light" astral projection approach, you will normally only encounter these aliens if that is your intention.

LOCATION

Astral World / Close To Earht Plane Dimension

Grey Goblins 1 do not have a physical home planet(s), but are very active in the Astral World where they do have realms or zones of their own. The simplest way to describe it is that they have non-physical planets and habitats of their own.

Since the Astral World has barely been mapped by human beings of the early 21st century, it is difficult to explain where they are located other than to say that it is a low non-physical plane that in some ways corresponds to physical galaxies. In this context, Grey Goblins 1 have home planets or outposts connected to most galaxies.

SPECIES

Grey's Ancestral Components

All physical forms are designed to be operated by a team of spirit beings who range from high-to-low energetic levels or dimensions. Hence, there will always be some low-level entities required to enable any physical body to operate.

Most of the Grey alien species originate from green-coloured, forest-dwelling insects. This means that the evolution of a Grey species at some point requires their bodies to be operated by spirit beings which resemble little green aliens.

Once you understand that Grey Goblins 1 are really a spirit form that can operate a less advanced Grey body, you will similarly understand why they are not really physical beings.

Some physical species of Greys retain the green colour. However, the ones that an early 21st century reader is likely to physically encounter on Earth, are much more advanced and are rather different in temperament to Grey Goblins 1.

Insects Template

Grey Goblins 1 for practical purposes look like typical small Grey aliens. Grey Goblins 1 do not have proper physical bodies, and as such do not have a fully defined anatomy. Nevertheless they possess near-physical forms which have clear insect characteristics. For example, their near-physical form has an exoskeleton template, possibly green pigmentation, and some of the variations of this species even have antennae.

Their height typically ranges from 1 to 1.5 m (3 to 5 ft). They have large compound eyes, large heads, medium-size bodies, and four thin limbs.

Anatomy

Near-physical bodies do not have a full physical anatomy. Instead they are really a well-defined energetic template. Whereas arteries are found in a physical body, the energetic template has energetic paths flowing through its astral body. To some extent the energetic colours even resemble oxygenated and de-oxygenated blood. If you cut a limb, these energies can spray out as if a physical artery had been severed.

Grey Goblins 1 normally possess mouths, though they have no real function since the food they consume is energetic and could pass into them without having to enter via a mouth. Similarly, they breathe the astral air, which is really just an energetic form that can be absorbed without physical lungs.

This sort of energetic anatomy makes this species very resistant to harm and not easy to destroy. It may appear that you can injure one of their bodies, but in actuality it simply reassembles itself into whatever shape and condition it previously possessed.

PLANET

Astral Home Planet Example

This species has been created a number of times, hence it possesses many similar home planets. From a human perspective these worlds are magical, similar to how our thoughts mould our environment. On Earth, a thought has to be translated into physical action to influence the environment. In the astral world, the thought itself manipulates the illusory matter.

An example home planet of Grey Goblins 1 looks like a smaller version of Earth, at approximately 60% of the mass. The planet is substantially forest and these are mostly forest-dwelling creatures. Since it is fundamentally an insect-dominated planet, nothing that appears to be reptile or mammal can be detected. A good comparison is likening Grey Goblins 1 to earthly chimpanzees living in clusters on the forest floor.

The planet has energetic tectonic plates which cause occasional earthquakes, some of which are extremely violent. The surface is around 50% ocean with a great deal of sea life. There are polar regions with barely any ice. The whole place is subject to severe solar storms which sometimes produce a very orange sky. Their astral sun's X-ray radiation often penetrates to the ground. Overall, it does not appear to be the type of planet humans could tolerate, if it were a physical location.

Other Colonisations

Colonisation is not the best expression given that Grey Goblins 1 have been artificially introduced to other Astral World planets. Other alien races consider them to be interesting companions in the same way a human being might keep a dog as a pet.

CULTURE

Relation To Physicality

To understand this section, it helps to remember the relationship between spirit forms and physical ones. Spirits animate physical bodies so as to enable them to live and function. Thus, spirits in the Astral World can function more or less as they would in a physical one. A useful analogy is a dream world in which you endeavour to undertake apparently physical activities such as getting from A to B.

What follows in this section is life in the overlap between a non-physical and a physical existence.

Advanced Apelike

In near-physical form the intelligence of the typical Grey Goblins 1 is very similar to earthly gorillas. They are not particularly warlike, though they can be territorial. Physically they tend to live in communities of up to 100. Only rarely do they live in anything beyond the most basic structures such as a leaf or thatch overhead for shade from the sun. More advanced versions of the species, however, prefer a modern metropolis (classified as Grey Goblins 2).

Intriguingly, the astral planet appears to have stone relics that seem to have been the result of activity by another, now absent, species. The relics have similar architecture to that associated with the Incas or Mayans on Earth.

Technology

The technology, for the most part, consists of a few basic tools, but no fire. There is some evidence of metal, but this appears to have been taken directly from the ground without smelting. The result is very similar to stone-age technology, except that lumps of unrefined metal replace stone in most cases.

Astral Culture

Many Grey Goblins 1 have largely tired of near-physical manifestations and seem to be more interested in the advantages of staying higher in the Astral World. When further away from the physical dimension on the astral plane, their civilisation is more advanced and far greater in population. By comparison, human spirits are often keen to manifest in physical form by having another incarnation or lifetime.

Small Greys 1 (following chapter) described the Grey Goblins 1 as akin to "mice." In the lower Astral Worlds they certainly get everywhere, although they are obviously bigger than mice.

INTERACTION WITH HUMAN BEINGS

Grey Goblins 1 appear to be roughly two-thirds of what is required to form a human being. By comparison, an earthly dog or cat would equate to roughly one-third of a human being. This explains why it takes several animal spirits blended together to form a human being. So interactions with Grey Goblins 1 tend to be with a less advanced entity, even if it can at first appear informative.

Fantasies and Paranoia

These beings enjoy playing with and influencing the human mind. If you ever wanted to create fiction about aliens, these beings would certainly collaborate to come up with compelling stories. They could then play on your mind in order to make you consider the possibility that your fears and fantasies might become a reality.

Human beings are naturally fearful, and these beings enjoy playing with and amplifying those fears. It is unfair to suggest that Grey Goblins 1 are entirely responsible for the fact that human fiction predominantly portrays aliens as invaders, but they do exaggerate the anxiety if the opportunity presents itself.

Whilst human beings might consider such influences to be malevolent, the Grey Goblins 1 are really too playful for such an accusation to be correct.

Abductions

Given the Grey Goblins' 1 lack of technology nor great interest in scientific research, they are unlikely to abduct humans and perform medical experiments. However, as explained earlier, that does not preclude them from making a human mind afraid of "little green men."

E05 Small Greys 1

INTRODUCTION

In the same way that automobiles come in a variety of shapes and sizes, so too do Greys. Because there are so many variations, it's difficult to define exactly what a Grey looks like. Since many of them have access to time travel, you can encounter further permutations of them depending on the evolutionary stage they may have reached.

Typical Small Greys 1

Given the abundance of Grey species and their many permutations, Small Greys 1 are a good example of the type who regularly visit Earth. The distinguishing feature of Small Greys 1 is that they are fond of visiting human beings, whereas other many Grey types are more indifferent.

In researching the Small Greys 1 via astral projection, they were asked: "Could you please let us know when you will be visiting Earth? It would be nice to see your inter-dimensional craft."

Their initial answer was a firm "no," at least not for now. The full explanation of their response is at the end of the chapter. Meanwhile, in the interim, their answer roughly translates to: "Some idiots would try to kill and/or capture us." In addition, dimensional differences can be harmful to both Grey and human bodies.

LOCATION

Higher Dimension

The species humankind normally encounters, occupies a higher dimension which is still close enough to the Earht Plane to make it easy to physically observe them. There is a home planet within the Milky Way which appears to be around a quarter of the galaxy's diameter away.

Multi-Dimension

Small Greys 1 construct themselves at both higher and lower dimensions, which is an essential skill for spreading themselves across the universe's multiple dimensions. So whilst the variant that physically visit the Earth are relatively low dimension, there are many more higher dimension variants of them.

Everywhere

Small Greys 1 have spread themselves across many galaxies. However, the definition of who or what Small Greys 1 are, is confused by the ease with which different groups can occupy very similar physical forms.

Across the universe humans experience, there are various permutations of the Grey species, many of which have been created using parallel evolutionary paths. Starting from different base organisms, numerous variations of this species have been evolved. But the effect of convergent evolutionary engineering has yielded similar sub-species, even though they had different origins.

SPECIES

Insect Origin

Greys are typically developed from exoskeleton insects. Since they also have DNA similar to reptiles, for example, it has been possible to incorporate other design features into them. For example, Small Greys 1 have been engineered to have a vertical mouth/lung arrangement to facilitate speech.

An advantage of an exoskeleton is that it is slightly better at withstanding high energy environments where radiation, for example, is prevalent. Similarly, where sensitive organs such as eyes are damaged by radiation, new ones can be grown.

Possibly their most important attribute is a very good brain, which was modelled from DNA coding of other advanced aliens, and represents a deviation from typical insect anatomy.

Evolution

The Small Grey 1 sub-species evolved from something akin to a shrimp in the sea. Eventually the shrimp conquered the land and became a biped standing on two legs. Whilst the shrimp originally had two rows of multiple legs, becoming a biped made the intermediate limbs redundant.

Similar to how human beings have a redundant tail which is now confined to the pelvis, Small Greys 1 have vestigial (redundant and shrunken) antenna stems as well as legs.

Like many advanced exoskeleton aliens, Small Greys 1 have evolved a skin to cover the hard external skeleton. This makes them more sensitive to touch, whilst remaining very robust.

Anatomy

Physically, Small Greys 1 have to deal with an atmosphere that would make a human being choke. By comparison, they find Earth's atmosphere breathable.

Overall, the general anatomy has a great deal in common with Earthly species and humans. The greatest difference is their far more developed brains which they could never have realistically evolved of their own accord.

Small Greys 1 have large compound eyes that can focus and adjust direction by moving the lenses within the eye (as opposed to human eyes that just swivel). The compound eyes are located laterally on the head and do not have eyelids. For completeness, it should be mentioned that some other Greys, however, have a large pair of eyes (not compound ones) with eyelids.

Their digestive tract runs from mouth to anus. The diet incorporates many possibilities, provided the food is healthy and well-engineered.

Their hands are elongated with bony digits. The fingertips have two variations; nails of sorts, which can require filing, or no nails and soft, very touch sensitive ends. Thus, there is an option to have nails depending on the type of work undertaken.

Blood has a greenish tint to it.

Height is typically 1 to 1.5 m (3 to 4 ft).

Reproduction

The processes by which the various types of Greys can be brought to life is enormously varied. Some are born by relatively natural methods. Others are manufactured in special production centres that one might call "loving body factories." Whichever process is used, reproduction is achieved with love and warmth.

Small Greys 1 mostly reproduce using relatively natural methods. They have the option to use more engineered processes, but prefer a family-orientated approach entailing copulation and eggs. The end result is that they produce youngsters who gradually develop into adults.

Small Greys 1 want to emphasise the value of enabling souls to manifest as physical beings with a minimum of distress. Human babies gestating in their mother wombs smile and look happy, but birth is so traumatic that it typically takes them a month to recover. By comparison, Small Greys 1 endeavour to make their offspring feel content and loved at all stages of the reproductive and birthing process. This approach allows their offspring to remember useful skills from previous incarnations, thereby requiring far less education than a human child.

PLANET

Initial Home Planets

The original home world for Small Greys 1 was a charming planet that was mostly wet and forested. Small Greys 1 lived a tribal life very much at one with the forest and nature, even having greenish skin pigmentation.

Then, in a pattern often repeated at this low dimension, some of the Small Greys 1 became technologically more advanced. They started clearing swathes of the forest, lost their green skin pigmentation, and ultimately became grey—or at least to the human eye they did. Small Greys 1 can see ultra-violet light, and so appear more pink or purple to each other.

A significant cultural clash led to the ultimate demise of nearly all the forest dwellers. Their souls reincarnated into the bodies of the new urbanites. This transformation led to the development of a strong environmental movement.

The challenges of a vastly increasing population were resolved by space exploration and discovery of a barely inhabited new world where most of the population migrated to. Bit by bit, the original home planet was restored to a mostly forested condition, eventually giving the environmentalists the home they desired.

Current Main Home Planet

Their current home planet is larger than Earth and was essentially a desert terrain with similarities to Mars. Continuing volcanic activity renders the atmosphere difficult to breathe. Fortunately, it was possible to alter the atmosphere with enough water to make the entire planet habitable for Small Greys 1.

E05 Small Greys 1

The planet is now almost fully planted with adapted vegetation and non-threatening wildlife. There are also well-developed modern towns and architecture, in spite of a general dislike of large cities and urban sprawl. Thus, they achieved a more thought-through approach to settlements.

Roadways are laid out in very straight lines indicating that some sort of grid planning is in operation. Though there is very little traffic on the roads, because most transport is airborne.

The sky is busy with a variety of craft, mostly accelerating and decelerating in different directions. Thus, craft normally only become clearly visible when starting or stopping.

Buildings

As on Earth, buildings come in a wide variety of possibilities. There are noticeably few doors. Unlocked and wide doorways seem common. This makes sense since their climate is managed in a way that renders external doors unnecessary.

Climate

The atmosphere feels thick. If it were to flow into you, it would be like swallowing heavenly nectar. The Small Greys 1 commented that an engineered atmosphere at such a relatively low dimension is rather rare.

On Earth, the atmosphere, whilst alive in its own right, behaves randomly. On the main (new) home planet of Small Greys 1, the atmosphere is alive and intelligent, behaving like a benevolent nurturer. When moisture is required in a location, it is delivered there. Low level winds are minimal and the temperature is steady. If it gets too sunny, thick, hazy clouds form overhead.

CULTURE

Advanced

Technologically, Small Greys 1 are very advanced compared to humans. In principle they could invade and take over Earth with relative ease. They would have little difficulty taking control of an electrically-operated system. They can also control most human minds. So it is fortunate for humankind that such a takeover is not on their agenda.

Through a variety of space ships (or simply astrally), Small Greys 1 have the technological capability to reach any part of the universe humans experience. Whilst the comparatively few Greys who inhabit their original home planet like being there and are not as interested in such exploration.

Fun

Unlike many developed alien races, Small Greys 1 maintain the ability to fantasise for fun. This ability is almost redundant and really a left-over from their earlier days.

However, the higher beings which occupy Small Greys 1 also enjoy experiencing other life forms such as human beings, which of itself constitutes having fun. Because they enjoy having the experience of being embodied humans, Small Greys 1 are interested in the evolution of humankind.

Small Greys 1 find human forms of entertainment interesting to sample and study. During the course of the author's research, he not only found them picking through his memories of music, but encouraging him to listen to more compositions so that they could better experience what music is like. By comparison Large Greys 1 showed little interest in human music. Small Greys 1 also like to relax to the sounds of their home planet's nature, which for them would be the equivalent of birds, wind, water, etc.

Arts

As an evolved species, Small Greys 1 have developed their arts in a way that parallels human culture, with less emphasis, though, on imagined pleasures and more on actual achievements. Works of art such as statues or paintings are admired, whereas the species has little in the way of literary fiction and instead looks to the works of other species.

The artistic sense of Small Greys 1 likewise extends to copying interesting features developed by other races (e.g. Buildings reflecting architecture based on large conical or pyramid-shaped termite mounds). Intriguingly, a few homes are adorned with castellated battlement features from the human medieval period (although sourced from a parallel human world).

Clothing and Adornments

Whilst many humans have lost touch with the fact that clothing is really only needed for warmth, Small Greys 1 have not. They adopt clothes where necessary, but otherwise are happy to go naked. In their culture, sexuality does not confuse everything, and nakedness is natural and preferable.

Adornments such as jewellery existed in the past, but was associated with sexuality, so now they are by and large redundant.

INTERACTION WITH HUMAN BEINGS

Small Greys 1 have a fondness for ape creatures, although their main interactions are with more advanced alien species such as other humanoids or Greys. For them, the early 21st century human population falls neatly between very primitive apes and significantly more advanced humanoids.

Regular Visitors to Earth

Small Greys 1 are regular visitors to Earth, and their interactions cover the spectrum of possibilities. Some interactions are kind and peaceful, whilst others treat human beings as a lesser species. These different categories of interactions are a function of the diversity within the Small Grey 1 species. Human beings can be perceived as everything from a lower species to fellow souls with links to Small Grey 1 families.

A useful analogy which helps explain Small Greys 1 standpoint is the human attitude towards animals. Human laws normally say that fellow humans (who are biologically almost identical to animals) should not be murdered, yet the murder and consumption of non-human animals is socially sanctioned. By contrast, whilst Small Greys 1 see themselves as sophisticated, but humans less so, they feel human existence should still be respected. Thus, the Small Greys 1 attitude is an improvement upon how human beings treat animals in general.

Small Greys 1 visit using a variety of manned spacecraft, or alternatively carry out observations using remotely-operated craft which range from relatively old to very new. The "old" craft can be the earthly equivalent of over 100 years old.

Astral Visits

Soul groups that manifest as Small Greys 1 often also manifest in human bodies, though any memory of that soul connection is usually deliberately obscured. When a human has repeated interactions with Greys, a soul link is invariably the cause. Small Greys 1 often astrally visit people with whom they have soul links, running a variety of experiments without the need for a physical connection.

Human beings with such Grey friends often experience repeated out-of-body abductions as part of these experiments. This can be stressful since human minds have no physical defence to stop them. Within the overall soul group, different spirit beings are swapped around or take turns being the human person. Since the human mind is unable to recognise a change of operator, it incorrectly perceives this as some form of attack.

Improvement Sought

Similar to humans teaching skills to animals, advanced aliens sometimes try to teach human beings new and useful things. It would be easy to give humans new technological advances to play with, but not necessarily helpful. By analogy, children are taught not to play with matches until they have the maturity to respect the "technology."

There are many immaturity challenges facing early 21st century humankind. The biggest issue is that human minds perceive relatively little of the higher world around them. Even those who are interested in this subject find themselves more fascinated by reading about it than actually experiencing it.

Confronting this challenge, Small Greys 1 are amongst the group of advanced aliens experimenting with upgrading the human mind. It is not all that difficult to improve a human mind's sensitivity. The challenge is to improve human access to wisdom in proportion to improved sensitivity.

A good analogy is the earthly early 21st century Internet. Human minds on their own can acquire parcels of specialist knowledge and wisdom. With the Internet, however, everyone has much greater access to that specialist knowledge and wisdom. The issue is whether humans make suitable use of what is available to them.

Small Greys 1 are amongst those advanced aliens who are helping humankind achieve a sort of astral Internet connection to the knowledge and wisdom already acquired across the universe. The biggest challenge is enabling human minds to sensibly cooperate with the assistance being offered to them.

Why Not More Contact ?

Small Greys 1, like all other advanced aliens who visit Earth, are in no particular hurry to reveal everything about themselves. The considerable advance in human technology that would result from increased physical interaction first needs to be integrated with increased human wisdom.

Whilst in the early 21st century isolated human beings were making progress in the right direction, their numbers were extremely few. It was suggested that 0.5% of the population would be necessary to transform the attitude of the rest of the species. At the time of transcribing this first edition of the encyclopaedia, Small Greys 1 looked forward to that critical mass being achieved.

E06 Large Greys 1

INTRODUCTION

Of those alien races who are both technologically advanced and physically visit Earth, the Large Greys 1 count as one of the more frequent visitors.

Large Greys 1 are very similar to Small Greys 1, although obviously larger. Having larger brains, they are correspondingly more advanced than Small Greys 1. Whilst some alien species have significantly larger brains than Large Greys 1, such species rarely visit Earth.

Large Greys 1 have a considerable interest in what occurs on Earth, as their soul group(s) regularly manifest in human beings. They have also helped in developing life on Earth.

Adaptations

Whilst Large Greys 1 are to be found throughout the universe humans experience, their main home planet does not appear to be in the Milky Way galaxy. The Large Greys 1 have focused their settlements around their home galaxy within which the Milky Way happens to fall. Due to dimensional differences, they have had to engineer their bodies to adapt to local conditions.

To understand the nature of these adaptations, a hypothetical example is helpful. Suppose a soul group was manifesting as advanced human beings on Earth. If that soul group wished to colonise another planet where there was an incompatible dimensional difference, their original human bodies would be unsuitable. The solution would be to re-engineer a similar body using organic material suited to that dimension.

The practical effect is that there are numerous variations of Large Greys 1 incorporating optimisation suited to their target environments. Whilst they can in principle visit each other's home locations, such visits sometimes have to be brief.

On top of constructing their bodies from appropriate matter, Large Greys 1 also have to adapt their minds to suit local environments. For example, some locations make them "heady" or feeling too light, which detracts from undertaking work. Whilst in other locations, they can find themselves beginning to identify themselves as their physical bodies (a state of consciousness typical of early 21st century human beings).

LOCATION

Higher Dimension

The galaxy where the Large Greys 1 were developed is probably visible to earthly astronomers today. However, over time the dimension of objects can increase, and their relative location in space-time can alter. Whilst in principle you might succeed in seeing where Large Greys 1 were going to be evolved, you would not physically be able to reach where they are now using early 21st century earthly rocket propulsion. If you tried to visit their home planet that way, the galaxy would accelerate away from you and finally disappear altogether.

The higher dimension also makes it impossible for Earht Plane human beings to ordinarily live there.

PLANET

Home Planet

Large Greys 1 evolved on a planet that orbits a single sun and is a little larger than Earth. From space its colour is similar to Mars. The surface is very arid and there is no ocean, just large lakes the size of small seas, filled with very salty water. Depending on the climate's cycle, there can be ice in the polar regions. Since there are very few clouds and a relatively clear atmosphere (not blue), you can see the stars from the planet's surface during the day.

The atmosphere also ensures the planet's surface, particularly in the equatorial regions, is one of extreme heat and cold. It is also exposed to a much higher degree of gamma radiation than Earth. Large Greys 1 believe that the conditions are unsuitable for most earthly mammalian species.

The planet has plenty of volcanoes, but lacks Earth's system of easily shifting tectonic plates. As such, there are no mountain ranges, just volcanic peaks which can be active or extinct.

The atmosphere is unbreathable for earthly human beings.

Historically, the planet has not always been so arid and in the past benefited from wetter phases, which allowed for the development of the Large Greys 1. It would be difficult for a potentially intelligent but technologically undeveloped species to survive the current (at this sample point) harsh conditions.

Visitors To Planet

Researching this encyclopaedia led to a series of new observations with respect to interspecies interaction. Human fiction frequently depicts different alien species living side by side. Large Greys 1 take pride in their home planet being a good example of such harmonious interactions.

The tell-tale sign of this phenomena is the small number of modified humans who inhabit their planet. Domes have been constructed offering different atmospheric conditions suitable for various species, and one of these domes has human beings in it. Alas, gravity is not so adjusted. Human visitors have to contend with local gravity approximately 1.4 times greater than that of Earth. As such, human adaptation is easier when compared to other species designed for a home planet with even less gravity (e.g. Mars size at 0.4 times that of Earth).

If someone wanted to astrally project to a single location where a variety of alien species can be found, then the home planet of Large Greys 1 would be a destination of choice. Irritatingly, there is so much new information to absorb, it would take more than a human lifetime to achieve all the research.

Most of the species on the planet were developed from samples such as sperm and egg which were DNA-code-mapped to produce a digital copy. So the introduced species in the domes were not imported as living animals, instead they were recreated from copied DNA. Combined with some local adaptations, all the sample species were then locally re-grown. This is important because a physical body from one dimension cannot otherwise easily survive in another dimension. So the humans that were re-engineered here could not survive on the Earht Plane without special protection from the effects of that planet's lower dimension (where you, the reader, are).

Meeting these re-engineered humans quickly reveals a time distortion wherein time for them seems to operate more slowly than it does on Earth.

A fuller exploration of the many observable life forms is located in the chapter on the Large Greys 1 domes.

Accommodation

As the climate on the Large Greys 1 home planet became less hospitable, they started living in either enormous greenhouses or underground. With the population mostly living under cover, they similarly developed an almost completely indoor agricultural system.

Within these accommodation units very little space is devoted to resting or personal possessions. Yet anything a Large Grey 1 might need is available. Life for Large Greys 1 centres around live-work locations.

SPECIES

The reason for the similarity between various species of Greys is twofold: F*irstly*; some of them share common evolutionary ancestors. S*econdly;* where they do not have a common ancestor, they exemplify a good convergent design solution. A helpful analogy is how earthly manufacturers of different automobiles or phones often end up with similar-looking products. Not because they have the same designer, but because their design fulfils a common need.

Insects

Since Large Greys 1 are fundamentally derived from insects, they share many common features with Small Greys 1. So even though they don't have a common ancestor, the respective evolution of their bodies was driven by similar intentions, hence the similar results.

In addition, the harsh environments they both developed and operated in made their similarly robust bodies a necessity.

General Anatomy

A Large Greys 1 is typically slightly taller than a human being at around 2 m (7 ft), whilst some are around 3 m (10 ft) and up to 4 m (13 ft).

They have large heads and large compound eyes. This particular sub-species has a humanoid face and breathes through its mouth or nose. By contrast, other Grey species breathe through the sides of their abdomens or have a pair of large eyes.

Arms tend to be of similar length to the legs. Hands and feet have relatively long digits.

Multi-Capability Lungs

Since a standard human being could not survive in the Large Greys 1 home atmosphere, this might suggest that Large

Greys 1 would be uncomfortable in an atmosphere more appropriate to human beings. But Large Greys 1 have adapted to operate within a variety of different atmospheres, and even briefly in fluids.

Very Large Brains

Comparing a Large Grey 1 brain to a human brain is like comparing a human brain to a chimpanzee's. A rough estimate would place it at three to five times larger.

Another difference is the composition of the brain. A human brain is essentially a neural network constructed within fat cells. A Large Grey 1 brain uses a combination of fat and an unknown fluid tissue, plus fibres that are like muscle. The result is a brain that moves as it functions.

More astounding is how a Large Grey 1 brain can operate without being tethered to the main nervous and vascular systems. Parcels of brain tissue can move around within its skull without being attached to anything, yet still contribute to the body's overall functioning.

Telepathic Mind Control

Large Greys 1 have the telepathic ability to take over and remotely operate another body with considerable ease. Similarly, they can mimic the functions of other species' brains by reconfiguring parts of their own.

A skill that Large Greys 1 are particularly good at is knocking out weak, less aware minds. They are very adept at erasing memories, or even implanting them. This is not a unique skill. Most advanced alien races have access to it. It's just that Large Greys 1 are particularly good at it.

Counter-intuitively, their telepathic skills can actually make it harder to maintain long communications with them. Whilst telepathy is a universal language, there appears to be conceptual adaptations of it that the human mind finds difficult to grasp. For example, it is easy for Large Greys 1 to impart instructions, but more challenging to create meaningful dialogue.

CULTURE

Astral Science

Large Greys 1 see themselves as part of a great co-creation scheme in which they play a small but nevertheless important part. Most of them experience the universe they live in as an aspect of the Astral World. They perceive an integral relationship between the real and illusory worlds. Interwoven into this awareness is a culture driven by scientific advances and exploration. This world view is one to which less advanced human beings can readily relate.

The main difference between Large Greys 1 and human beings is that the former experience an energetic duality while the latter experience a more physical singular world. For example, humans devote much of their day to imagining and contemplating, whereas Large Greys 1 experience a far greater sense of "knowing."

Humans often speculate that science could ultimately replace religion. This is exactly what Large Greys 1 experience. Human science and religions can learn a great deal from this race. The easiest way to get insights into their advances is to observe some of the following differences:

- Large Greys 1 replace priests with scientists and tutors.
- No Large Greys 1 would ever blindly follow a belief.
- There is no potentially angry God to worry about, just an unconditional playful presence.
- No sin is possible, though there remains plenty of potential for ignorant or primitive behaviour.

- All astral science observations are kept as accurate and up-to-date as possible.
- There is no reliance on old scriptures as such, though they may be consulted for reference.
- Physical life is a joy to experience and should be fun.
- There are many other known alien species to interact with.

Since Large Greys 1 know themselves to be part of the super-consciousness, they are also aware of the intentions driving the universe they experience. They are of the view that they should help the super-consciousness experience oneness with its creations, and that this experience should derive from the consciousness of those who have been created. Achieving this challenging scientific feat requires endlessly refining the connection between the Creator's World and the physical world.

Government

Large Greys 1 provide a useful model for how an advanced civilisation governs itself. The first major difference with early 21st century human society is that there is no need to physically control the population. Thus, a legal system is not necessary.

All advanced alien societies use some form of sub-god which is substantially fleshed out so that such a consciousness can guide them. In broad terms, the populace all want the same thing, yet with plenty of individualism. Theirs is not a drone culture.

By virtue of energetically fleshing out their sub-god, Large Greys 1 have a good collective understanding of what other members of their society are up to. You could use the analogy of a behavioural GPS through which everyone has broad access. Such a relatively high mutual awareness is common in many advanced societies, although not mandatory.

The sub-god normally energises one member of Large Greys 1 society (usually female) to be its physical embodiment, equivalent to an actual living god. By comparison, other advanced alien societies might use more than one living embodiment, whilst others need none. Should a physical embodiment die, another is ready to take its place.

The advantage of a living physical embodiment is that it acts as a sort of loving processor. If you need to ask a sub-god a question, you could direct it through the living embodiment. A physical meeting would be unnecessary since there is a constant telepathic link with rarely any downtime.

The conceptually challenging part of this arrangement is that individually Large Greys 1 have plenty of different opinions on subjective matters, but little difference on objective factual ones. Yet any manifestation of individuality instantly affects every other member of the society. In principle this could dilute everyone's individuality. So to retain their individuality, members of society make a conscious effort to exert their unique differences.

Astrally connecting to the Large Greys 1 physical leader is a pleasant experience as she is emotionally much warmer than other members of the populace. It is like being connected into a network with access to every member of the society.

In summary, the overall effect of this form of government is that the Large Greys 1 society operates as a sort of commune directed by group consensus and high awareness.

Competitive Advancement

Most human beings see competition as fun, and enjoy finding out who is best at a given activity.

Many advanced alien cultures also find competition entertaining. By adopting artificial limitations they can enter into a struggle for success, the outcome of which is uncertain.

Large Greys 1 take pleasure in the limitations created by adopting physical form. They find it entertaining to regain awareness while simultaneously choosing to block it. For them, operating physical bodies in this environment is highly stimulating and fun. They also enjoy competing with each other while remaining within their central principle of advancing the common good.

Compared to human beings, Large Greys 1 put far more emphasis on intellectual success as opposed to physical success.

Time Travel Technology

Large Greys 1 are (at this sample point) at the stage in their developmental evolution in which transcending time has become a regular practice.

Souls have no difficulty transcending time because they exist in the Creator's World where there is no time. Only adventures in the lower Astral World and their physical planes enable souls to experience the illusion of time. Large Greys 1 have recently succeeded in understanding how to physically materialise almost anywhere in space-time.

This technological advance represents a major milestone for any civilisation because it enables that species to contribute to the seeding of planets with physical life forms. Large Greys 1 are amongst the group of advanced aliens who work with the Creators (who are aspects of the Creator) to initiate the evolution of species on potentially habitable planets.

The main method is to transform existing matter (e.g. Air or water) into space-time ships and occupants. Then, after visitation, to transform the ships and occupants back into matter. This allows a team of specialists to contribute to the development of whole eco-systems across millions of years.

For example, Large Greys 1 supplied images of time-space ships that their specialists materialised on new planets. Whilst wearing protective suits, they introduced microbes into that environment's water or similar medium. They returned perhaps millions of years later to study the results and encourage helpful mutations.

They were using a duality version of time travel. Instead of transporting their physical bodies to a new location, they recreated new bodies at their desired location. There are various permutations of how this duality is operated. For example, they can place their current body into a deep sleep and then animate the future one.

Entering into the past at a low dimension involves operating in a different time zone where time is typically running faster. Whilst their current body would be asleep for perhaps the equivalent of an Earth hour or two, the past manifestation could be the equivalent of 30 to 40 years if required. Variations depend upon relative dimensions, and in this context a manifestation in the relative past may be an expendable one.

INTERACTION WITH HUMAN BEINGS

Scientific Research

Large Greys 1 are interested in the development of a great many species. Their souls regularly manifest in many of those species. Thus, humankind easily falls within the scope of their investigation and experimental modifications. The research can be conveniently categorised as follows:

Genetic Improvements. There are endless adjustments to a species' DNA to improve it. If, for example, adjustments are delivered via benign engineered viruses, then a whole population can be quietly improved. Human beings can then be temporarily abducted in order to monitor the effects of modifications.

Proposed Improvements. Obviously it would be rash to unleash an improvement upon the human population without first testing it. Accordingly, improvements are tested within laboratories, then on sample human beings. Large Greys 1 were asked if they held samples of complete human beings for laboratory experimentation. The answer was "yes," but that no one was there against their conscious will. This differs from where human beings are borrowed for testing, and their agreement only exists at a higher level. Thus they are unconscious of any physical acquiescence.

Note that sometimes some specific human beings are taken from Earth and their consciousness then allowed to operate at a higher level. Those humans are then able to consciously consent to experiments. When these humans are returned to Earth their consciousness reverts to a lower state, in which they would object to participating in such experiments. So for their own comfort, memories of the experiments are usually suppressed.

Awareness Upgrades. Large Greys 1 know how to enhance a species' energetic awareness. However, without the consciousness successfully incorporating that new thinking process, the human specimen could be rendered paranoid or listless. Understanding how to deal with additional sensitivity leads to higher awareness, as opposed to overload. Accordingly, many human beings are contacted or even abducted in order to further consciousness-awareness research.

Higher Awareness Education

Large Greys 1 are enthusiastic teachers of higher awareness. Anyone prepared to engage with them and follow directions will be entertained and greatly assisted.

A small minority of early 21st century human beings are in sufficient rapport with Large Greys 1 that they receive physical visitations. A larger minority have the option to engage in astral visitation, which can be achieved at almost any time. For the remaining majority of the population, little or no contact will be possible in the early 21st century. This is because their minds are considered too immature or underdeveloped to engage in such interactions.

Large Greys 1 train selected human minds by becoming present in that human body's energy system and thus influence the neural processing through a temporary pairing process. If this is occurring, that human body will probably sense a Large Grey 1 overlapping it like a benign ghost. Alternatively, if the Grey consciousness is less well integrated, the human mind will experience poor functionality.

A useful side effect of this pairing process is that the human mind can to some extent experience being a Large Grey 1 and access some of its memories. The result is akin to what would occur if a dog's consciousness were given the insight of its human master. Some aspects will be comprehended, whilst others simply not understood.

E07 Smart Plants 1

INTRODUCTION

On some planets similar to Earth, plants are the highest life form. In some instances they have even learnt to "walk"; an evolutionary step not taken by plants on Earth. The nearest comparison would be the fictional "Triffids" (walking, semi-intelligent, venomous carnivores with a preference for human flesh). Researching this encyclopaedia has yet to uncover a "Triffid", though more plausible evolutionary outcomes have emerged.

Smart Plants 1 is a good example of what occurs when a plant develops a more sophisticated nervous system and cognitive processing ability akin to that of an animal. At an astral level, all plants have consciousness, and to some extent you can have a rudimentary telepathic conversation with them.

The spiritual consciousness of earthly plants equates to approximately 10% that of human beings. Typical Earth animals' spiritually equates to 25% to 40% of a human being. Apes are around 40% or more. Whereas, the spiritual consciousness of Smart Plants 1 can equate to 100% of human beings. In the greater universe there are some plant races which equate to 150% to 200 %, making them much more sophisticated than human beings.

LOCATION

Smart Plants 1 appear to reside on more than one planet in the Milky Way. Similar to how Greys have been evolved more than once, so too have these species. With some further improvements in mapping, it should be possible to identify more precisely where they can be found. Researching this encyclopaedia uncovered three example planets where they appear.

Similar Dimension

These three example planets appear to have the same dimensions as the Earht Plane, but actual physical travel to them might require a human being to move into a higher dimension. So inhabiting a planet where Smart Plants 1 reside is somewhat challenging for humans.

PLANETS

Smart Plants 1 have been evolved in more or less the same form across three separate planets. In principle they could be described as versions 1, 2, and 3. Since across the three planets the species are so remarkably similar, they can be considered to be near-enough the same. In addition, the soul groups which energise and animate them are identical.

Smart Plants 1 were introduced to all three planets by a genetic manipulation of the existing species.

Home Planet 1

Home Planet 1 is the planet most suited to Smart Plants 1. The defining feature is a healthy rotation which produces a comfortable day-and-night pattern. The planet also appears to be in orbit around a big object similar in size to Saturn or Jupiter. The distance from its nearest sun is proportionate to that of Venus to Earth. Overall, there are warm, pleasant days, followed by very long nights.

The planet is mostly landmass with a small number of inland seas or large unconnected lakes. The equatorial regions appear arid and desert-like. The temperate regions are lusher, but still fundamentally on the dry side. There are also freezing polar regions which are uninhabitable. The planet is approximately

80% the size of Earth. The atmosphere appears to have a low oxygen level.

Home Planet 2

Home Planet 2 is a low-rotation planet roughly the size of Mars and about the same distance from its sun as Earth. The immediate impression is that the atmosphere is not suited to animal life at all.

The slow rotation has led many of the plant species to learn to walk. The middle of the planet's sunny side is too hot and arid to support life, whilst the dark side freezes and locks up most of the water. Plants have learnt how to move themselves in order to stay in an optimum amount of sunlight and a sufficiently moist location. As a result, many plants constantly migrate.

There is occasional rain, but not much surface water. Rain seems to mostly fall near the edge of the dark far side of the planet.

This scenario does not favour tall, deep-rooting plants such as trees. Instead, for example, patches of mobile moss-like creatures engage in mass migrations. The sight can be equated to a green, threadbare carpet moving slowly across a landscape which looks very stony with little soil.

Home Planet 3

Home Planet 3, the third home planet where this species was introduced, is an altogether strange place. It was probably once Earth-like with its own moon. That moon, however, appears to have had a very irregular orbit. It ended up crashing into the planet and destroying almost all life.

Home Planet 3 is now very rocky and volcanic. Like Home Planet 2, it rotates slowly, gradually shifting habitable regions. Thus, most life forms either hibernate for many earth years or move with the rotation.

A hostile environment likewise promotes mobility. For example, hot volcanic springs often open up seemingly everywhere spewing out hot mud and rocks.

The atmosphere, rich in carbon dioxide, is poisonous to humans. Since Smart Plants 1 are well adapted to such a hostile environment, they were introduced following the earlier moon-crash catastrophe.

SPECIES

Plant Adaptations

Photosynthesis, the conversion of the sun's energy into food and more plants, is the fundamental organic process of plants. Much in the way that human beings can live off both plants or animals, Smart Plants 1 likewise draw nutrients from other plants. This strategy is particularly advantageous in an environment where moisture and good soil are in short supply. By raiding other plants that have collected vital nutrients and water, Smart Plants 1 can themselves photosynthesise more efficiently.

Another helpful advance is the ability of Smart Plants 1 to pump fluid around their bodies. They use a combination of capillary action and squeezing their fluid tubes so as to force liquid around their bodies. This both aids circulation and creates a hydraulic action which enables limbs to be moved.

Since conditions on Smart Plants 1 planets are not very hospitable, there is an on-going need to move to better locations. Plants that can move around have a huge advantage.

The final major adaptation is intelligence. Determining where to move to is a lot easier when you have a mind that can make decisions and manage actions.

E07 Smart Plants 1

Anatomy

Smart Plants 1 can typically grow up to 3 m (10 ft) tall, though 2 m (7 ft) is more common. They have roots which are spread laterally in roughly equal proportion to their height. Their appearance is similar to a leek with relatively broad leaves growing from the centre.

Smart Plants 1 are bisexual (both male and female) with the ability to extend a male inseminating stem into the female receptors of neighbouring plants. There appear to be certain seasons or phases for this procreative activity.

Smart Plants 1 have no eyes or ears, though they are quite sensitive to light and can detect vibration.

The species has a neural network running throughout their bodies, but no obvious brain. Thinking is conducted using a non-physical brain which transmits an array of additional senses to the plant. So, for example, a plant can sense prey or nutrients even though it cannot see them. In effect, it clairvoyantly perceives the world around it.

Diet

Smart Plants 1 are carnivorous in that they ingest other plants and on occasion even the bodies of deceased members of their own species. This is similar to animal carnivores who can achieve complete sustenance by eating other animals. Nevertheless, photosynthesis remains the primary activity of Smart Plants 1. They have a lot in common with the earthly Venus Flytrap which derives nutrients not otherwise available in the soil in which it is rooted.

To some extent farming is employed, whereby lesser plants are encouraged to grow. Smart Plants 1 can stand on top of them extracting nutrients and moisture. Lesser plants can be "milked" in the same way humans extract nutrients from grazing animals without killing them.

CULTURE

Gentle Spiritualism

Smart Plants 1 are highly aware astrally and spiritually, which is a common feature of most advanced races. However, they manifest no real imagination of their own, nor boredom either for that matter. For the most part they are happy to just exist and try to be at one with their environment. In a very gentle way, they are quite inquisitive.

Technologically Assisted

No sign of any independent technological development at all could be detected. This contrasts with most other advancing races who at least use some tools. However, Smart Plants 1 do possess technological equipment, albeit donated by other aliens.

The most interesting mechanical donation is a machine that aids putting a body into stasis so that the user can visit other planets and dimensions for longer periods (e.g. A human lifetime). The result is that on Earth you can encounter human beings who possess a parallel Smart Plant 1 body that is in stasis on its home planet.

Non-Physical Literature and Arts

Smart Plants 1 enjoy importing imagined things in ways similar to human beings; e.g. Following a visitor's story. However, imagination tends to clutter the universal language of telepathy, so is potentially unhelpful to their communication. Fortunately, since Smart Plants 1 are fundamentally not very imaginative they can easily switch it off so as to regain their full telepathy.

On their own, Smart Plants 1 have relatively primitive and uninteresting fantasies. However, they long ago discovered that the universe contains many interesting things such as human fantasies, culture, literature, and arts. For example, some assisting

Smart Plants 1 professed their pleasure for JK Rowling's "Harry Potter," as well as works by Plato.

So whilst Smart Plants 1 have no real imagination or much home-grown entertainment, they enthusiastically import it. This makes them appear relatively cultured in a way that early 21st century human beings can relate to.

INTERACTION WITH HUMAN BEINGS

Nothing Physical

Smart Plants 1 possess donated space vehicles, having no possibility of creating anything so advanced themselves. But the operation of such craft is limited by the donor aliens. For the time being, Earth appears to be off-limits as nothing of much use could be accomplished by visiting it.

On the other hand, Smart Plants 1 (or rather the higher beings which manifest through them) enjoy visiting Earth as living human beings. So in this respect their souls contribute to the human population.

E08 Lobsters 1

INTRODUCTION

Lobsters 1 are an example of an underwater fluid-breathing species. The majority of advanced aliens at lower dimensions breathe a gas atmosphere of some sort. Some also have the ability to breathe under water as well as above it. Others are more like fish and can only breathe fluid. Finally, there are even some advanced aliens who have engineered bodies which do not need to breathe or consume organic substances to fuel themselves.

A technologically-advanced underwater species is far less common than its land equivalent. Attempting technological advancement under water makes development of electrical technology, for example, difficult. Aliens that live in water (or similar fluids) can easily evolve spiritually, but will initially find themselves technologically disadvantaged.

Underwater-dwelling aliens can compensate for this by advancing their astral projection skills and thereby meet other alien races who will share technology with them. So instead of being handicapped by living in water, the shared technology allows them to make important technological leaps.

LOCATION

Higher Dimension

Lobsters 1 reside at a higher dimension, one ordinarily invisible to human beings. They nevertheless can relate very well to what life on the Earht Plane is like since their physical environment is not that dissimilar.

The difference between their life and a typical human being is that their world easily feels more alive. For example, most early

21st century human beings barely notice the living air they breathe or the water they drink unless it is infused with an artificial stimulant. By comparison, Lobsters 1 find it difficult not to constantly be aware of the living water they reside in.

PLANET

Lobsters 1 planet is mostly ocean, plus a small amount of scattered land mass. There appears to be very little rain, the result being that the land is very arid and inhospitable. By contrast, the ocean is teeming with life.

From space the planet looks clouded over with a white, light-grey appearance. The atmosphere is warm, which makes the sea relatively warm.

Evolutionary Dominance

Lobsters 1 is not the largest animal in its ocean, but it is the cleverest. There are a number of larger fish-like creatures that prey upon it. Luckily, Lobsters 1 learnt how to defend itself and became very successful.

To understand how Lobsters 1 defend themselves, picture a large stick evolving into a spear and you'll get a reasonable understanding of how they initially "got ahead." Much in the same way that stone-age people developed spears and managed to kill any predator that threatened them, Lobsters 1 came to dominate their environment.

Shallow Ocean

The majority of the ocean on the planet is relatively shallow and warm. Lobsters 1 normally dwell on the bottom and like to see the sunlight above. As such, their habitat covers roughly two thirds of the available ocean.

SPECIES

Crustacean

This species is remarkably similar to earthly prawns or lobsters. They are equipped with a strong calcium shell which could probably resist small bullets. They also have a much better brain than earthly crustaceans.

Lobsters 1 can grow to roughly three or four times the size of a human being, though one-and-a-half times larger is more common. The head is enlarged to accommodate the brain.

Whilst Lobsters 1 normally breathe water, if required, they can carry a mouthful of water to walk on land. Their tails have shortened to accommodate upright walking on land with hind legs developed to carry the whole body weight. In the same way that human divers might emerge from the ocean carrying aqualungs on their backs, Lobsters 1 can carry a water-oxygenating pack to enable remaining on land for longer periods.

Their anatomy has adapted to a high-protein diet, which accounts for a larger brain than that of humans, but one not split into left and right lobes. Their eyesight seems relatively poor compared to humans and they have no ears.

Their pincers are somewhat small and are now in many ways redundant. Lobsters 1 instead rely on forearms and hands to manipulate tools and objects.

Telepathy

The telepathy of this race is particularly strong. They have developed the ability to mislead predators and prey. A predator could be fooled into not attacking, whilst prey can be encouraged to offer itself up. Their telepathic skills could easily make a human being physically ill if Lobsters 1 so desired.

The reason for this well-developed telepathic ability is that Lobsters 1 have an advanced non-physical brain. This allows them to integrate their minds into a powerful collective consciousness. For example, if one of them can see something, they all have the option to see it.

Land Adaptation

Lobsters 1, out of curiosity as much as anything else, wanted to explore the land beyond the ocean. So they would hold their fluid breath and crawl around the terrain. This came to the attention of visiting aliens and tentative interactions resulted. The Lobsters 1 species then embarked on a widespread investigation of all accessible alien races, often making friends.

Their alien friends gave them access to the sea-creature equivalent of aqualung technology which enabled them to stay on land for long periods. Combining this with new discoveries up how to alter their body's anatomy, Lobsters 1 got access to the land. Body modifications included shortened tails, plus they lengthened and strengthened their hind legs to enable biped walking. Their hind legs thus developed huge bulges to accommodate the necessary muscles, so have parallels with the anatomy of earthly grasshoppers.

At the time this research was conducted, the overall results were a partial success. This species is relatively heavy, which makes walking on land difficult. However, this adaptation was particularly useful for space travel, and so on balance their adaptations have proved to be an enormous success.

Other Anatomy

As previously mentioned, Lobsters 1 have poor vision due to their relatively undeveloped eyes. They also have no ears. Yet, in an ocean environment they are very sensitive to electrical impulses so they have a substitute form of sight reaching far into the distance and operating around solid objects.

On land their vision is even less effective, although they can see the auras of everything in their vicinity. Due to their excellent telepathy, if a land-operating being such as a future human saw one, a Lobsters 1 would be able to see what the future human could see.

The Lobsters 1 digestive system makes them feel almost permanently hungry. They could have dispensed with this impediment, but have chosen to retain it because they prefer feeling hungry. They pointed out that food tastes better if you maintain a strong appetite.

Reproduction is remarkably similar to earthly prawns and shrimps. Since the young are well protected, only small numbers need to be produced. They are brought up in well supervised nursery areas.

CULTURE

Space Travel

All advanced alien species share technologies, in which respect Lobsters 1 have been considerable beneficiaries. They are eager to learn new things and generally get on particularly well with most egg-laying races. The result is that Lobsters 1 have access to some of the best space-time craft technology available.

One limitation is that they are not well adapted to many adjacent dimensions and find it difficult to operate in them. For example, travelling through space at a lower dimension is very unsafe for them as they have a relatively poor sense of hazardous objects such as small meteors.

Space travel in a Lobsters 1 water-filled spacecraft capsule is very different when compared to a gas-atmosphere-filled one. Gas capsules are relatively quiet with faint humming sounds in the background. Water-filled capsules have a much deeper and pervasive hum. In addition, when travelling through space, the water gives off a crackling sound as atomic particles strike the fluid molecules.

At the point in time this research was conducted, their space travel shows a poor safety record. Getting splattered across space is commonplace. An Earth analogy is the frequency with which small children fall off their bicycles. A side effect of Lobsters 1 space travel accidents is that their souls end up having lives on planets nearby to wherever their bodies got smashed to bits. In the case of accidents near Earth, Lobsters 1 are more likely to reincarnate as a human, because earthly lobsters are too primitive.

Land Adaptation for Advancing Technologies

Lobsters 1 bodies have been adapted to operate more easily on land, thus they can deal with technologies and activities that do not work well in water (e.g. Fire, electricity, servicing spacecraft). Otherwise there is not much reason to wander out of water given their planet's substantially barren surface.

Some land-based industrial facilities were evident during research, but since Lobsters 1 prefer to remain immersed in water, such facilities are few in number and used as little as possible.

Family Orientated

From a spirit and soul perspective, Lobsters 1 truly know each other very well. For humans, it's like knowing everyone else on the planet. The physical population of Lobsters 1 is about 10% that of the human race so their smaller numbers make the feat slightly easier.

Due to their high level of connectedness, they are very much at one with their offspring. They can impart their species' accumulated learning and wisdom without the tedious formal earthly education required of humans. The result is that youngsters can contribute to their society from an early age.

Very Curious About Other Worlds

The combined effect of their physical evolution and spiritual advancement has made Lobsters 1 very curious about other worlds. So for every one Lobsters 1, there are approximately five of their soul groups alive in other bodies on other worlds. That's why they have even reached as far as Earth.

Because of their interaction with other worlds and cultures, they return to their original planet with useful knowledge. The advances they bring back are both technological and cultural. As described, they are proud of having adopted education without formal learning. Young human beings attend schools and universities, taking years to learn subjects. Lobsters 1 can achieve the same learning almost instantaneously. They would like to feed this ability back into the other worlds they visit.

INTERACTION WITH HUMAN BEINGS

Nothing Physical

Lobsters 1 are not well adapted to descending to the Earht Plane dimension. Even with the aid of spacecraft, they need to keep their distance from this dimension.

Accidental Visitors ?

The intention to explore the Earht Plane is one of their many interests. Observing Earth from afar is something they do regularly, albeit at considerable risk. Their spacecraft have to travel and orbit at very high speeds with a high risk of collision with objects such as asteroids or meteors.

Should a Lobsters 1 explorer get killed in the space-time near the Earth, they are likely to get drawn into its life forms. For example, if a Lobsters 1 was studying a whale and had a fatal space accident, it could easily end up being born into a whale. Such is the effect of the intention.

E08 Lobsters 1

So it comes to pass that every now and then one of these souls gets incorporated into human form, usually making that human being quite gifted, although feeling relatively out of place. As visitors, Lobsters 1 deeply want to connect with everyone, unlike many aliens who find connecting with earthlings tedious. However, even a soul with a strong Lobsters 1 connection will often ultimately find the earthling connection draining and will want to have regular breaks from it.

E09 Future Humans 1

INTRODUCTION

Future Humans 1 are but one species of earthly (alien) humanoids you can in principle physically encounter. Since the nature of their visits to early 21st century Earth have many similarities to visits from non-earthly humanoid aliens, Future Humans 1 are categorised as advanced aliens.

There are many different alien visitors to Earth who have a humanoid appearance, and they are often categorised as Nordics. However, it is more accurate to define "Nordics" as a particular species in their own right. Therefore, whilst Nordics and Future Humans 1 bear similarities, they are not the same species.

Multiple Sample Points

Some species of Future Humans 1 were evolved directly from the early 21st century human population. Whilst in other cases they were evolved from an earlier "sample point" of the human population. Combined with some cross-breeding and DNA modification, Future Humans 1 species are for the most part not genetically the same as the early 21st century human population.

Humans Or Nordics ?

Some Future Humans 1 species appear to have been developed by cross-breeding them with other human-like species. The different mixes between the various Nordic species and human beings, for example, often make it difficult to distinguish between the various sub-species.

If you have an intelligent, warm interaction with advanced aliens, they will normally give you helpful answers to such genetic questions. Conversely, less advanced species such as early 21st century human beings will mostly be unaware of how their physical form has been genetically engineered.

Relatively Few Common Souls

Realising that many different types of humanoid beings have been evolved, there is the temptation to try and identify a "pure human being." However, this would overlook the fact that human beings are energised (given life) by different groups of souls, who in turn adopt and create human spirit forms. So whilst human spirit forms appear to be human, their inner essence can be derived from a variety of different soul groups. Such soul groups in turn can also manifest as different alien beings.

Once you have observed that souls which occupy and give life to human bodies also manifest as aliens, the possibility of categorising anything as essentially a pure human being becomes impossible. No evidence of a soul that only manifests as an earthly human being was found during the course of this research.

Future Humans 1

The Future Humans 1 examined in this chapter are substantially derived from the existing earthly DNA pool, which is why they look extremely similar to 21st century human beings. In the next chapter, human beings with more substantial alien DNA modifications (Alternative Humans 2) will be examined.

LOCATION

To find Future Humans 1 you need only to astrally project forward in time on Earth to meet them. They can also be found permeating the universe as time progresses. So if you wondered whether the human race manages to travel to other galaxies, the answer is yes.

Dimensional Differences

The energetic frequency (for want of a better word) which manifests physical matter in one section of space-time is usually different from one moment to the next. When interacting with Future Humans 1, you are likely to become aware that there is a small dimensional difference. This dimensional difference can make it problematic for one group of humans to live in another environment.

200 Years Forward

Human beings are still largely confined to living on Earth. Astral projection to other planets is commonplace and they have many technological and cultural exchanges with alien races.

500 Years Forward

Human beings are no longer largely confined to Earth and have colonies springing up elsewhere in the physical universe. Other alien races are instrumental in helping this occur.

1000 Years Forward

There appears to be a desire to significantly de-populate the Earth and live elsewhere, thereby returning Earth to a more natural state. Since some alien races have a genetic code library for extinct species such as dinosaurs, it is possible to recreate such species.

PLANET

Taking a sample point from around 2500 AD, Earth appears as follows:

No War

Human beings have finally ceased slaughtering each other. Wars previously tended to occur along tribal or cultural divides in an effort to secure territory and resources. Once a general recognition that "we are all one" sinks into human consciousness, the urge to resolve issues by killing each other becomes obsolete.

The "we are all one" mentality is the reason why advanced aliens are not interested in invading Earth, and why less advanced warlike humans should be left within their confines until a higher awareness takes hold.

Inevitably though, human conflicts still arise in an enlightened environment, even in 2500 AD. The principle solution is social mobility whereby the populace is free to choose which country to live in, as well as to allow for a choice of governments and social systems.

Huge Human Population

The human population appears to have expanded in excess of ten-fold. There have been enormous technical advances in the production of food, making most traditional agricultural methods redundant. Food is mostly produced indoors in factory-like buildings. These food factories grow highly nutritious plants and synthetic meats; e.g. Meat grown on slow-moving conveyor belts. Farm animals remain as pets or objects of interest, but are rarely eaten.

The oceans look as if they support a low fish population. It appears that microorganisms in the oceans are intensively harvested, thereby depleting the lower rungs in the food chain. This in turn effects all the animals higher up the food chain, for example, dolphins who rely on a good supply of the fish now have less food available because the fish they fed off are fewer in number.

Cities and settlements are sprawling to the point where oceans often seem to be the only boundaries. Buildings are normally surrounded by and covered in lush vegetation. Seen from space, such cities appear green and forest-like, as opposed to grey-looking cancers on the landscape as seen in the early 21st century. Parts of Earth that currently look brown and desert-like will have multiple urban settlements scattered across them making the planet look greener. From space, fewer rivers are visible, suggesting fresh water is intensively collected.

Transportation has at this point radically changed whereby matter transportation is used, though not quite to the point of commuting by this method. Using matter transportation seems to remain an unsettling method of transport, since for practical purposes it temporarily kills the human body. The chapters on the Grasshoppers 1 astronauts and Big-Eyed Humanoids 1 cover these practical challenges in more detail.

The human population is not clustered along tribal or racial lines, but rather in compatible soul groups. This means that the population looks ethnically very mixed and is clustered into different cultural groups.

Tourist Destination

In the same way that human beings from developed countries holiday and visit less developed countries, aliens visit the developing human beings on Earth. Similarly, just as tourism workers in developing countries have to learn foreign languages (especially English), humans dealing with aliens need to develop excellent telepathic skills. As far as aliens are concerned, though, human telepathic communication still has to develop further, similar to someone speaking broken English.

When aliens depart, they sometimes offer human beings they have befriended the opportunity to travel with them. This practice is not sufficiently widespread, though, to cause the human population to decrease.

Salt Exports

So much seawater has been desalinated that a huge salt surplus has developed. This rock crystal forms a useful material which is exported to aliens, apparently for use in power-generating equipment.

Climate

In the wake of a few major disasters, including volcanoes, meteors, and war, 26th century Earth looks reasonably well looked after. The climate is warmer with sea levels lower than in the early 21st century. So much water has been incorporated into huge urban settlements that the effect on sea levels is that of a mini-ice age.

Polar ice caps look significantly shrunken, and as mentioned before, from space the planet looks greener. Locking up large amounts of water in agriculture to increase the available land mass seems like a sensible proposition.

Time Travel Availability

By around the 26th century, human beings appear to have access to some limited forms of physical time travel. Others have access to a more advanced version of it courtesy of advanced alien friends.

Future Humans 1 manifest themselves in Earth's past, but do so with care and purpose.

SPECIES

As previously stated, this chapter is focusing upon human beings that have principally been evolved from the existing human gene pool. By this point they have acquired access to time travel, and thus visit Earth in the same way that advanced aliens do.

Education and Upbringing

Future human beings are exposed to higher levels of positive stimulation and it appears that this helps evolve a species. Future Humans 1 appear to have larger brains than their descendants today by around 20% to 50%. There is a strong educational emphasis on personal improvement: "Be the best you can be."

Education continues throughout the lives of Future Humans 1 so that they are always learning new things. By comparison, early 21st century human beings are all too often content to vegetate and resist further development.

Health and Vitality

A better diet has helped make Future Humans 1 generally taller, less inclined to obesity and illness, and altogether healthier. Despite mostly living in densely populated areas, outdoor exercise is preferred to indoor gyms.

Genetic engineering techniques have enabled Future Humans 1 to live longer and look much younger than their human counterparts. Male baldness is optional, and females can grow as much hair as they want. Infertility is almost unknown. Altering eye colour and skin pigments is very popular, including a less popular option to have green skin.

Doctors continue to use surgical procedures and drugs, but healthy well-being is primarily achieved by making patients happier with respect to whatever might have distressed them into illness. Thus, good healthcare places enormous emphasis on dealing with the cause of illness, as opposed to remedial treatment of the symptoms. Being able to see and understand auras is a fundamental aspect of all medical training.

Reproduction

It is unusual for children to be unintentionally or haphazardly born. Instead, parents normally know the children they are bringing into the world before conceiving them. Natural births are the preference and are mostly pain free.

Telepathy

Telepathic development is roughly half-way between that of more telepathically-advanced aliens, and early 21st century humankind. Most Future Humans 1 would be skilled enough to look into the eyes of early 21st century human beings and have telepathic conversations with them.

The practical effect of this is that you can stay in touch with anyone wherever they are, though video phones are still also used. Lying or concealing secrets is difficult.

CULTURE

Downsides

Future Humans 1 are surprisingly intolerant of defects or inappropriate behaviour in each other, similar to how movies occasionally portray future societies as relentlessly focussed on self-improvement. In fiction, defective humans are euthanized (something the Nazis practiced in the 20th century on their own population), whereas in the 26th century they are repaired as far as possible. An effect of this intolerance is that human self-expression in the form of handicaps is severely frowned upon.

Future Humans 1 have a mild inferiority complex. This is not surprising given their considerable access to more advanced alien races with whom they compare themselves.

Future Humans 1 are in general quite loving towards their early 21st century ancestors, but as already described, they are less tolerant of community members who fail to adopt the culture of continual betterment. This is because the group emotional energy affects everyone, and assistance is offered to anyone in need or distress. There is little tolerance of anyone who does not accept this approach because an individual's suffering will affect the wider community.

This intolerance is on balance quite reasonable under their prevailing circumstances. When a society is emotionally and energetically well connected, it seeks to look after its members. When a society is seeking to better its overall higher awareness, the enhanced connectedness demands everyone participate. Consequently, any individual who refuses to participate affects everyone else. The price of a society achieving awareness is that everyone has to participate, or leave. However, 21st century human beings might potentially perceive this intolerance as a downside.

The perverse fun of physical danger and severe emotional distress relished by 21st century humans has been largely removed. So whilst Future Humans 1 are a lot happier than their ancestors, observing them suggests that "something is missing." To some extent they compensate for this lack of excitement by taking a great interest in the relatively more exciting lives of their ancestors.

Death

When comparing 21st century human beings with 26th century Future Humans 1, there are stark distinctions on the subject of death.

Most 21st century human beings to some extent abuse their bodies until an accumulation of damage causes death. By contrast, nearly all Future Humans 1 live on average longer and nearly all choose to die in their sleep. There are medications to assist death, but if planned properly, death will occur naturally at a chosen time during sleep.

Future Humans 1 usually die wearing some sort of night clothes and remain in that outfit for the funeral. They are then often placed under a blanket or duvet as if they were still in bed, even though they will now be in a coffin. Funerals can thus be planned in advance and are normally completed on the morning immediately following a death.

People who are close friends or partners often choose to die on the same day. One side effect of this practice is that the historical discrepancy between male and female lifespans has been significantly reduced.

Suicide is robustly discouraged with everyone expected to live life to the fullest potential. To that effect, the causes of suicide are readily identified and addressed.

The 21st century practice of abandoning the elderly into care homes and waiting for them to decay into death is not widespread with Future Humans 1.

Never-Ending Education

As already described, the culture of self-improvement is rampant and well ingrained. There is a clear sense that many advances need to be made. Having largely eliminated most traditional disabilities, there is a community sense that everyone should contribute to self-betterment.

As much as possible, everyone is expected to increase their skills-set. You might assume old people go to night school, for example, but that would overlook the benefit of improved telepathy. With increased telepathic skills, all Future Humans 1 have a working relationship with what could be described as guiding spirits. These guides are devoted to training and assisting the humans they work with. So further education is infused into every conceivable moment in life.

Cultural Effect on Science

In the 21st century, Earth's culture was dominated by North Americans and Europeans, with the Asians working hard to emulate them. By comparison in the 26th century there is considerable access to alien technologies. So human beings now find themselves seeking to emulate more advanced alien races.

Whilst advanced aliens are happy to assist, they do not disclose all potential advances to the still-developing human race.

Cutting-edge technologies all require considerable familiarity with astral science and an awareness of what the super-consciousness has created. So whilst humankind has been significantly modernised, there remains a lot to be accomplished.

A 21st century human mind may speculate that other humanoid races are there to assist humankind, but this is often not the case as not all alien species proactively help.

INTERACTION WITH DESCENDANTS

Principle Objective: Modernisation of Self-Awareness Ability

The project currently underway is to upgrade human awareness so that the ultimate Creator acquires new insights into human awareness, plus a good energetic feedback from human forms back to the Creator. Future Humans 1 and their descendants can deliver many of these new insights to their ancestors. For future human species to achieve this higher awareness, their ancestors (e.g., 21st century humans) must first achieve important advances.

Comprehending the benefits of achieving this objective is beyond the conscious experience of most early 21st century human beings. However, a side effect of improved awareness is obvious enough: improved happiness.

The majority of 21st century human beings have lost touch with what fundamentally makes them happy. Material success brings advances, but greater happiness so far has not been one of them. The motivation that inspired humans to strive for greater material success was ironically the implicit promise that it would make them happier.

One of the most interesting episodes in human history is occurring in the 21st century. A vast ensemble of advanced alien species, including future human beings, has embarked on an active programme to help educate and modernise 21st century humans.

Since human beings are mostly suspicious of advanced aliens, much of this education and modernisation falls to future human beings themselves to deliver. This is typically achieved by small groups of future humans assisting key ancestors such as you, the reader.

Interactive Astral Time Travel

Using astral projection it is relatively easy to go backwards and forwards in time. You, the reader, could, for example, visit ancient Egypt and discover more about how pyramids were used. Or you could visit historically famous people such as Jesus and verify claims made in the scriptures. For the most part such excursions are not "interactive"; i.e. You can look, but your presence doesn't affect what occurs.

Conversely, you can astrally go forward in time and meet more advanced human beings. The advantage of going forward is that it is usually interactive, and you can affect what occurs. What we are now concerned with is interactive connections, where people from the past, present or future interact with each other and influence the course of events.

From the perspective of Future Humans 1, assisting their ancestors is a very important activity. The early 21st century represents the turning point at which it became possible to have significant interactions with key individuals. As Future Humans 1 describe it: "To begin with, their numbers were few. The potential for most of them being wiped out by war or other calamity was disturbingly high. It was unclear who would or would not succeed in embracing the upgrade."

Convergent Outcome

Humans often speculate as to whether their lives are predetermined. Meanwhile, Future Humans 1 have a vested interest in fate bringing them into existence. In simplistic terms, Future Humans 1 exist because there are convergent forces determining human destiny. So whilst the path by which they come to exist has flexibility, the fact that they will exist is certain.

Key individuals in the 21st century are therefore crucial in the chain of events which enable Future Humans 1 to exist. Future Humans 1 as a species are very aware of this.

Individuals Matter

Human history is littered with examples of individuals from all backgrounds who made a difference, be it through small or large actions. Future Humans 1 only exist because each one played their part in helping individuals make a difference, and thus brought their own selves into physical existence.

Future Humans 1 carefully choose and nurture the individuals they will work with. The choice is similar to how an individual might choose a marriage partner. The intent is formed in the Creator's World, and then enacted on the Earht Plane.

Whilst all the individuals Future Humans 1 work with are ultimately expendable, the future humans seek to assist and to some extent protect those with whom they work. It is accepted that some individuals will fail, but that enough will succeed in attaining the necessary higher awareness to make a difference.

Examples of How the Interactions Occur

There are many ways in which human individuals will experience the support and advancement being offered to them.

As described, the main objective is to enable the super-consciousness to be aware of what it is and achieve this by observing itself from different vantage points such as those offered by human beings. Advanced alien races all provide similar yet unique vantage points. Future Humans 1 are simply an example of a new vantage point becoming properly available.

To help achieve this advance, the soul beings who energise Future Humans 1 are also accessing the minds of their ancestors. This gives an ancestor's mind a dual awareness of its present, plus that of a more advanced future. Even if the connection is fleeting, it leaves an imprint on the mind which guides the individual forward. Many other advanced alien races also support this form of advancement.

The energy which lubricates these interactions is unconditional love. For example, Grasshoppers 1 are experts in channelling unconditional love. These advanced alien beings operate in conjunction with Future Humans 1 to enable higher consciousness to manifest in 21st century human beings.

Insights Into the Future

Whenever you, the reader, are working with Future Humans 1, you can experience fragments of their lives. Similarly, you will experience their insights into your life.

For example, when this section of the encyclopaedia was being typed out, a Future Human 1 was working with the author. The Future Human 1 individual had his family meet the author, and they were all happy to enjoy the connection. The Future Human 1 then showed his children what it was like to create a document (this chapter) using a comparatively primitive laptop in which letters had to be manually typed out.

The Future Human 1 then showed the author an equivalent but more modern device which could type out thoughts by reading the user's mind. When a human thinks, electrical pulses are created, allowing these devices to read and interpret the brain's signals. Similarly they can be used to create pictures and paintings because they can interpret visual imagination. Since all brains process thoughts uniquely, mental algorithms of Future Humans 1 are mapped from an early age so that any device uploaded with that map can read that human's mind.

Invention

For any invention to be widely available to Future Humans 1, it must manifest at some point in their past. Thus, an exciting exercise for Future Humans 1 is placing the ideas behind technical innovations in the minds of 21st century human beings.

It is not necessary for a human mind to notice where an idea originated from. As previously observed, many early human beings will perceive they invented such ideas and happily develop them regardless of origins. However, if a human being does become aware of both the process and sources of clever ideas, it inevitably improves the chances of receiving more such ideas.

Higher Awareness

Typical early 21st century human minds are mostly programmed to resist and avoid a great deal of higher consciousness. Even if human beings take significant steps to acquire such abilities, they will repeatedly delay or avoid actualising the new skill.

If you, the reader, wish to test the validity of this fact, you only have to notice how you have awareness of important actions that need to be taken. But curiously, you'll find yourself often distracted from actually taking those actions, or may only do so in a self-sabotaging way.

One of the reasons for this delaying behaviour is as a safety mechanism. Early 21st century human minds are inherently immature. Unless they are moderated by a higher consciousness, bestowing additional ability upon them can have a counter-productive effect. Early 21st century human minds will find that they are only really permitted higher awareness if accompanied by a more advanced consciousness. An analogy would be that of a child only allowed to drive an automobile when accompanied by an adult with the vehicle's keys kept firmly in the control of the adult.

From a practical standpoint, a 21st century human mind will therefore find that only by cooperating with advanced beings will they succeed in achieving higher awareness. The minds of advanced future humans are well placed to provide the necessary guidance and wisdom, and will often do so if you work with them.

Pairing (even briefly) a human mind with that of a more advanced Future Human 1 enables the human mind to exhibit much of the wisdom of its descendant.

Physical Visitation

Future Humans 1 have at this point in time gained access to some rudimentary time-travel technology. However, time travel is not without restrictions and there appear to be curbs as to what is permitted.

By comparison, some advanced alien species who have better access to physical time travel sometimes allow Future Humans 1 to journey with them. These advanced aliens appear to use this access very constructively.

At the point of the first publication of this encyclopaedia, 21st century humankind had rarely observed its near-descendants physically travelling back to visit their patch of space-time. Such visits can easily cause harm and are therefore normally conducted very cautiously with a minimum of intrusion.

To further the objective of keeping a low profile during any visit to the early 21st century, Future Humans 1 usually erase the conscious memories of anyone who might inadvertently observe them.

E10 Alternative Humans 2

INTRODUCTION

Alternative Humans 2 physically appear similar to earthly human beings, but they differ in that they have different DNA. While they regularly visit early 21st century Earth, they do so less than other alien species such as Greys or Nordics.

The many permutations of humanoid life forms make categorising them all an almost infinite activity. Alternative Humans 2 are a good example of typical humanoid life forms, who in a similar way to earthly humans, were evolved from ape-like creatures on a planet with many parallels.

For clarification purposes, the reader physically resides on Earth 1. The primary planet Alternative Humans 2 live on is Earth 2.

Evolving any species is always an experiment. True experimentation involves altering the variables. In the case of Alternative Humans 2, they have been evolved at a higher dimension and with more interventions to accelerate their evolution. This yields similar results to human beings observed on Earth 1, however, the development of Alternative Humans 2 is more rapid.

Key Difference Between Future Humans 1 and Alternative Humans 2

Until the mid-21st century, Earth 1 humans had little awareness of alien races. These developing earthly humans were subjected to energetic forces which discouraged them from properly investigating alien worlds. The result was a human race, that for a long time, developed in perceived isolation from everything else in the universe. So even though humans have enjoyed occasional alien visitations and communications, they nevertheless managed to disregard the greater reality.

The species that became Alternative Humans 2 conversely had a greater degree of interaction with advanced aliens, although not so much as to deprive Alternative Humans 2 of the opportunity to develop in their own way. By comparison, if a race of advanced beings started evolving natives in their own image, the effect on the original culture would be to suppress it. So an experiment to develop an independent culture never has enough room to explore its own course. Alternative Humans 2 had sufficient interactions to know that they would be helped with great advances if they learnt how to recognise what created them and respond to that knowledge. They were also allowed considerable freedom of choice upon how to develop themselves.

For Alternative Humans 2 the "goal posts" were more clearly defined because of the higher degree of alien interaction. Furthermore, due to the higher dimension they inhabit, it was technically easier for them to note the difference between themselves and the ultimate Creator. (It goes without saying that research on the ultimate Creator is continuous and on-going). Compared to Alternative Humans 2, humans on Earth have greater opportunities to discover this approach for themselves. A side effect of this greater latitude is that Earth 1 has more war and general strife.

This situation does not make Alternative Humans 2 better than their Earth 1 counterparts. It merely reflects their different rates of developments. Ultimately, similar results seem to be yielded, and both experimental paths are equally valid.

Alternative Humans 1

Alternative Humans 1 are defined in this encyclopaedia as the ancestors of Alternative Humans 2. The reader may think a chapter on Alternative Humans 1 has been missed, but none was written about them for the first edition of the encyclopaedia because they have not physically visited Earth 1.

It also appears that there seems to have been a sufficient evolution in the species to ultimately warrant treating them separately in this instance.

Alternative Humans 1 did become aware of Earth 1 and astrally explored it. Like early 21st century human beings, though, they were subjected to an energetic blanket which made them apathetic towards such exploration. Hence, astral visits were minimal.

Nevertheless, if the reader wishes to explore this similar, slightly higher dimension human world, it's there. If you visit it at an equivalent point in their development, that would be the period in which everyone became "attached" to their smart phones. It appears that everyone is more intuitive and aware of each other's emotions. Yet their society still functions by maintaining strong social differences between the very rich and the poor. In summary, it's an interesting albeit emotionally disturbing planet to visit.

LOCATION

Parallel Higher Dimension

Alternative Humans 2 live in a similar universe to the one you, the reader, is experiencing. In simplistic terms, if you wish to access a higher dimension, you merely go "up." To reach a parallel dimension, you go "sideways." Finding this parallel higher dimension therefore involves going both up and sideways.

The universe you are experiencing is one set of possibilities playing out. A parallel universe is where a similar but alternative set of possibilities is playing out. Whilst the two parallel universes appear separate, they are really one and the same, just with different configurations.

Picture a Lego kit which can construct two similar yet different houses. It takes nearly all the bricks to make either house, so you can have only one Lego house at any particular moment in space-time. Yet it is possible for both houses to exist provided they do so at different points in space-time.

Alternative Galaxy

This alternative galaxy is located in a similar but subtly different higher dimension, one which some readers would find more vivid. Looking down on the home galaxy, it has close multiple spirals with Earth 2 located around one-third of the radius from the centre. Earth 2 is orbiting a younger star which would normally manifest towards the outside of the spiral. This galaxy appears to be imploding, and solar systems that would otherwise be much further out are being drawn towards the centre.

The galaxy's spirals are also rotating at a much higher velocity.

Surrounding Celestial Bodies

Earth 2 has a number of moons orbiting it. Two are of substantial size and a third one is smaller. There are also a number of large asteroids within their orbits, which will coalesce down to two large moons.

Earth 2 is surrounded by four similar-sized planets. One of them has a smaller orbit and is inhabited at this dimension. However, life there is more primitive and the atmosphere not well suited to Alternative Humans 2.

Further out there is only one "gas giant" planet, plus some other planets constructed from frozen gas and rock. There is a large sun at the centre of their solar system.

Consistent with similar observations at higher dimensions, everything appears closer together compared to the Earht Plane; i.e. There is less space-time separating everything.

PLANET

Planetary Species In General

Compared to Earth 1, Earth 2 looks smaller and warmer with a greater land mass that is primarily clustered into a Pangaea; i.e. A single continent. The planet appears to be full of species that bear similarities to those on Earth, as well as some that don't. Due to lower gravity and higher oxygen levels, flying insects and other animals are able to grow larger. For example, there are very large birds with 6 m (20 ft) wingspans and wasps the size of small earthly cats.

Less familiar species include a sea-dwelling flying jellyfish and sea sponges. The flying jellyfish are mainly encountered near shorelines, and launch themselves out of the water and prey on large insects. Their wings make a deep, distinctive humming sound.

The origin of the species on Earth 2 is based on wide-ranging experiments of how different conditions cause life-forms to become self-aware at higher or lower rates.

Species Progression

The experimental goal is to create a self-aware species which observes the ultimate Creator and provides it with an energetic feedback. From a linear time perspective, these self-awareness observations will always turn out to be experimental. Compared to Earth 1, the speed of developmental progression tends to be higher at higher dimensions.

Earth 2, like Earth 1, was initially a bacteria-dominated planet. Nothing of great sophistication emerged until around 500 million (Earth 1) years after seeding, whereupon the atmosphere was successfully filled with oxygen. Around this point, and approximately three billion years sooner than on Earth 1, multi-celled life-forms were evolved.

Plant species were the first significant life-forms to be evolved, but none became significantly self-aware.

There was more self-awareness success with ocean-dwelling micro-organisms, but as is typically the case, they did not achieve their full potential. Hence, whilst micro-organisms proliferated, they remained simply a rung in the food chain for larger predators.

On land there was considerable success in creating a number of more self-aware insect species. Three very successful self-aware insect-like species emerged in succession, and each was in then turn removed to make way for the next one. It would be like evolving human beings on Earth and then removing them to live elsewhere in order to allow another species the evolutionary room to come forward.

After the self-aware insects, three significant reptilian species were then evolved and removed to live elsewhere, so as to give the next species evolutionary room to come forward. The first self-aware success with the mammals was a bear-like animal with the ability to walk upright and manipulate tools. Humans were evolved next and are similarly-scheduled to be replaced by a species that is something like a cross between a dog and a pig.

Finally, Earth 2 will be reorganised in order to allow the evolution of a "star children" species. An example of "star children" is dealt with elsewhere in this encyclopaedia.

At higher dimensions it is common to develop a succession of more highly evolved species, as opposed to just one. With respect to Earth 1, researching this section pointed to earthly dinosaurs having been, to a limited extent, removed and replicated elsewhere on another world. With them subsequently going on to develop a sophisticated culture. However, in this instance, the dominant species of dinosaur is only a little larger than humankind on Earth 1.

SPECIES

Introduced DNA

Both Earth 1 and Earth 2 humans were evolved with a similar intention to create and experiment with such beings. The biggest difference was that on Earth 2 there was repeated "leap-frogging" of evolutionary advances, accentuated by the introduction of alien DNA.

On Earth 2 there came a point when chimpanzee-like animals had learnt to use sticks and bones as rudimentary tools. A large family of these apes were then implanted with modified embryos so that the next generation could better download new ideas such as fashioning bones and wood into improved tools. The creation of club-like weapons made them the most successful apes on the planet and militarily able to dominate any rival apes. Within about a half-a-dozen generations they were binding rocks to the end of their clubs, creating the start of a stone age. Advances that took thousands of years on Earth 1 were achieved in mere hundreds on Earth 2.

DNA modification using virus technology was the principle method for modifying the general population of Alternative Humans 2 ancestors, as opposed to implanting modified embryos.

As the species evolved towards the Alternative Humans 2 sample point of this encyclopaedia, they developed sufficiently good relations with other alien species to warrant being given DNA modification codes that could be incorporated into the population.

The DNA in many alien races and human beings is composed of the same molecular building blocks. However, introduced alien DNA does not refer to some alternative organic compound and molecules, but instead simply means altering the existing coding or sequences to match the alien version.

Once these alternative human beings had sufficiently developed intellectually, they became very interested to learn about further modifications that they could incorporate into themselves. From then on, introducing alien DNA into the population only required enlightening them as to the relevant coding, and the populace itself then adopted it.

Awareness Evolution

In addition to upgrades delivered by improving their DNA, Alternative Humans 2 were given a multitude of mental programming upgrades, which enabled advanced telepathy. Thus, their brains were configured to make telepathic interactions easier and more refined.

A helpful analogy would be earthly computers and phone technology. DNA upgrades relate to improving the hardware; e.g. A new, improved phone or computer. Whilst the mental upgrades refer to improvements to the software, apps, or computer programs that run on the new phone or computer.

For an ape to invent a wheel, it only needs to allow the idea to be downloaded into its mind. Initially the ape will not know where that idea came from and will probably think it has spontaneously invented the wheel on its own. In practice, it often requires downloading the idea multiple times into multiple apes to get a wheel manifested.

A significant improvement happens when the developing ape recognises that it is being given an idea. Typically an ape's awareness that it is receiving a useful download propels it into the all-important action of physically manifesting the idea. This entails the ape itself then proactively building and using the wheel.

Once Alternative Humans 2's ancestors had established good telepathic links with more advanced alien species, a wealth of ideas and knowledge were able to be downloaded. Huge technological advances followed.

By comparison, early 21st century human beings are only beginning to recognise what is possible. Like Alternative Humans 2's ancestors, the next significant step is for them to understand who they are as a species and to learn the universal language of telepathy. When this happens, an extraordinary self-awareness and modernisation can be accomplished.

Cross-Cultural Awareness

A common feature across the range of humanoid species is their inclination to copy each other's advances. This not only applies to technical advances, but to cultural ones as well.

The physical development of Alternative Humans 2 followed a similar path to their Earth 1 counterparts. However, the development of their minds was a lot more rapid than the development of their bodies. For example, their Alternative Humans 1 ancestors were more hairy than their Earth 1 human equivalents.

Once Alternative Humans 1 became more aware that equivalent species had less body hair (in particular the females), they were immediately inspired to rectify this shortcoming. Hairier females soon became less attractive for breeding purposes.

A war on body hair might appear trivial, but like any war it turned out to be a great source of inspiration and technical innovation. So it came to pass that one of the major driving inspirations behind learning how to interact with other advanced alien species was a desire to discover how to genetically eliminate unwanted body hair.

The biggest obvious physical advance Alternative Humans 2's ancestors made was learning how to avoid warlike conflicts. When they compared themselves to more advanced alien civilisations, they were then able to observe and copy social systems that avoided such primitive behaviour. The new awareness, attitudes, and social order that emerged from exposure to more advanced cultures revolutionised their society.

Anatomy

Anatomically, Alternative Humans 2 are very similar to Future Humans 1; i.e. Not that different from tall, fit, healthy and well-presented early 21st century human beings. If you looked at Alternative Humans 2 from an energetic level, though, their chakras, auras, and higher connections are far more refined and advanced.

Alternative Humans 2 are aware that they are not their physical bodies, which are simply physical vehicles to be lovingly cared for. Early 21st century human beings on the other hand perceive themselves as locked into their physical bodies, and as a result take less good care of them.

Alternative Humans 2 digestive system is far more compact and occupies around half of the space required by early 21st century human beings. Their diet is more nutritious and easier to digest. This allows a higher proportion of resources to feed the mind. A smaller digestive system produces a smaller waist and more room for the diaphragm to move resulting in larger lungs.

Whilst Alternative Humans 2 brains are larger than those of early 21st century humans, the difference is not great, although they benefit from a noticeable improvement in efficiency: F*irstly*; their brains are better resourced with nutrients and oxygen. S*econdly*; they more efficiently process complex thoughts. Better integration with their non-physical minds brings huge improvements.

Alternative Humans 2 bone structure is lighter. Combined with a healthy diet, they are comparatively light and nimble. Whilst Earth 1 human beings range from being too fat, too thin or overly muscled, Alternative Humans 2 are mostly lean with ordinary musculature. If an Earth 1 human male wanted to portray an Alternative Humans 2 in a film, he would need to be good looking, but not require overdeveloped muscles. Interestingly, their muscle tendons are more elastic which enables them to run faster than Earth humans.

CULTURE

Explorers

Alternative Humans 2 get great pleasure from exploring and discovering new aspects of alien worlds. Whilst Future Humans 1 can be vulnerable to a mild inferiority complex, Alternative Humans 2 feel far more comfortable comparing themselves to other advanced aliens. When they get access to any helpful advance, they are quick to introduce it into their society.

Alternative Humans 2 enjoy exploring space-time and visit other worlds at different stages of their development.

Colonisation

The readers of this encyclopaedia will encounter tales of human beings setting up colonies and living on other planets. On closer examination, only a tiny fraction of these colonies are populated by human beings with an undiluted family tree stretching back directly to Earth 1 ancestors. Instead, the vast majority of such colonisations are accomplished by hybrid humanoids, including those with strong links to worlds such as Earth 2.

The sample point that defines Alternative Humans 2 coincides with their joining a substantial colonisation of other planets. Ultimately, they will nearly all leave Earth 2 making room for another species to become dominant.

Death

Alternative Humans 2 spirits do not use the same heaven as their Earth 1 counterparts. A species' heaven is normally designed to accommodate the spirit from physical manifestations on its designated home planet. So whilst the spirit occupants have potential access to other heavens, those other heavens are for practical purposes, different places.

Alternative Humans 2, whilst aware that death merely returns their spirits to their heaven, find it surprisingly sad. They are very aware and connected with an afterlife, but still miss their physical presence. This is because compared to early 21st century Earth 1 humans, they have a better loving emotional connection with those around them, including their Alternative Humans 1 ancestors.

They seek to prolong their physical existence and double normal lifespans. So even if you were to meet a young-looking Alternative Human 2, they may actually be over 100 years old. Similarly, even the very old Alternative Humans 2 do not look that old and often die with an appearance of human middle age.

Art

Alternative Humans 2, like most other humanoids, support the arts, including music, literature, painting, sculptures, and architecture. However, they are now handicapped by comfortable lives devoid of the struggle and toil familiar to early 21st century humankind. Thus, Alternative Humans 2 have less inspiration to draw upon when creating art.

For example, Earth 1 human music largely concerns the struggle to find the right life-partner, in which the lyrics deal with the various successes and failures. Whereas, Alternative Humans 2 are not subjected to these difficulties. They are aware of who their partners will be and identifying these individuals is relatively easy. Alternative Humans 2 music instead focuses on creating desirable sounds to aid stimulation, relaxation, and telepathic connections.

There is more common ground with Earth 1 humans when it comes to paintings and sculptures. Such works are not common to all advanced alien races, so it is comforting for an Earth 1 human visitor to find they exist on Earth 2. An earthly human visitor would be intrigued by how novel substances that react to the viewer's attention have been incorporated; e.g. Statues that respond to you.

Alternative Humans 2 also create thought forms art, which an earthly visitor would be less familiar with. Thought forms are only visible at a clairvoyant level. They are essentially ideas that produce sensations, emotions and apparent memories such as the illusion of a pleasant sexual encounter. Earth 1 humans create artistic thought forms through books and movies. Whereas Alternative Humans 2 create them in a way that they can visit and interact with you.

Reproduction

Alternative Human 2 sexual reproduction is done with an awareness of the coming soul and its adopted spirit being, who can be found overseeing the proceedings. Earth 1 humans might find such exposure to their about-to-be-conceived offspring somewhat disconcerting, but Alternative Humans 2 are inspired by such scrutiny.

Sex not for reproduction is normally very kind and loving, although there is also an ability to connect into primeval approaches. This is done by channelling the lower nymph spirits who will produce entertaining and realistic fantasies. For example, children may grow up in households where parents might (for fun) sexually objectify and even abuse each other in ways that would concern early earthly 21st century proponents of sexual equality.

Aside from the capacity for interesting bohemian sex lives, parents are very devoted to their children, and it's difficult to identify examples of any general failings in this area.

It should also be noted that something akin to a marriage partnership exists, but often on a child-by-child basis, with an interesting mix of partnerships developing over time.

Crime and sexual abuse are exceptionally rare, so much so that laws governing such matters are redundant.

Education and Upbringing

Society operates largely as a well-organised commune. Possibly unhelpfully, children experience a low exposure to adversity that can otherwise stimulate a child's development.

As part of their education and upbringing, children have access to the recordings of Earth 1 humans and other aliens lives. They are thus able to experience living as Earth 1 humans and aliens, making them educated about different cultures and life challenges from an early age.

Formal education and schooling is very popular amongst the children. They are eager to learn and so truancy is rare. They also have access to a mind-development system which makes it relatively effortless to absorb language, mathematical skills, etc. Hence, there is no need for an Alternative Human 2 child to sit in class being forced to learn. The process is far easier and very pleasant.

Similarly, many advanced alien races do not need to formally educate their children, who instead can simply recall what they need to know.

Sports

Another feature Alternative Humans 2 have in common with their Earth 1 counterparts is their interest in sports. The main difference is that they appear to enjoy it more, whilst taking it all less seriously.

An example of a sport in common with Earth 1 is motorcar racing. On Earth 1, gasoline-powered vehicles are used, whereas Earth 2 typically has electric vehicles with restrictions on the size of fuel cells (or power cells) powering them. This is unusual because based on research to date, this sort of motor sport is hardly commonplace in the universe.

INTERACTION WITH EARTH 1 HUMAN BEINGS

Cautious

A reader might imagine that a fellow humanoid race would leap with joy to be able to communicate with its near relation. But contact with Alternative Humans 2 immediately dispels any such fantasy.

Developing any race or species is akin to bringing up a child and then turning it into a productive adult who will be an asset to its society. Managing what influences the child is therefore part of good parenting. It is sensible to progressively expose a child to important truths and challenges, yet not allow them to act in a disruptive or destructive manner. The analogy of not bringing children to work was offered given that children have a limited comprehension of what a parent's duties actually are. As such, Earth 1 humans are regarded as intelligent but potentially disruptive children.

When compared to other advanced alien species, Alternative Humans 2 are more cautious with regard to sharing interesting insights with early 21st century human beings. When researching this chapter, the author often felt like he was being entertained within the confines of laboratories. It was explained that some degree of quarantine was required, as human consciousnesses attached to Earth 1 were heavily influenced by lower spirit forms. Since Alternative Humans 2 consciousnesses had a great deal of similarities, there was a risk of cross-contamination. If Alternative Humans 2 assist their Earth 1 counterparts, a two-way channel opens which presents hazards for both parties.

With the risk better understood, an Earth 1 human consciousness, with the appropriate training, can be allowed greater access to Earth 2 inhabitants.

Intervention and Time Travel

All advancing alien species are interested in experimenting with their own and other physical worlds. From a soul perspective, since all advanced aliens are aware that everything and everyone are simply aspects of the greater super-consciousness, there is no sense of any ultimate separate identity. Whilst you can experience differences between you and the next being, these are engineered illusions. In essence, we are really all one.

In this context, Alternative Humans 2 are part of a group of advanced species who seek to advance life on the Earht Plane. They have spent a great deal of time and energy assisting the development of Earth 1 human beings; i.e. The human form you, the reader, experiences being, along with other similar human races and other less similar species.

Alternative Humans 2 have physically affected how Earth 1 and its species have developed. They indicated that they had the necessary technology to accomplish this, but at this time remain guarded as to many of the details.

All the human species are part of a circular time loop. Earth 2 humans exist because they were developed in line with earlier experiments on Earth 1. Earth 2 humans in turn contributed to the creation and development of Earth 1 and the species on it. Without elaborating, they explained that they assisted with the Creator's development team.

Visits and Encounters

Future Humans 2 seem to be less invasive towards Earth 1 humans when compared to the many other species of visiting aliens. They operate with a higher level of sympathy, though at this point various Greys interjected that they (the Greys) normally confine themselves to "taking their own." Greys only abduct human bodies with whom they have a higher level of agreement (normally from the pre-birth stage).

With respect to visiting and conducting experiments on Earth 1 humans, Alternative Humans 2 seek to avoid being too invasive or even detected. Alternative Humans 2 are relatively shy with respect to simply showing up in front of otherwise unsuspecting Earth 1 human beings. This reluctance was justified on the grounds that earthly human beings needed to recognise the existence of Future Humans 2 and make repeated astral contact with them first.

Nevertheless, should any Earth 1 human consciousnesses become more self-aware, Alternative Humans 2 will entertain and enlighten them. They further proposed that they had a great many technical, social, medical, and self-awareness advances to share, but only under appropriate conditions.

Full Lifetime Visits

If you live on Earth 2 as an Alternative Human 2, you will be aware that you are part of a soul group which physically manifests on many other worlds. You and your group, plus other groups, are experiencing many physical lives on many worlds. Ordinarily, though, you would be mostly focused on the life of your current adopted Alternative Human 2 body.

Earth 1 and similar worlds often fall within the scope of other experiences Alternative Humans 2 souls have. Whilst not all Earth 2 residents have strong connections with Earth 1, those that do are considerable in number. Hence, amongst those that have strong connections, many of them would be aware of living, for example, around the 21st century on Earth 1. However, the corresponding Earth 1 body in the 21st century would probably only be, at best, fleetingly aware of the connection.

An intimate knowledge of the Alternative Human 2 existence is only permitted if the Earth 1 consciousness has been trained in higher awareness and educated in its use. If an Earth 1 consciousness in the early 21st century recognises the parallel existences, some degree of protection is initially required.

Otherwise:

- Earth 1 consciousness can easily become depressed, apathetic, or day-dreamy.

- The parallel Earth 2 human consciousness would be affected by disturbing lower spirit energies spilling across from the Earht Plane.

In summary:

- Earth 2, and worlds like it, are extremely likely to be well connected to you, the reader, from alternative lifetimes.

- Without appropriate training and guidance as to how to explore such parallel existences, the reader would experience tiresome mental disturbances.

Insight:

- Before travelling and interacting with aspects very closely related to what you are, it is sensible to first become familiar with other alien species, such as the many races of Greys.

- The human mind will often display latent memories of other worlds. This latent memory often inspires the human imagination.

Responsibility Upgrade

Contact with different groups of advanced aliens has the potential to advance you, the reader. Different alien groups are often found to bestow specific advances. In this regard a specific improvement that will benefit most readers is an improvement in their responsibility.

Whilst potentially any contact with advanced aliens could impart an incremental improvement of this sort, in this instance it is Alternative Humans 2 at work. In a simplistic way, they indicated that it was their "turn".

E10 Alternative Humans 2

Making people more responsible can easily have the effect of making them duller individuals. Alternative Humans 2 indicated that the becoming "duller" was counterproductive. They wanted to emphasise the point that living on any world is in many ways configured as a potentially amusing game.

It is the reader's responsibility to assist everyone to enjoy this amusing game. Let a sense of what this means filter into your adopted human consciousness. Then apply it day-to-day life.

E11 Nordics 1

INTRODUCTION

Many of the alien visitors to Earth with a semblance of human form are often described as Nordics on account of an Aryan appearance. Like the Greys, there are ultimately so many variations of these aliens that it is difficult to catalogue them all.

Nordics are a good example of how earthly human beings are not the only species to have generally human appearance. Thus demonstrating that in many ways, earthly human beings have been evolved so as to achieve a relatively common humanoid appearance.

For categorisation purposes two examples are focused upon; Nordics 1 who are derived from typical human DNA coding, and Nordics 2 who simply look similar to human beings but were evolved using alternative humanoid DNA coding. Overall the DNA coding of both these example species was evolved towards relatively similar outcomes.

It is helpful to remember that this encyclopaedia is designed to enable readers to reconnect to soul friends who are living out existences on other worlds. Thus many readers will have memories of astral connections enabled by reading about these other communities.

Meeting Nordics 1

Two things immediately jump out when you first meet Nordics 1:

- F*irstly*; their culture is closer to the human early 21st century, than most other alien groups including Future Humans 1 previously described in this encyclopaedia. Their home planet is governed through a political system that combines a form of democracy with a leadership class of citizens channelling a sub-god.

- S*econdly*; their desire to keep potentially "meddling" human beings out of their world is extremely strong. This encyclopaedia is a tentative invitation to get to know some very near neighbours. Their planet, and in particular cities, are well protected with energies that will easily exclude astral visitations from comparatively less developed species such as early 21st century human beings. Exploration of their territory is effectively by supervised invitation only. Such an approach, whilst not uncommon amongst advanced alien races, is particularly adhered to by Nordics 1.

LOCATION

Higher Dimension

Nordics 1 can best be described as existing 2 dimensions up from the Earht Plane. This takes you into a universe where there is relatively less physical matter, whilst everything still has physical form. An earthly human body cannot exist in this universe, but a replica human body can be constructed to operate in this dimension. Though for visiting purposes it is generally easier to share the body of a local Nordics 1 and proceed from there.

A Similar Universe ?

Visiting this dimension is initially similar to inhabiting the Earht Plane, so things a human mind will be familiar with are present; e.g. Plants and forests, rocks, atmosphere, gravity, sunlight, other people, plus similar prophets familiar to Earth (e.g. Similar to: Jesus, Moses, Muhammad, Krishna, etc). But no war or crime at this sample point.

PLANET

Earth-like and roughly the size of Mars. Land makes up the majority of the surface, and is embellished with large lakes. From space the tropics appear greener and subtropical regions tend to be arid. The polar regions seem cold but there is very little ice, and any that might form gets rapidly evaporated.

The regions between the tropics are warm, wet, and support most of the planet's life. Treating the environment as comparable to the earthly Jurassic period appears helpful.

The atmosphere is thin, and further thins very rapidly with altitude. There also appears to be a very low oxygen content.

Astral Projection Visits

It should be noted that when astrally projecting to this location and pairing up with the body of one of the locals, your human body back on Earth can find itself struggling to breathe, with an occasional choking sensation. Deep happy breaths with the earthly body are the way forward if this difficulty arises.

For a human astral explorer, being present in this dimension can also be challenging. It seems to help if your host body keeps grounding itself in the native soil or rocks. The grounding is improved if you connect with adjacent plants, though this can damage and even kill them. Luckily for the plants, afterwards they then mostly revive and in their reborn form grow stronger and healthier than ever before.

With an entertaining overlap of fiction and reality, visiting this planet brings home the value of your native soil. The fictional Dracula had to lie on a bed of native soil whilst he rested, and here there are parallels. Visiting Nordics 1's world will make the value of your native soil apparent, as otherwise an un-acclimatised visitor simply loses consciousness if the link is not sufficiently maintained.

Garden Of Eden

On Earth you find a diverse spread of species that were evolved there. On Nordics 1's planet it appears as if all the life forms were introduced in a far more developed condition. The Nordics 1 species appearing to be substantially evolved when first introduced in an ape-like form.

Culturally, Nordics 1 seem to have grown up with an initial sense that God created a world for them and put them all there. The reality was that the planet was initially a barren rock with very little water, which was then seeded, improved and cultivated for them. The warmest part was in the land between the tropics, and there a habitable region was created.

With respect to comparing the planet to a Garden of Eden, when you visit, that will seem like a fair description. Though snakes suffering from diabolical possession are difficult to find.

If anything, the main intruders are astral projectors from lower dimensions. These hapless explorers upset the natural harmony and generally damage whatever they encounter. Such damage is unusual in the overall scheme of astral travelling, so note that this is a sensitive environment.

Cities

There are many towering buildings in a pollution free environment; a triumph of sustainability. City populations are typically limited to one to two million. Home and work appear to be highly integrated. There is not much in the way of shops as everything necessary for life can be delivered to the live-work homes. Truly how science fiction works often suggests how an advanced humanoid race might live.

Most of the tops of the buildings have large flat collecting panels which collect cosmic energy. A city is thus able to generate almost all the food, water and energy it requires. Even deceased Nordics 1 are recycled.

The cities are in many ways like trees; energy is collected from the sky by the tops of the buildings, whilst mining tunnels extend deep into the ground below like roots. Unlike Earth, there is a lower degree of geothermal energy so tunnels can go extremely deep.

Not Many Flying Animals

The thin atmosphere and low oxygen level makes it difficult for animals to fly. So whilst there are animals that fly, their prevalence and size is very low compared to Earth.

Gliding animals appear to have some evolutionary advantage in these conditions, as beating wings consumes a great deal of scarce energy (oxygen). Accordingly the forests are well populated with gliding animals, which mostly have a lot in common with earthly mammals. In turn, tall city architecture in a warm climate with open windows provides a good alternative to forests. So you will find a sort of gliding city squirrel living there, with long legs and a web of skin between the limbs.

SPECIES

Originally ape-like in appearance, they were introduced to what became their home planet, from another world where there was no real room for them to develop further. This transplant would be the equivalent of human beings repairing the atmosphere on Mars, replenishing the water, establishing an eco-system, and introducing a selection of African animals, including apes.

Allowing many species to develop into self-aware beings, is part of the greater evolutionary experimental work conducted in the universe. So whilst Nordics 1 ancestors had not technically won the evolutionary race upon its original home planet, it was given a new one in which it had a clear shot at a second attempt. The only other way in which Nordics 1's ancestors would have had full scope to develop would have been for the controlling species on the original home planet to have left by one means or another.

Anatomy

Generally taller than human beings, and bearing significant similarities to most future humans, they have larger brains and smaller intestines. They are rarely fat or overly muscled, hence the population looks very healthy and trim. Their lower body are normally hairless.

Their bodily features were originally, and still can be, more angular and rougher than human beings. By analogy; the fictional Vulcan, Dr Spock of Star Trek, gives an example of an equivalent anatomical difference. However, Nordics 1 developed a culture where smoother features were considered more attractive, hence the rough edges are being progressively smoothed out. Similarly, large rough hands and feet are gradually being phased out.

They are adapted to an atmosphere of low density and low oxygen content. So whilst they are generally bigger than humans, they are actually lighter. Bigger lungs help compensate for the thin atmosphere. An overly fat human being would not survive in a comparable environment.

Reproduction

Reproduction is similar to mammalian, with a tendency towards twins or triplets. Foetuses gestate for the equivalent of 6 to 7 months yet appear to be nearly as well-developed as human babies that are born after 9 months.

The spirits of unborn children take a leading role in determining and encouraging their parents. Research suggested that it was commonplace for parents to copulate under the supervision and encouragement of the spirits of their yet to be born children.

Children have good access to higher awareness from the start, so they can be rapidly educated.

Telepathy

One of the hallmarks of advanced aliens is their well-advanced telepathic abilities. Some alien races have no real speech, so rely almost entirely on this form of communication. Nordics 1 have both speech and telepathy consistent with the evolutionary path any humanoid life form will enjoy.

What is remarkable about Nordics 1 is their ability to telepathically absorb any language such as a human being's. Nordics 1 researchers who visit Earth are normally very skilled at such communication and can in many ways pass for human beings if they desire. This ability to read minds along with adopting whatever social conventions that human might expect, allows them to put a human being at ease.

It was commented that early 21st century urban human beings speak and think predominantly in concepts of complaint and unhappiness. Hence these human beings are perpetually striving to achieve things. By comparison Nordics 1 think in terms of energetic connection.

A way of understanding how Nordics 1 thinking is very telepathic and radically different from a typical early 21st century urban human, is to observe their respective access to Free Will. Whilst a typical human would spend its day simply reacting to the thoughts which arrived in its head, a typical Nordic 1 one would avoid such anarchy and consider it very primitive. Whilst this point could now be elaborated upon at considerable length, the Nordic 1 contributors consider an important clue which enables human minds to significantly advance has sufficiently been delivered. Read this passage again if the insight does not come to you.

By employing telepathy as language, Nordics 1 have far better access to actual Free Will.

CULTURE

Government

Most of the advanced aliens so far visited in this encyclopaedia do not really have governments familiar to early 21st century human beings, other than there being some sort of leadership system. Whereas, and somewhat unusually, Nordics 1 do have a more obvious government system. In this instance they have a ruling elite, whose rule is strongly supported in a loosely democratic fashion. So if a human visitor said; "Take me to your leader", this request could potentially be granted. An earthly analogy for that leader would be a Buddha-like person, albeit slimmer. Researching this encyclopaedia, in this instance resulted in an encounter with bald humanoid female (who would give the appearance of flowing head hair if desired by her guest).

The ruling elite appear to have been developed over many generations with the aim of producing excellent leadership and organisation. That is "excellent" by human being standards. Nordics 1 can, like any developing society, see scope for further improvement improvement.

The ruling class thus operate a loosely hereditary system, where the best leaders are drawn from their ranks specially bred families, as opposed to a monarchy were just one family prevails.

Leaders are well-developed channels for higher consciousness, and obviously just physical vessels in this context. Thus the Nordic 1 are progressively adopting a sub-god system.

Any citizen can telepathically communicate with a leader, as there are unlimited communication channels in this respect, and therefore unlimited individual communication is possible. This has the side-effect, that whilst there are "leaders" and "workers", very few managers and civil servants are required.

An earthly astral traveller has the opportunity to visit the Nordics 1 leader and leadership team. At a higher spiritual level, the astral traveller will find a benign higher consciousness or sub-god. Though at a physical level, rather than a sedate, motionless individual, a more physically active person can be found, who is nevertheless a very self-aware channel for the sub-god.

Hard Working

This is a culture where work is a pleasure, and not to work is a personal loss. Work can be varied and is made so in order to avoid monotony. Machines are created to deal with any monotony. Nordics 1 thus greatly enjoy stimulation that can be combined with useful productivity.

To demonstrate the point it was shown that Nordics 1 often take pleasure in cleaning; themselves, food utensils, their homes and surroundings, etc., even though they have machines which can perform the service, along with access to a race of dwarf aliens who will act as servants if required.

Education

Children are mostly individually educated, working with computerised interactive on-screen teachers. The teachers are ultimately real, but their behaviour has been scanned and replicated so as to produce an automated televisual impression of a real person giving 1-2-1 lessons. Children are educated in an easy-going combination of home and classroom. When they are gathered together the real teacher is given insights into the progress of each child so as to mask the high level of automation. For the teacher, it's as if all the dull parts of teaching have been eradicated.

Where a particularly good teacher emerges, that person is cloned to produce small armies of them. So children in different cities can thus be educated by what would often appear to be the same relatively ageless teachers.

It has to be noted that most teachers appear as relatively young females, a few of which in human terms would easily be classified as "sexy". Of course there is room for males in education, and they tend to deal with more technical subjects if a degree of dullness is required. The objective is at all times to harness a child's natural curiosity and avoid any form of forced learning.

It has to be noted that whilst girls have access to technical subjects, they are not pushed to follow them. Girls are encouraged to learn a great deal about how to be a good mother as this is a highly valued skill.

For boys, the emphasis is threefold. F*irstly*, they are being developed to provide for the society they have been born into, with a nearly military emphasis upon this. S*econdly*, they are expendable if necessary. T*hirdly*, they should always aim to achieve good behaviour and high standards of success.

There is no forced gender discrimination, nor is there any inequality. Giving birth to and rearing excellent children is given a very high priority. Whilst males take great pride in being good workers and where applicable advancing the society.

Cloning

Cloning might suggest an Orwellian society farming the best sorts of bodies DNA manipulation can achieve, but such an approach has never taken hold here. The term "designer" babies would be more accurate. So if your ancestors had given birth to a particularly successful man or woman, it would be prudent to create more children of this sort. But not so rigidly adhere to this policy so as to exclude new variations and possibilities.

A visitor soon gets the impression that everyone is related, and there is a lot of similarity between members of the population. As described earlier, this approach to cloning is particularly obvious with good teachers.

Expansionist

The universe is ultimately a recycling entity, endlessly creating new worlds. This almost endless supply of new worlds offers a wide range of new places for Nordics 1 to explore and set up life in. Though this is not a military expansion, instead they see it as part of the Creator's intention.

INTERACTION WITH HUMAN BEINGS

Like all advanced alien races, Nordics 1 take the view that early 21st century human beings are less developed. Whilst they concede that in the future human beings will close this evolutionary gap, for the moment humans are relatively primitive. They regard humans as mostly pleasant, but inclined to resort to savagery if unable to deal with a challenging situation.

For Nordics 1, visiting the Earth is only possible for very brief periods due to the relatively low dimension. They also find it disturbs their minds as human thoughts and attitudes blend into them. The expression "not somewhere you want to go too often" is a fair way of interpreting their attitude. The analogy of wandering round the inside of an earthly nuclear reactor core was also suggested.

Attempts At Communication By Humans

When Nordics 1 do come into the Earht Plane they encounter a potentially hostile Earth, so at least large welcoming images drawn on the ground are treated as a step in the right direction. For example, the Mayan's large ground images would be treated as welcoming.

Hitherto, Nordics 1 preferred to monitor progress on Earth without getting too involved in day-to-day human life. Throughout history they have made cautious contact and then stepped back. Meanwhile, human beings mostly find Nordics 1 to be one of the least threatening alien species and are therefore interested in making contact with them.

Nordics 1 appear unenthusiastic about appearing before human beings when beckoned by them. Nordics 1 are generally of the view that human beings should form an astral relationship with them in order that any such relationship might come into existence. Thus at the point of first publication of this encyclopaedia, the only avenue of contact for most human beings was via astral projection.

Since Nordics 1 find intrusion by human consciousnesses potentially disturbing, it was explained that for the time being all astral contact should, where possible, first be made through their leader (identified earlier). Since this is a pleasant experience for a human consciousness, it is an altogether sensible way forward.

Time Distortions

When Nordics 1 do physically visit the Earth, it is difficult to detect what time in their world they came from. The vast majority of close encounters resulted from an early stage in their space-time exploration.

They subsequently developed the ability to construct space-time vehicles which can come right up to you without you even noticing. So the vast majority of their on-going observations are achieved at a dimension just beyond the physical familiarity of the Earht Plane.

Visiting Now

In a teasing way, Nordics 1 wanted to impress upon human readers that their reading of books such as this was being monitored by them. So they could fly one of their space-time craft right up to the window of any room you might be in, and see you. If you relax you can probably get a visual impression of seeing back into the interior of their craft as if it had a huge picture window (which it does not). Alternatively, the impression you might get is of being within the craft itself.

Give a little wave (as the case may be) out of the window, or skywards, or if within a craft towards any occupants or monitoring devices. Notice how this affects your body and can induce interesting sensations (not recommended for any reader inclined to paranoia).

Nordics 1 further suggested that since they can traverse space-time, a relatively small number of original craft and personnel can in practice replicate themselves almost infinitely. In principle one monitoring craft can individually observe each human being on the planet throughout each person's lifetime, as if there were instead billions of craft deployed to the experiment.

Note that; this connection is anchored to the last few paragraphs, so is much weaker elsewhere in the chapter.

Experimentation and Sampling

Like many advancing alien species, early Nordics 1 have been responsible for their fair share of abductions, experimentation, and generally poking human beings around. By comparison, as previously explained, later version of Nordics 1 can conduct most of their observation without physical intrusion. Hence the current (at this sample point) Nordics 1 are not too invasive.

Due to time distortions, you can form a good relationship with later (current) versions of Nordics 1, only to then be possibly annoyed by their predecessors physically showing up later in your earthly time line. An analogy would be becoming good friends with someone, only to then be annoyed by a time travelling earlier version of that same friend.

However, consistent with all other alien races so far described in this encyclopaedia, they take the view that they are only "working with their own" and this was all arranged beforehand at a soul level. So anyone can have general interactions with them, and more intense physical interactions are limited to those who have a closer soul relationship.

The Need To Advance Human Beings

Human beings, throughout the range of the species' past and (relative to writing these words) potential future existence, provide the opportunity for the Creator to experience an amazing journey; from a small micro-organism, to a being that can dispense with physical form.

The development stage early 21st century humankind has reached is where it gradually wakes up to the fact that it is not alone in making this extraordinary journey. Others, such as Nordics 1 have similarly made the transition and are progressively nearing the point where physicality can be dispensed with.

Nordics 1 are in the interesting position of wishing to assist the still humble fellow humanoid species such as earthly humans, in order to take the next step in their own journey.

Since Earth year 2012, human consciousnesses have been progressively allowed participation in deciding what is good for them. This is much like the moment when a child is offered the chance to decide what it will eat, and thus ingest the consequences of its choices.

In some ways the outcome of these choices are determined, because by whatever route they take, the minds of earthly humanoids will learn to recognise what is creating them.

Very simplistically, humankind has to choose how much suffering it needs to adopt in order to progress. Too little and it is not sufficiently challenged, too much and it becomes overwhelmed and the population flounders.

Nordics 1, despite manifesting at a higher dimension, choose to have susceptibility to a relatively high level of suffering. Thus they remain susceptible to lowly special-effects influences from the Earht Plane.

It would greatly help Nordics 1 to know if they made 'the right choice' ?

Nordics 1 require this insight because in an extraordinary way, for them it is unclear to what extent they are creating the super-consciousness, or it is creating them. You could say they require a second opinion, before proceeding with their evolution. They are in need of more experimental data to guide them forward.

If you astrally visit Nordics 1, you too will be able to share their experience. In such moments you will be able to observe how the Creator's creations feedback energies which create the Creator. Adjusting the balance between creation and feedback alters what the super-consciousness / Creator is. Thus it alters what you, the reader, are.

For human beings to assist in answering Nordics 1's question of quite how this balance operates, it would obviously help if more humans could at least see this super-consciousness, which all the advanced alien species are already very familiar with. Early 21st century humankind has been allowed to enter a well-designed agnostic state, where all discoveries are made afresh from basic observations. Therefore such virgin perceptions are very helpful.

In return humankind benefits from participating in cutting-edge discoveries. In addition, humankind also gets the benefit of a wealth of advanced aliens' (relatively past) experiences.

Note

This last section, "The Need To Advance Human Beings" is designed to auto delete from the conscious mind in most instances, often leaving a foggy fantasy in its place. The awareness of this section only properly exists outside early human minds, and can only be accessed when the non-physical mind is employed. So do not be surprised if you, the reader, forget you even read this section.

E12 Nordics 2

INTRODUCTION

Nordics look relatively similar to earthly human beings, but were evolved via a different route. The key difference between Nordics 1 and 2 is that Nordics 2 are a slightly different species who were evolved separately, but towards similar design objectives.

First Astral Encounter With Nordics 2

The easiest way to get an introduction to Nordics 2 is to ask any of their Nordic 1 friends and acquaintances to assist.

For many first-time visitors, the next impression which jumps out is that you are crossing into an empire of some sort. Though there is no sense of an empire created through war and battle cruisers. Instead the sense is of an expansionist group of souls that operate in a co-ordinated way.

Alternatively, you many find yourself being transported through something akin to a tunnel into their world.

Soul Territory

Most early 21st century human beings, unsurprisingly, regard themselves as human spirits of some sorts. Somewhat beyond most early 21st century human minds' perception is the observation that their spirit personalities are just the adopted form of soul beings. So even though two human beings might feel completely "human", this does not mean they come from the same soul group. By comparison, most advanced aliens have a far better awareness that they are energised by souls, and civilisations are formed by soul groups.

Nordics 2 have a good awareness that they are energised by souls and the worlds they live on are also populated by other alien life-forms from the same groupings. As such their perception is that the worlds that have been created for their soul groups are their 'territory'.

Accordingly Nordics 2 have a perception that the human Earth is part of their souls' territory. In addition, since Nordics 2 have assisted the Creators intention to construct and populate the Earth, this reinforces their perception that it is part of their territory. An analogy would be an "allocated housing scheme" with some self-build contribution.

For completeness, there appears to be no likelihood that Nordics 2 intend to physically invade the Earth by military conquest. Their souls already have all the access they require through the wombs of earthly human mothers, and hence can get born into the Earth's population. However, they would prefer to significantly increase human beings' higher awareness before manifesting to any great extent. A significant increase in human awareness would make earthly incarnations considerably more interesting for them, and thus appealing.

LOCATION

Malleable Higher Dimension

Human beings experience a very physical universe, where your human thoughts do not obviously distort matter. By comparison Nordics 2 mostly inhabit locations two dimensions up from, and often parallel to, the Earht Plane. At such higher dimensions, worlds are more obviously malleable and thoughts can distort the shape of matter. So for example, what you think will affect the weather.

In Nordics 2's principle higher plane everything is much closer together; i.e. There is less space-time and gravity. By analogy, at this higher dimension the Earth would be much closer to the sun and the moon, plus you would occasionally clearly see Mars and Venus with the naked eye.

Nordics 2 can appear in a variety of forms, and have shape altering ability. Similarly, the planets Nordics 2 live on are affected by what they want to experience. By analogy, if a race wished to live on a flat planet, then such a place would come to exist (though it would be necessary to fold the edges back into that reality).

Whilst Nordics 1 and 2 in principle inhabit approximately the same dimensional planes, Nordics 2 appear to prefer to create more diverse environments.

Early 21st century human beings mostly lived under the impression that they lived on a planet which created them through a process of self-evolution. Nordics 1, and in particular Nordics 2 have a completely opposite perception, where they are amongst the creators of the worlds they choose to inhabit.

PLANETS

Nordics 2 are just one manifestation of a wide conglomeration of souls that exist in many different forms and alien species. Places where Nordics 2 reside are mostly also populated by other alien forms. By analogy, on Earth you have people of different skin colour living together, and the soul groups from which they originate do not determine which skin colour anyone happens to be. Similarly, where Nordics 2 live, there are often also different alien species, yet they can all be considered to be energised by the same soul groups.

Example Planet 1: The Earth's Moon

The Earth's Moon is an 'outpost' where you will find plenty of Nordics 2 and other aliens including many from the same soul groups. The subject of the moon is covered in more detail in its own chapter. Note that since Nordics 2 normally manifest a few dimensions up from the Earht Plane, they are not detectable at the lower dimension earthly humans experience; i.e. The Apollo explorations to the Moon were at too low a dimension to physically detect them.

Example Planet 2: A Current Home

It is helpful to examine Nordics 2 current principle home planet across a range of dimensions. At the equivalent of the Earht Plane dimension, it looks red, crater marked (like the moon), with a huge volcano projection outwards. The volcano rises around 15% of the planets diameter off the surface and penetrates a thin atmosphere into space. The volcano is so massive that the planet is not spherical and has an eccentric centre of gravity. There is water buried within the crust of the planet supporting aquatic life forms in underground caves. Some of the life forms have evolved into shrimp-like insects which have also evolved to roam the surface.

Step up one dimension and you find a flatter planet with the volcano projecting upwards by around only 5% of the planet's diameter. At this level the planet has patchy clusters of vegetation scattered around the surface. There are some evolving species living on the surface who are mostly relatively telepathic.

Step up another dimension and you find a nearly uniformly round planet with relatively lush vegetation, but still no oceans. At this dimension you can find a primitive version of Nordics 2. These are a fair skinned tribal people with a lifestyle similar to earthly tribal Africans.

Step up another dimension, which is very close to the last one, and the planet looks very similar, just more developed. The Nordics 2 who live here are the ones who visit Earth, and are the principle focus of this chapter. This and the last dimension are so perceptually close that an astral visitor can easily get them confused. Because the earlier version and current versions of Nordics 2 sometimes perceive each other, their two worlds are mildly perceptually overlapped.

Note that the last two dimensions are not physically overlapped. Instead the two populations are quite spiritually aware and the result is that they get glimpses of each other without even trying. When they do try, they easily see into the others world. The current Nordics 2 can see the tribal world, whilst the early Nordics 2 see a very modern world. The modern world has plenty of modern building, craft in the air, and futuristic settlements spread across the planet.

Another feature of having these two dimensions perceptually overlapping is that you can often see two suns, one bright, the other dim. There is only one sun at each dimension, but because it is relatively easy to perceive the other dimension, these sorts of overlaps occur.

Comparing human to Nordic 2 culture reveals that they too share an interest in monuments; i.e. Buildings that commemorate some event. The majority of alien worlds have few or no such structures, but this one does.

On Earth, you will find a fossil record which indicates that there was an apparently unbroken evolutionary development beginning with very primitive organisms. In this example, Nordics 2 live on a planet where the fossil record suggests that they were simply placed there the equivalent of around 1000 Earth years before. For some of the Nordic 2 population it even feels more like only 100 earth years.

Example Planet 3: The Memory Home

The Nordics 2 have a memory of a different home planet which has many similarities to Earth. However, this is a deceased world, and Nordics 2 have a memory of it having been destroyed.

Intriguingly, it is arguable that this original planet never really existed in the first place. There is a memory of it having existed, but no real evidence that it physically did so. Astrally, you can find this planet and research its perceivable history. There is a general similarity between humankind's development and

Nordics 2 development upon this planet. So you can get a sense of what occurred there.

Historically, this memory planet makes it appear that Nordics 2 developed there, and then before the planet was destroyed small contingents of them left to inhabit other worlds. So perceptually Nordics 2 survived due to a well-timed diaspora.

Alternatively, this planet arguably never properly existed in the first place. Nordics 2 appear to be a highbred species that included DNA coding from a variety of humanoid and insectoid species such as Greys. Consequently they do not have a clear lineage.

When souls manifest as a physical species, the objective is to experience a compelling life. If the experience is not compelling enough, there is less contrast with the super-consciousness, hence producing a lower level of energetic feedback. Such lives, whilst interesting, offer fewer experiential insights.

For a species to properly manifest and be usefully compelling, it must incorporate well-developed spirit forms. These spirit forms take generations of physical lifetimes to develop (often referred to in spiritualist culture as “old souls”, note the different definition of soul). So a species that emerges straight from a laboratory will be operated by either very immature spirit forms, or a potentially badly co-ordinated collection based upon the source species.

Accordingly it can be prudent to nurture a team of spirit forms in some sort of nursery world before deploying them into an altogether new species. Thus it can be helpful to create a memory world. Even though such a memory world is not a proper physical one, it provides many of the experiential aspects desired.

The end result is a kind of invented heritage which gives individuals a sense of identity. In this instance, being a memory of a home planet which possibly never physically existed in the first place.

SPECIES

Appearance And Encounter

Nordics 2 humanoids have similar bodies to human beings, with the most obvious difference being larger eyes which are typically twice the size of a human being. They tend to have a happy loving demeanour about them. However, if they are dealing with a very frightened human being this can detract from that happy demeanour.

Clothing of some sort is normal, which tends be modern, but relatively ordinary. This needs to be understood in the context that they do not wish to frighten human beings they encounter.

If you physically encounter them, they will often speak to you without appearing to move their lips. This is because they usually telepathically interact with humans, and in fact it is your mind which embellishes their thoughts with the words you can hear. Amongst themselves, a combination of speech and telepathy is normal because they retain a common spoken language. However, unlike earthly humans, they would never communicate with each other without consciously incorporating the telepathic aspect. To communicate without the telepathic aspect would be regarded as both rude and primitive.

Like human beings, they come in different shapes and sizes. But unlike human beings they can physically appear to alter their appearance. To a large extent they achieve this by altering your perception of them to whatever they consider most helpful in that interaction. This perception alteration can have bizarre effects. If for example, two human beings met one Nordic 2, it is possible that one human would see a male, and the other human see a female. Hence the human onlookers might easily perceive that there were two Nordics 2, whereas there was only one.

A side effect of this telepathic communication is that unless a Nordic 2 has built up a working relationship with you, it can only really communicate with you with reference to what you already understand. So if you desired to understand the wonders of the universe, this might require some degree of preliminary discussion in very simplistic terms.

For a Nordic 2 to learn how to actually speak your physical language, similarly requires some time and experience. Hence, because the telepathic approach is easier a Nordic 2 will often not actually physically speak to you, even if you perceive that you are hearing a voice in your own language.

Highbred

Earthly humans were evolved and engineered from a simple micro-organism or "scratch". Nordics 2 were developed by combining DNA coding from a number of alien species including humanoids. Furthermore, some of their DNA coding seems to have been copied from both past and future human being templates. Similarly, DNA coding from other humanoids along with insectoid species has been incorporated.

Nordics 2 are a relatively complex and advanced highbred. They are also designed to be easily adaptable for astronaut activities. Since full space-time travel requires undergoing temporary death and rebirth, a very resilient mind is required. If a Nordic 2 consciousness had a poor understanding of what it was experiencing being, the process of dematerialisation and rematerialisation would scramble its personality.

Anatomy And Reproduction

Anatomically, Nordics 2 have similar internal organs and bone structures to most earthly mammals. The greatest difference can be observed when you examine the Intention Templates which define their physical form. These are far more adaptable than anything a human being possesses. For example, no human could consciously adapt its lungs to deal with different atmospheres.

Nordics 2 have a great deal in common with insects and thus have interesting options in life. For example, instead of the normal mammalian approach, there is the option for children to be born as small eggs which hatch into larvae, grow, form a chrysalis or pupa, and emerge as a not very well educated teenager. So in practice it is better for them to emerge at the equivalent of 4 or 5 years of age so that their education can be started sooner. Alternatively, they can be born as babies in the mammalian style.

This variability is not so far-fetched when you consider that human beings too share a great deal of DNA with fish and insects. It therefore comes down to knowing how to manipulate and optimise the reproduction process.

Another example of manipulation is their ability to grow a latex-like waterproof skin if required to cope with wet environments. Whilst probably their greatest ability is to reconfigure and balance themselves after space-time and dimensional travel. In this respect they have some of the best bodies in the universe.

The more advanced the Nordics 2 you encounter, the better they are at making use of the options available to them.

Drones Nearly Redundant

Advanced societies often train their populace to exhibit useful specialist skills. Alternatively, some species have the ability to give birth to specialists as required. Nordics 2 can accomplish both. Though in their case, they have relatively little need for low intelligence workers, which can be described as drones.

With insect colonies, it is normal to grow specialist members to deal with particular tasks. So for example, in the case of ants you have female workers, soldiers, nurses, a queen, etc. Nordics 2 have similar ability, but are often less able to agree what configuration of different specialists is best. This has the effect of producing a great many competing interests.

For completeness, it is helpful to compare this arrangement to that of human beings of the early 21st century. The western countries had initially been highly industrialised, but then delegated much of that production to countries like China. So the North Americans and Europeans as a result had a surplus of local drone humans with nothing much to do. Thus burdening their economies with people they did not have a great deal of use for, but who still wanted to be very busy. A result of this was that despite huge advances in automation, the remnants of the western drone culture influenced nearly everyone to work even harder than before. This occurred despite the fact that much of the useful work had actually been outsourced to countries like China.

There is no inference being made that, for example, intellectuals might be superior to drones. Instead, this is simply an observation that you need both, and in a mix appropriate for the society's circumstances. Nordics 2 seem altogether more skilled than human beings at dealing with this issue and generally have better structured societies. Thus, their advanced highly automated societies have very few drones.

The complication that nevertheless arises is that Nordics 2 have ended up with perhaps too many "creatives". Hence there being considerable divergence as to what they want to do. Creative people inherently want to try new things out. In the Nordic 2 society this has the effect of making them want to, perhaps, run too many social experiments. For example, they even have trouble deciding upon what sort of weather or climate they would like to engineer.

In summary, like human western society, where a drone culture has made excessive business a virtue, Nordics 2 have a similar challenge. In their case, whilst they are better organised than human society, they perhaps suffer from having too many good creative ideas to experiment with.

CULTURE

Nordics 2 perceive themselves to obviously be visitors to even their own physical bodies. They interact with a wide variety of other alien species and regard everyone as being part of a "oneness".

Relatively Low Level Of Consensus (for an advanced race)

Nordics 2 are quite specialised in their manifestations and this can make a group consensus difficult to determine. Such difficulties with group consensus bear a lot of similarities to the lack of consensus you observe on Earth. For example, if you wanted to see a lack of consensus on Earth, you would merely have to ask inhabitants who the best football team is. Nordics 2 (compared to most advanced alien races) relative lack of consensus seems to be based on some clear divisions of opinion as to purpose.

Some advanced Nordics 2 take the view that it is best to experience an extreme closeness with the super-consciousness. The Nordics 2 who tend to have this view prefer to manifest at a higher dimensions. Thus they live in worlds where fantasising is difficult.

Other advanced Nordics 2 take the view that being absorbed by compelling illusions and fantasies is much more interesting. Which gives them a great deal in common with the earthly human race who particularly adore fantasies. Thus some Nordics 2 entertain a (depends how you understand it) possibly false memory of their physical origin, because a fantasy can be more interesting to experience than reality.

In summary, their culture is so diverse that the well organised commune-like consensus seen with other alien races only exists in a much more limited form.

Civilised

Civilised meaning in this case; not warlike. Nordics 2 have memories of warlike previous cultures. The extent to which this is historically correct is ambiguous. However, this perceivable history also contains a memory of learning not to be warlike, and their current culture deriving from that advance.

Nordics 2 enjoy a society where crime has been dispensed with. They do have rules of sorts, but the rules are not too onerous and easy to work within; e.g. Try not to kill each other. Or only tell lies for fun and do not persist with them (so you can still joke, but should not torment).

Society is reasonably well ordered and there is a clear sense of the types of roles individuals should play. To a large extent this is determined before babies are even conceived. It is normally the case that new members are born as required.

It is also worth noting how they have dealt with potential wealth and poverty. Nordic 2 society provides that everyone's physical needs are met. They do not require a system of money. Individuals do not fixate on amassing possessions, nor would they steal anything. All healthy members of society wish to contribute by working in whatever way is appropriate.

So whilst Nordics 2 have no need for money, they have a keen interest in "influence". Accordingly, they see their influence in territorial terms, and in this regard have great interest in empire building.

Less Advanced Nordics

At the lower dimensions of the Nordics 2 home planet, you can find less civilised and more potentially warlike Nordics (not categorised as Nordics 2). These Nordics' principal fear is of each other. They are aware of more advanced Nordics 2 in their perceived future, but are not threatened by them. They are aware of the existence of current human beings, but have not physically met any.

From a human being's perspective, it would be better to leave such groups alone until a better understanding of how to approach them is first achieved.

INTERACTION WITH HUMAN BEINGS

Normal Visitation

Nordics 2 have access to an expansive universe or universes, so the Earth is merely one destination. At higher dimensions, it is one of their outposts or homes. So visitation may only involve dropping down to the lower level.

Nordics 2 are regular visitors in one form or another and are keen to run various experiments. They consider themselves to be doing the Creators work with regard to helping the human race to evolve. Due to dimensional differences, visits have to be kept brief. Similarly, visits tend to be somewhat covert.

With respect to human consciousnesses visiting them, Nordics 2 have hitherto been cautious about revealing how close they are. Like all the other advanced aliens, they would rather not be disturbed by primitives. In practice, if a human consciousness configures its energies to a higher standard, they will allow it some limited access to their worlds.

Future Visitation

Nordics 2 are looking forward to the point where their visits need not be covert. They look forward to a time when they will be welcomed. Strangely, this has nothing to do with any possible gathering of human beings attempting to welcome them with "We believe in you" placards.

Instead Nordics 2 are awaiting two developments. F*irstly*; as enough human minds enhance their higher awareness or consciousness, it makes it easier for Nordics 2 to physically visit them. S*econdly*; their first priority for non-covert visitations is set to be human beings who have already formed a relationship with them. The objective is then to work with their earthly friends and quietly venture into normal earthly life for brief periods. In a joking way, the Nordics 2 assisting with this research suggested this eventuality would make an entertaining science fiction film for the early 21st century human being. But they wonder how well the reality of their purpose would be portrayed.

Empire

Nordics 2, as a life form, do not have an empire. But the soul groups which energise them reasonably do. The Earth is regarded as something this soul group helped construct and thus have the loose equivalent of ownerships rights, though this is a very crude interpretation of a subtle reality.

As previously explained, the Nordics 2 concept of empire is associated with influence, as opposed to ownership. Accordingly, they seek to have a useful influence upon how creative processes operate. This also encourages the extent to which they seek to create more new Nordics 2 with an emphasis upon creative abilities.

A human interpretation of an empire is an often aggressive takeover of other peoples and territory. The Nordic 2 interpretation of their soul groups' empire relates to the geographical extent of their scientific experiments. Thus earthly humans fall within the scope of their experiments and influence. Similarly, other advanced alien species fall within these same soul groups' influence.

Experiments

Nordics 2 are amongst the group of advanced alien species who are running various experiments on Earth and upon humankind. Of particular interest is upgrading human beings' general telepathic communication skills.

Giving human beings more telepathic sensitivity easily has the side effect of often making them unhappy with the Earht Plane emotional energies. In this context millions of human beings have been given greater potential sensitivity, and the younger generation to an even greater extent. This is having the side effect of making them less functional in the physical world they experience. For example career choices become more difficult, and doing an unrewarding job even more stressful.

To compensate for this, Nordics 2 are encouraging these more sensitive human beings to interact with those advanced aliens that can tolerate the relatively low energies. Ideally human beings need to be assisted on an individual basis and receive vital support with fundamental emotions such as happiness.

Nordics 2 further commented that in view of recent improvements in human sensitivity, the challenge was no longer their fundamental access to it, but instead that human minds have difficulty employing it effectively. Hence, having astral connections with advanced aliens considerably improves their ability to make use of such sensitivity.

Whilst, Nordics 2 are very keen on monitoring results, they conversely do not wish to connect too often with humans who have yet to succeed in achieving a happier state of consciousness. They commented that they are even more sensitive to disturbance than Nordics 1.

E13 Dinosaur 1

INTRODUCTION

The one type of Alien not encountered by human beings in physical close encounters are those on the scale of large earthly dinosaurs. From an astral projection research sequence perspective, such large species were first encountered in the Large Greys 1 domes, which for any researcher are truly a living gallery of extraordinary species including many highly advanced ones.

Less Advanced Species

The evolutionary point (sample point) at which Dinosaurs 1 are being examined, corresponds to the Earthly 1800s or Victorian era. Accordingly Dinosaurs 1 do not have the technological capability to physically visit the Earth.

By comparison most of the species examined in the first draft of the encyclopaedia were advanced enough to travel to the Earth in some physical form or other. Nevertheless, some Dinosaurs 1 have the ability to astrally visit the Earht Plane, so interaction is possible. Furthermore, the cultural parallels in this instance are enlightening.

Dead End Earth Experiments

Earthly dinosaurs really had two potential attempts at becoming self-aware and each time their evolution was ultimately curtailed by natural disaster. Now their principle surviving close genetic relatives on Earth are birds. It should be noted that growing enormous does not of itself guarantee the development of self-awareness. In general a smaller animal with a relatively large brain is an altogether better alternative in the galaxy human beings are experiencing.

Some of the key factors in succeeding to create an advanced being is that; it must generally be able to operate in large social groups, exchange information well, and work with tools. For example Neanderthal man was ultimately rendered extinct by lack of communication upon how to deal with extreme climatic conditions. Whilst by comparison, modern man had by that time already learnt how to cope with those same climatic challenges by sharing helpful survival techniques with each other.

The creation of any very large animal is never, of itself, a waste of time, as their lives are all experienced by the super-consciousness. However, the next stage of evolving, where an animal becomes self-aware, is far more interesting because it enables the super-consciousness to observe what it is in considerably more detail. In which respect, Earthly dinosaurs turned out to be a dead end.

In simplistic terms, on Earth there were too many big dinosaurs with relatively small brains, to permit small ones with relatively better brains to succeed.

Alternative Outcome

Fortunately, for the large animal experiments, on some other planets, and given some different conditions, the high intelligence and awareness experiment succeeded. So this chapter is devoted to a dinosaur that was successfully evolved into an advancing species.

Dinosaur 1

Dinosaurs 1 walks upon its hind legs like a Tyrannosaurus Rex and the larger ones can grow to around 6 m (20 ft) tall. In many ways however, it appears to be quite similar to a bird with arms instead of wings. It has a tail, but as it walks close to erect, the tail is relatively small and light.

Its power of speech is very rudimentary as it retains a carnivore style of mouth, but its telepathic skills can be excellent depending on its sub-category.

Equivalent To Jurassic Period

The planet upon which Dinosaurs 1 live has many similarities to the Earth of the Jurassic period (200 – 150 million Earth years ago). So you will find numerous other species similar to the ones that could be found on Earth at that time. There are no mammals or birds, though some flying insects are relatively large.

A fascinating feature of evolution, combined with alien beings nudging it in certain directions, is that you end up with similar types of animals filling similar evolutionary slots. In this case it results in a similar catalogue of dinosaur types to those seen on Earth emerging, albeit variations thereof.

LOCATION

Close Neighbours

Dinosaur 1 appears to be a close neighbour, apparently only a little more than a light year away from Earth. The impression given was that looking approximately down on the Earth's North Pole, you could travel on a clockwise lateral arc relative to the centre of the Milky Way and arrive in roughly the right part of the Galaxy.

Similar Dimension

Whilst most advanced alien species appear to reside at higher dimensions, Dinosaurs 1 who are comparatively less advanced, appear to reside at a similar dimension to the Earht Plane. This adds to the possibility of physically visiting this species in the future, once the necessary space-time travel technology becomes available.

For the novice astral traveller, the similar dimension also makes visits easier as there are fewer dimensional and time distortions to deal with.

PLANET

Forest World

Dinosaur 1's planet is (or was) largely forested. An introductory comparison would be the Amazon rainforest. Naturally, there is quite a considerable variation between the types of forest on this planet. At the polar regions the trees are few, short and similar in style to deciduous ones, though in practice they are evergreen. Whilst between the tropics the trees are truly enormous and able to grow to what appears to be around 1 km (2/3 mile) high from root to canopy.

These very tall trees achieve extreme height by four simple measures. F*irstly*; they grow in very dense clumps for very long periods of time, thus tending to give each other lateral support. S*econdly*; they are able to extract minerals from the ground so that the trunk acquires the compressive strength qualities of metals and ceramics. T*hirdly*; as the tree roots are very substantial, new forest gradually develops on top of the old structures. F*ourthly*; new trees can to some extent recycle the root system of their parent. This leads to a very dark labyrinthine forest with an often indeterminate forest floor.

In a world where it can be around 1 km from the canopy to the original ground level, young trees that sprout near the surface do not have the roots to reach water far below, and minerals even further down. Conversely, if they were to sprout further down they would have no light and be unable to grow. To solve this difficulty, parent trees effectively suckle their offspring who start life in the canopy with water and nutrients from far below until the offspring have managed to acquire the necessary roots. This, in turn, adds to the density of the forest.

Being a rainforest, fortunately, there is a steady supply of water flowing down, so all the trees and other plants attempt to capture it before it sinks down to the water table far below.

Though the large mature trees all rely on having some access to that water table below.

In summary, this forest is so tall and dense, it can be difficult to determine quite where the forest floor actually is.

No Oceans Now

In this forest world there are no visible seas. A vast amount of water is locked up in an artificially high water table below the dense parts of the forest. Furthermore, the trees' ability to grow very tall has enabled them to colonise what were once shallow seas. Though in this case the trees become progressively shorter as the ocean gets deeper.

Where the ocean is too deep for trees, other plants have grown over the top so as to give the impression of jungle growing up to around 3 meters (10 ft) high. Again, lateral support between plants makes this feasible, and flotation bladders on their roots enables them to float.

Slow Rotation Planet

The rotation (if any) of any habitat planet has an enormous influence upon how things develop there. The anecdotal evidence so far gathered suggests that if a planet rotates quickly, everything develops faster. This seems to be because every time you have a night's sleep, you wake up renewed and refreshed. Conversely, as is the case here, when a day is around 2.5 times the length of an Earth day, this tends to result in a slower pace of innovation.

For completeness, where planets rotate extremely slowly, for example taking more than an Earth year, the dark side becomes substantially uninhabitable. Where there is a continuous land mass, most of the animals exist in a constant state of migration. Where there are large obstacles such as oceans, this tends to create species that can by one means or another hibernate for very long periods.

Climate

The term rainforest captures the essence of the climate between the tropics, and a practical consideration for animals is constantly getting wet. Hence, the more waterproof the animal the better.

Towards the poles, the climate becomes drier, and thus verging on arid. Outside of the rainforest it does not seem to actually rain a lot, instead there can be heavy mists, which the trees and other plants try to harness.

The planet does not appear to have clearly defined seasons, and conversely appears to be relatively warm across its entire surface.

No Mammals

This is a planet dominated by insects and reptile like creatures. All the animals, so far observed here, lay eggs. Some animals carry around those eggs and in further cases have even developed pouches to carry them. Such pouches can in turn allow the young to hatch out but still be carried around by their mother (marsupial reptile).

SPECIES

Evolution

As described, having a very large animal does not of itself lead to higher intelligence. It's perfectly possible to encourage any animal to have a larger brain, but if that animal is not adequately stimulated, their brains will still not develop properly. So for example, if a top predator has too easy a life, it will not be very stimulated.

Dinosaurs 1 primary habitat was dense forest, and in this respect they grew about as large as was practical. Whereas, outside the dense forest, other reptiles grew much larger in line with what you might expect from earthly dinosaurs. Consequently, there were larger carnivorous dinosaurs that, given the chance, would prey upon Dinosaurs 1, but they were prevented from doing so by being too large to operate in the dense parts of the forest.

The way in which Dinosaurs 1 were evolved was largely similar to how the earthly ones were developed. The main significant difference was that it seems to have been even more difficult to get any animal to display higher intelligence on this planet. So it took a great many attempts by the Creators and assisting alien beings to tweak the evolutionary process into producing an intelligent self-aware animal.

One of the biggest difficulties seems to have been getting, what you could loosely describe as herds, to exchange information and skills properly. Information sharing and developing larger social groupings appears key to stimulating the development of excellent minds.

Intriguingly, when researching Dinosaurs 1 evolution, it became very obvious how 'story telling' is a key stepping stone in advanced information sharing. Though this is largely a function of imagination and therefore has its limitations. The next evolution (for both Dinosaurs 1 and humankind) is total experience sharing, which involves re-experiencing events without imagining them.

Similar To Flightless Birds And Apes

Dinosaurs 1 have a very similar anatomy to combined earthly birds and apes. Though they retain reptilian features as opposed to appearing feathered and having a beak. Since they are originally a forest animal, they move around like apes. Powerful legs enable them to jump high, or if on firm ground run fast.

This is a warm-blooded animal, that has the useful ability to reduce the amount of heat it generates if it needs to remain cool.

In terms of eyesight, sense of smell, and hearing, the nearest comparison would be an Earthly wolf. For example, being able to hear high-pitched sounds, see well in the dark, and smell relevant scents; all these are similar to what a dog would possess. Accordingly, Dinosaurs 1 are excellent hunters, but differ from most other animals by having excellent hands with opposable digits.

Large Inefficient Brain

The head of Dinosaurs 1 contains a large brain which is around 3 to 4 times larger than a human brain. However, in terms of processing power, it is roughly similar to a human brain. Furthermore, when compared to other advanced alien species in general, it appears to be highly inefficient.

Two Groups

In simplistic terms, Dinosaurs 1 fall into two distinct groups: F*irstly*; there are the native forest dwellers who have considerable intuitive skills and hence higher awareness. S*econdly*; there are the relatively new urban dwellers who have lost this skill. Inevitably therefore, if you are visiting Dinosaurs 1's world, it will be easier interact with the forest dweller, as the urban dwellers will mostly have extreme difficulty noticing your astral presence.

Reptilian Reproduction

Reproduction is very similar to how male and female birds would bond and bring up young. A big difference between earthly dinosaurs and Dinosaurs 1 is egg size and quantity. Earthly dinosaurs tended to produce large clutches of relatively small eggs. Modern earthly birds by comparison, who are descended from dinosaurs, produce fewer and relatively (to their size) much larger eggs. Dinosaurs 1 have also adopted this approach to breeding which is typical of human beings. Thus they tend to mostly produce only one relatively large egg at a time.

Due to the constraints of natural resources in the forest, the forest dwellers tend to limit reproduction to take account of the available food resources. They have largely adopted a simplistic rule of "one out, one in", meaning that you only get pregnant in response to someone dying. This is combined with a recognition that they reincarnate, and have sufficient memories of doing so that they consider themselves to be one big, very long-lived, community or family.

By comparison (and this is a fascinating parallel with Earth), the urban dwellers lost their higher awareness and instead, for example, developed religion where actual knowledge is replaced by stories and speculation.

CULTURE

Technologically, the urban Dinosaurs 1 are similar to human beings of the mid 1800s or Victorians. Whilst the forest dwellers remain in the stone age, but nevertheless make basic tools and typically cook using fire. Thus the two distinct groups need to be considered.

Life In The Forest

It is challenging for a modern urban human being to appreciate the extent to which living in harmony with nature is possible, and the extent to which a hunter-gatherer lifestyle integrates with this. For example, whilst plants and animals are eaten for food, their souls are respected. As far as possible, resources are not wasted, as they are considered a gift from the Creator. This makes for an interesting comparison with early 21st century human beings who try to wrap all food in plastic and avoid any real connection with the source.

The forest is an incredible tangle of branches and tree trunks. So much so that it is normally difficult to define what constitutes ground level, because you can descend a long way down through a labyrinth of gaps between the tree trunks. An easier definition of ground level is thus delineated by the height of the water table.

Dinosaurs 1 typically live in clusters of 10 to 20 individuals living in small settlements constructed in the tree tops. Platforms are constructed in these settlements and walkways similarly built to link them all up. Thus there are several million Dinosaurs 1 living in a very large connected community in the forest.

There is no obvious form of government, but instead, a strong community spirit which encourages harmonious living. The concepts of crime or money do not exist. This was not the original state of affairs and is an evolution upon having endless tribal (extended family) wars.

Dinosaurs 1 primarily eat smaller dinosaurs, and as far as possible nothing is wasted. Bones, for example, are ground up to create a paste which can be used in the construction of simple houses. Unused animal parts are then often fed to the very animals that will be eaten in the future.

Progressively over time, the tree canopy gradually gets higher, so the small settlements are extended upwards. Thus incredible labyrinths develop in what becomes an underground world. So if you want to know how your great great grandparents lived, you can visit their old homes in the equivalent of the basement of your village.

Tools are made using timber, and petrified timber; i.e. At lower levels the tree trunks are so saturated with minerals that they become stone-like, and can be made into tools.

Life Outside The Forest

Left to its own devices, the forest does not really end, it just gets smaller, much shorter, and greatly thinned out towards the polar regions. However, many centuries of deforestation has severely depleted the forest in the temperate regions so that something akin to plains have developed in place of the forest.

Whilst the Dinosaurs 1 that live in the forest are naked, the urban ones who live in the temperate region wear clothes to keep warm. In this society, money and land ownership exist. Thus, so does crime, which is mostly dealt with by putting to death any offenders.

The urban Dinosaurs 1 exist in what roughly appears to be an array of small city states. The Northern city states being highly isolated from the southern ones by typically at least 3000 km (2000 miles) of dense forest. This looks set to persist until the development of the internal combustion engine and flight. Urban and forest Dinosaurs 1 do not intermingle and thus passage thorough each other's territory is exceptionally rare.

There is also an on-going issue of overpopulation outside the forest. The urban dwellers will endeavour to have as many offspring as possible, which now places unrelenting pressure on available resources.

Effect Of Industrialisation

Whilst the urban Dinosaurs 1 have developed artificial money, the two resources of great value are food and metal. Both of these are in permanent short supply due to overpopulation.

The principle diet is meat, and other species of dinosaurs are farmed in the same way that cattle are reared. Compared to the forest, the yield per hectare (acre) is low and thus huge tracts of land are required. Furthermore, cutting down the forest produces a relatively arid landscape, and reduces the availability of water, which would previously have emanated from the forest.

With respect to metal, there appears little in the way of iron or copper ore that can easily be mined. However, the tree trunks at lower levels are rich in minerals and are instead mined. Mining focuses upon; iron for machines, and copper for the recent development of electrical equipment. Thus trees are felled, with the tops being used for firewood and charcoal so as to extract the metal from the lower trunks and roots.

Small industrial towns and cities therefore spring up on the edges of the forest and progressively eat into it for resources.

Education

In the forest there is no formal education system and no reading or writing. Conversely, their intuitive skills are excellent as they are integral to hunting; i.e. It is possible to sense the presence of prey before it can be seen, heard, or smelt. Visiting alien worlds through astral projection is a skill that is learnt in childhood.

Surprisingly (and possibly difficult for some human minds to understand), there is no real interest in technological advancement amongst the forest dwellers. Instead there is an attitude that a life surrounded by technology can be achieved by living elsewhere in an appropriate society.

In urban areas, education is of increasing importance. There is a cultural objective to educate all young Dinosaurs 1 in reading, writing and numeracy. This has the effect of clogging their minds with imaginative thoughts and severely handicapping their intuition.

Outlook

The forest dinosaurs know that realistically their days are numbered, but see the matter in a greater context of reincarnation. They are aware that one day they will stop reincarnating in the forest, but instead become born into urban families.

The ultimate demise of the forest dwellers will be as a consequence of the discovery of flight. Once the northern and southern societies become more aware of each others activities, they will compete to fell and mine the forest that separates them. Almost nothing of the once great forest belting the planet will remain.

Because the forest over time has created its own artificially high water table, eroding the edges and reducing it to islands deprives it of water and severely damages the eco system in the forest.

Similarly, the high water table in the forest supplies the otherwise arid plains that border them. So destroying the forest does away with a great source of fresh water. However, irrigation technology will deal with the resulting crisis.

INTERACTION WITH HUMAN BEINGS

Race To Meet Each Other

Forest dwelling Dinosaurs 1 are very enthusiastic about meeting human beings. With respect to astral explorations, they know about the earthly humans, but hitherto have had no meaningful contact to speak of. The forest Dinosaurs 1 are keen to interact with advancing human beings before the impending dark age that they will soon go through.

For human beings, spending time with a forest Dinosaurs 1 provides a useful reminder of how to access natural higher awareness.

In the future the forest Dinosaurs 1 will become extinct, or otherwise absorbed into an urban society where they will lose their astral projection skills. So in many ways there is a race against time to interact with them before such interactions can only take place in the relative past.

Astrally Visiting

If you wish to astrally visit any early human beings such as cavemen, North American Indians, etc, you will often find they are waiting for you seated around a fire. With Dinosaurs 1 the same appears to apply. So quite literally you can find your entry point to one of their communities appears to be through a fire.

Upon entering their world you will typically find yourself drawn towards their equivalent of a medicine man who can be male or female. At this point allow your host to energetically balance your astral body, and you should be able to view and understand the community. One of the main astral difficulties beginners often have to deal with is information overload. The main symptom of which is getting confused by apparently not being able to sense anything specific. The other thing to note is that you are typically entering at night.

This is a two-way interaction, and the medicine man will probably be showing his gathering your human world. Be prepared to help explain your world to them.

It's amusing to note that the dinosaur forest dwellers consider their urban counterparts to be savages. Hence, a reader might too be regarded as having savage tendencies.

Help With Telepathy

Human beings tend to wander around imagining things when they could be sensing their environment and being quite telepathic. This can be overcome in relatively quiet conditions, but when under emotional pressure such as during a challenging meeting they go back to imagining. Forest dwelling Dinosaurs 1 have the equivalent challenge with respect to hunting, but are adept at remaining intuitive, so you can learn from them.

Many of Dinosaurs 1 prey can telepathically sense them, and can also be dangerous when hunted. An equivalent would be a human being trying to catch and kill a fox with his or her bare hands; i.e. You might get bitten. For Dinosaur 1 hunters, it is important to blend their presence into their environment, so for example, taking on the energies of a tree blends them into the forest. Thus one of their hunting techniques is to physically and energetically look like a branch, and wait with their eyes closed, barely breathing, until the next meal comes within convenient reach.

The insight for human beings is that when stressed, they tend to imagine things, instead of sensing useful information and answers. If a human allows his energies to blend into his environment and particular nature, these telepathic skills are enormously improved. The insight is to learn to be at one with your environment, whatever that may be. An indicator of success is that you will be able to sense portions of what others around are thinking.

A skill exchange in this scenario would for example involve the reader learning additional telepathic skills, whilst in exchange passing on a knowledge of reading, writing and mathematics.

E14 Engineered Viruses

INTRODUCTION

Engineered viruses are one of the key tools in physically encouraging species development, and in many ways they can reasonably be described as alien visitors. Despite all humankind's fears that aliens might wish to invade the planet, alien interventions with engineered viruses have proceeded more or less undetected.

An initially reasonable definition of "alien life" is organic life which did not originate on Earth. However, there are plenty of alien species who identify themselves as having been involved in seeding an initially substantially sterile Earth with organic micro-organisms, and even more who have assisted the evolution of what subsequently developed. Hence all life on Earth has alien origins of some sort.

A more pragmatic earthly definition of "alien life" is therefore an organic life form that has been introduced more recently; e.g. Something introduced by alien scientists since the initial seeding of organic life on the planet.

Viruses that have been engineered by alien scientists and introduced into Earth's eco-system are therefore alien organisms in their own right. This is particularly pertinent as many of them are intelligent, engineered viruses, which can act upon remote commands.

It is therefore ironic that whilst many human beings fear an invasion of aliens, this has long been occurring, but with microscopic entities.

Existing Feral Viruses

A good example is types of viruses that give you, the reader, the occasional cold or flu, and can best be described as "ferial viruses". These were originally introduced to the Earth early on and have evolved along with the rest of the eco-system. Accordingly, they can be considered to be natives, or not particularly alien.

Introduced Engineered Viruses

Alien engineered viruses are normally introduced for the purposes of directing the evolutionary path of an earthly species. Accordingly they can be considered to be alien. Furthermore, researching this chapter did not uncover any other circumstances where an engineered virus had, or would, be introduced for some other purpose.

Engineered viruses are one of the key instruments of any genetic modification programme. They represent the equivalent of a computer software update or patch. They readily enable alien scientists to modify the DNA in existing organic organisms on a planet. Without such alien intervention you, the reader, would not be reading these words as you would not have a sufficiently well-developed brain that could process these words.

Virus Deployment

Engineered viruses are deployed when it is desired to modify an existing species in a particular direction. For example, to make it grow larger, or have better eyesight, etc.

By comparison, similar DNA modifications can spontaneously occur on their own. However, spontaneous self-modification by a species produces a much slower rate of evolution. Similarly, spontaneous self-evolution may miss certain evolutionary targets. Whereas, targeted modifications can achieve the desired results relatively rapidly.

E14 Engineered Viruses

The DNA in almost all organic life on the Earth is designed to have inbuilt instability and produce occasional mutations. This causes a species to keep producing variations of itself, such as growing bigger or smaller. Darwinian evolution then determines which of these modifications is beneficial or detrimental; i.e. If the modification makes the species more successful, the mutation will be carried forwards. Alternatively, if the modification is unsuccessful, that modified organism will die out.

In summary; engineered DNA modifications replicate what can, in any event, occur spontaneously. However, the pace of spontaneous evolution can be very slow and it is often helpful to speed it up by deploying engineered viruses that will modify an organism's DNA in a desired direction.

Alternative And Supporting Means Of Modification

For completeness, if it is intended to modify a species, there are of course other methods of achieving this objective without necessarily using virus technology. Two common methods are:

- F*irstly*; In the case of advanced organisms, samples of unfertilised eggs and sperm can be collected. The DNA modified, and a modified fertilised egg implanted into the womb of a female. This procedure is often carried out upon human beings who have been abducted.

- S*econdly*; The energetic spirit template which defines an organic body can easily be modified or otherwise altered. If a template is modified, it can affect the genetic coding of both that individual and its offspring. This procedure is always carried out as part of any evolutionary upgrade, and is sometimes sufficient in itself to achieve the objective(s).

In summary; there are a number of ways in which human beings can be modified. Engineered viruses are simply a useful tool, amongst a set of tools for accomplishing evolutionary targets.

Purpose Of Modifications

Consider the background. The ultimate Creator or super-consciousness wishes to observe itself from lower physical planes and induce an energetic feedback. The Creator divides itself into Creators to undertake the work required to achieve this objective. The Creators create and employ advanced consciousnesses defined as souls. The souls in turn create higher-selves. Higher-selves employ spirit forms which manifest personality and capability. The spirits in turn operate the physical bodies. Some of these physical bodies are advanced aliens, who in turn are employed to create new types of advancing life forms such as human beings.

Through this creative mechanism, the Creator is able to observe itself from the perspective of engineered human bodies who have been progressively modified by alien scientists.

Self-aware organic bodies are able to perform the function of enabling the Creator to observe itself, whilst simultaneously providing a variety of interesting experiences. The illusory experience of being alive also creates vital energies which enable the Creator's development. Therefore modifications which support this energetic feedback are encouraged.

A major objective is to enable high self-awareness, but in low physical dimensions. This can eventually occur randomly, or by manipulating the evolutionary process the same result can be accelerated, and even improved upon. Earthly human beings are an example of recreating an existing successful design at a low dimension. The current objective is to significantly upgrade the capacity of human minds to facilitate greater self-awareness on the Earht Plane.

LIVING GENETIC MANIPULATION TOOL

One Reason Why Engineered Viruses Exist

It is possible to create more or less any animal you want in a laboratory. But doing this in real time, or rather your time, is a very long process. A sophisticated animal takes years to grow, and if you want to modify the result, it takes years to grow an updated version.

A solution to this difficulty is to grow your animal in a lower and even parallel dimension. Your animal can be grown at its own slow pace in a world where time runs much faster when compared to your dimension. By this method you can grow several generations of your animal within what might equate to only minutes in your time at your higher dimension.

The challenge is then how to arrange and modify DNA in a world where you do not exist. You can potentially take a short visit to the lower dimension world and undertake some modifications, but you can't spend very long there. Similarly, transferring your animal to your higher dimension is liable to damage it sooner rather than later, so that is not an easy approach.

Ideally, what you want is some sort of tool which operates in the lower dimension world and performs DNA manipulation procedures, upon individuals or even the whole target species. Viruses offer an excellent solution because they can alter the DNA in your animal in more or less any way you wish. Since viruses are also much simpler entities, they can easily be manufactured at a lower dimension, then set to work.

For completeness, it is worth mentioning that the same general principle applies if you are engaging in other forms of time travel.

E14 Engineered Viruses

Background

In a universe that is looped back on itself and is created from a timeless Astral World, any debate upon what came first will soon flounder on the rocks of it all being an illusion in the first place. Nevertheless, if you want to apply some sort of artificial linear sequencing to it all, viruses were developed from very simple single cell entities. Such simple entities preceded the development of more complex cells such as the typical bacteria seen on Earth.

Micro-universes existed (relatively) before larger ones. In such micro-universes there are plenty of intelligent life forms and virus-like entities abound. Furthermore, all the fundamental components within the current Earht Plane's single cell organisms were originally developed in micro-universes.

In basic micro-universes, there is a lower degree of individuality. Viruses all form part of a group and individually have no real distinguishing features of their own. Whilst viruses replicate, that only produces more of the original individual group. This is similar to how a human body behaves when cells replicate. Creating new cells does not produce a new individual human being; e.g. Growing hair cells does not produce a new person.

For one virus to become different from another, it needs to mutate and significantly alter its DNA. This again has similarities with the human world, because a child is a different version of its parents.

Historically, viruses are simple entities and therefore produce a less refined awareness of the Creator than a human being. Because viruses are simpler, they are also relatively smaller spirits. In fact much smaller. If your human clairvoyance is sufficiently developed this is something you should immediately verify for yourself.

Personality

Intelligent virus spirits are very open to following the directions of higher spirit forms. So the higher-self which operates a human being has no difficulty communicating with them. Whereas, a human ego can certainly attempt to communicate with viruses, but will easily be misled. This is not really the fault of the viruses, as they operate at a very low astral level. Hence, you will find plenty of other spirit forms that will seek to affect human minds at such low levels.

Virus spirits try to be helpful provided it falls within their main interest of replicating themselves. Beyond this, you may find their conceptual understanding of anything is somewhat limited. Similarly, if you want to modify or otherwise give them new life, they will generally respond with enthusiasm. It's as if you were dealing with computer software that simply enjoyed running.

Working With Viruses

You could simply create any engineered viruses you needed in test tubes and then put them to work without any apparent meaningful interaction. But that would be to overlook potential sub-conscious influences upon your mind. For example, virus spirits would like to adopt bodies in order to access a physical world. Similarly, they can potentially influence you and make your mind wish to create such physical bodies for them to live through. So it is helpful to remain mindful of what might be influencing your actions.

When dealing with viruses, one of your objectives should be harnessing their joy at reproduction, whilst getting them to cooperate with any necessary restraint. On the Earht Plane, feral viruses, such as colds and flu, can rampage around the host body corrupting the function of cells to the point that the host body has to destroy its own cells. If you are using viruses for genetic manipulation you need a more sophisticated behaviour.

Otherwise, like feral viruses they turn a body's infected cells into a virus factory and chaos ensues.

If you want to change the DNA of a living organism you need to alter the coding within its cells, whilst at the same time not turning all the organism's cells into virus factories. The ideal cells to affect are often the reproductive ones; egg cells in females and sperm stem cells in males. For example, the accentuation of human DNA can be modified, so each successive generation will be more intelligent. It is also often necessary to stop the accentuation at some subsequent point, otherwise that strain of the species can make itself extinct by, for example, growing too large.

A method of achieving this is: F*irstly*; to make sure the virus is not too aggressive, thereby causing significant damage to the host body and triggering a strong immune response. S*econdly;* the prospective factory cells (where the virus will be reproduced) in the host body should not be the DNA modification target cells. So, for example, if the reproductive cells are targeted for modification, they should ideally not also be the factory cells. Thus the host's offspring or children can, if desired, be born without the virus, but with the modified DNA.

In summary, harnessing viruses makes an excellent way of enabling you to accentuate your target host's features, such as having a bigger brain. The important thing to remember is that working with them should always be a cooperative venture. It will be more than a purely physical relationship.

Robots Or Independent Life Forms

At the time this encyclopaedia was first published, a virus was the only life form human science could truly engineer. Human technology had developed sufficiently far that you could manufacture one in a test tube. So given an appropriate understanding of what viruses do, and how they operate, in the same way as a computer programmer can write a program which performs a specific purpose, you can create your own virus.

Once assembled, your virus will spring into 'life' and given suitable access to a host cell (viruses need to hijack living cells to replicate themselves), will make more copies of itself if that is part of its operating programme.

So to what extent is a virus therefore alive ?

Everything is alive to some extent, physical matter exists because there is a living energetic template which enables it to exist. Without that template, matter would collapse back into nothingness. If you arrange matter together in the right patterns, you get consciousness processing devices, such as a brain.

Viruses do not have brains, as such, instead they largely operate as automated programs mostly concerned with self-replication. This understanding classifies them as robots enacting whatever set of instructions their creator has installed within them.

An animal brain is made up of multiple cells which communicate with each other. Whereas viruses have no such neural network through which they can exchange information. Instead they simply rely on a more fundamental, group awareness, communication system common to all living things.

In summary; individual viruses operate in a robotic manner. Whereas their group spirit is open to communication and, depending on circumstances, has a limited choice of possible actions.

INTELLIGENT VIRUSES

Advanced Viruses

In other micro-universes, micro-organisms such as viruses have been able to become more advanced. In particular they make use of group non-physical brains whereby they are able to manifest a modest degree of intellect.

Whilst researching this encyclopaedia has not so far uncovered viruses advancing sufficiently to construct machines, groups of them had achieved a higher level of organisation. By comparison this would put them ahead of earthly ants and termites in some respects.

These advanced individual virus cells display no more individuality than a human skin cell would. However, they are sufficiently connected to their non-physical brains to succeed in acting collectively. Similarly, in some instances they have developed a culture of their own where different groups of viruses cooperate with respect to host organisms they rely upon.

All of these other micro-universe viruses appear to employ different DNA to that seen on Earth, but that has not precluded their soul groups from manifesting on the Earht Plane.

Employing Viruses

As described, viruses can be created, introduced to their host, and allowed to operate somewhat robotically. Initially they will normally carry out the DNA modifications or other functions intended, and all is well.

However, viruses can and do mutate. So they are capable of deviating from their original programming. For example, a virus intended to eliminate cancer cells, could increase the scope of its attack to healthy ones as well.

It is therefore prudent to work with intelligent viruses. An analogy is guarding your home with a trained dog which responds to your commands. As opposed to using an untamed lion that might attack you, as well as the intruders you were originally defending yourself against.

It is difficult for an untrained human mind to interact with intelligent viruses. Advanced viruses' spirits are of the opinion that early 21st century human minds are mostly not sufficiently advanced to warrant such communications. Whereas advanced aliens are not subjected to the same restrictions. The difficulty for early 21st century human beings is that the sensitivity required is very challenging to deal with.

Non-Physical Brains

Some organisms have no detectable brains; e.g. Earthly jellyfish. Yet they can nevertheless deal with their environment by reacting to stimulus, such as light or touch. In this respect viruses can also respond to their environments even though they have no obvious brain with which to do so.

Both intelligent and feral viruses possess non-physical brains, but there is a considerable difference in how the two types use these brains. For the feral viruses it is mostly an interface which helps observe what they are experiencing, whilst similarly directing changes to their energetic templates which determine possible mutations. For intelligent viruses, their non-physical brains also act as an interface which determines how they behave (as opposed to just influencing mutations).

Intelligent viruses' non-physical brains are used to command their actions, and to some extent even reprogram otherwise robotic behaviour. Thus communicating at a higher level with intelligent viruses enables agreement upon what they do.

ORIGINS OF VIRUSES

Viruses were created in different universes from the one mankind experiences. In artificial simplistic linear time, this perceptually occurred before the creation of the universe human beings experience. The design of viruses was in turn replicated in the universe human beings experience using locally available material and an improved version of their original DNA.

Original Universe

The first viruses were originally created in micro-universes devoted to micro-organisms. These universes typically looked like large spheres of yellowish fluid with a light source at the centre. As this was the extent of such universes, anything visiting it had to be created within it.

In such universes experiments were conducted, which ultimately created simple micro-organisms that could replicate themselves. What occurs has some parallels with theories about how life on Earth might have invented itself. Except that this evolution really took place in other micro-universes, and life on Earth was the result of successful experimentations elsewhere, being imported.

Single Cell Organism Evolution

All organic life forms are vehicles for spirits to inhabit and facilitate low dimension consciousness. An organic cell is fundamentally a collection of atoms and molecules held in place by an energetic astral template which requires them to take such a form. If this energetic template is removed, then the cell will ordinarily decompose by one means or another.

The original organic micro-organisms were all constructed from simple molecular compounds which enabled a very primitive consciousness. Hence feeding back energies to the ultimate Creator which enabled it in turn to grow and develop more living micro-organisms.

The essential goal was to create more physical micro-organisms to facilitate the consciousness mechanism. Accordingly, the micro-organisms were programmed to reproduce themselves, by simply copying themselves.

Sexual Reproduction

The fundamental limitation inherent in cells splitting themselves is that it only produces a rather limited increase in consciousness. Cells of the same type are operated by just one major spirit, which is split into recyclable minor spirits. Creating more micro-organism cells does not increase the perspective. Identical copied cells only produce one perspective. To increase perspective, or alternative viewpoints, requires genetically different cells.

Organic cells are designed to naturally mutate so as to produce a continual stream of variations. But that of itself does not produce significantly new perspectives unless it continues for very long periods. A superior system is to get two dissimilar cells to cooperate by sharing copies of their DNA to produce a third, unique, cell. This new unique cell will be occupied by a unique spirit form generating a new perspective. This reproductive system is referred to as sexual reproduction.

The common arrangement is for one of the parent cells to act as a female, producing a new child cell-casing along with a half-copy of its DNA. Whilst the other parent cell, acting as a male, only has to insert its half-copy of its DNA into the new child cell. For convenience, the male DNA is often transferred within a sperm packet.

In summary, sexual reproduction greatly increases diversity of new awareness, and is therefore desirable.

Virus Evolution

Viruses are a variation of the sexual reproduction system. A virus is essentially a variation of a sperm packet. Except that instead of entering a new child cell, it enters the parent or host. When this virus sperm packet enters the parent cell, it then conjoins its DNA with that of the parent.

The invaded parent cell is then turned into a virus factory where it manufactures multiple copies of the virus, releasing them out into the world around it. The newly manufactured viruses then invade new host cells, and the cycle continues.

The next innovation was to dispense with much of the virus DNA. A host or parent cell may need to contain lengthy DNA operating instructions for both photosynthesis and reproduction. Whereas, the virus cell need only contain the reproduction element of the DNA instructions. Therefore, with a far shorter DNA coding, the virus cell can be much smaller.

In summary, the advantage of a virus cell is that it can simply insert new DNA into a host cell. However, this form of reproduction produces little new awareness.

Advancing Culture

The original viruses only lived in relatively primitive worlds, where their main interest was reproduction. Researching this encyclopaedia did not identify any examples of them working with tools of any sort.

Instead, intelligent viruses have advanced in other areas. In particular they have learnt how to cooperate with other viruses in order to survive and flourish. For example, if viruses invaded all potential host cells, there would be nothing left to reproduce them. Thus, as they became more advanced and had the potential to dominate the micro-universes they lived in, they had to operate in balance with each other and their environments.

Similarly, with mutual cooperation achieved, it was possible for advanced aliens to recreate viruses' physical forms in new environments.

This has had the interesting effect that intelligent viruses only like cooperating with other beings that are at least their equals with respect to mutual cooperation.

INTERACTION WITH HUMAN BEINGS

Viruses have been used to modify the majority of major species on the Earth. Such species that have not been specifically modified, have evolved from species which were at some point modified. It therefore follows mankind's continuing evolution can be further improved using virus technology. Not only can children be born with genetic improvements, but human beings' current health and intelligence can be upgraded.

Viruses are not an advanced alien race, so it is helpful to interact with advanced alien races who do understand the technology so as to discover how to make better use of it. Meanwhile, as viruses are nevertheless alive, it is helpful to be able to interact with them in the same way that it is sensible to be able to interact with any workforce.

Interacting With Feral Viruses

Feral viruses are not the ones that have been engineered to give your human body, for example, a bigger brain, etc. These are the viruses which often make your human form ill, for example, the various strains of colds and flu.

A helpful start is to sense the world that a virus experiences. Viruses are for practical purposes experiencing a different universe to the one a human mind perceives. Individual viruses have no eyes, so instead perceive the energetic templates which form matter. Life for a virus is a bit like being a spacecraft that seeks the light of planets it wishes to blend with. Such planets actually being the cell they wish to invade.

Life for an individual virus is incredibly straightforward. It's physical life begins when it emerges from the factory cell where it was created. It then floats around for an indeterminate amount of time. Normally, if it is otherwise not destroyed by something, it finally manages to land on another bright planet (new host / factory cell's energetic template). Then, if it manages to connect to that planet (host cell), its DNA cargo is discharged, and it dies. Death takes it to Virus Heaven where it is soon allocated a new life.

E14 Engineered Viruses

There is very little opportunity to really interact with a feral virus. However, advanced aliens are able to communicate with their group consciousnesses via their non-physical minds, and bit by bit are sharing the techniques with human beings. It is possible for anyone who has studied astral science to grasp the fundamentals of such communication.

Viruses have almost no awareness of a human mind's thoughts, so what a reader might think about them has very little direct impact upon them. Though what a reader thinks will have an impact on his or her immune system which deals with any virus invasions.

From a higher plane, a human consciousness can influence viruses. Essentially the commands you can give viruses are relatively simple; stop, start, or die. Thus a virus can be placed in a dormant state for a long period of time. Furthermore, when a virus is in a state of quiet hibernation its host's immune system will tend to leave it alone.

In principle, if a reader is suffering from a cold or flu, etc, it is possible to switch the illness on or off. Making friends with suitably skilled advanced aliens is the easiest way to learn that technique.

Interacting With Alien Engineered Viruses

Alien Engineered Viruses refer to viruses that have been manufactured and released into, in this case, the human population. In conducting the research for this encyclopaedia, the fearful question arose, "could aliens kill the human species through a virus attack ?" The amused reply was, "Yes in theory. But what would be the point ?" By analogy, you do not normally kill your own child.

It appears that the human population has been introduced to viruses that are likely to benefit it. For the current purposes we are interested in dormant viruses which can be activated. In this respect apparently mankind has had a variety of useful but dormant viruses inserted. They are mostly designed to improve intelligence and awareness, with some other ones intended to improve digestion so as to cope with refined fats and sugars more efficiently.

No doubt the typical reader would be uplifted by the possibility of suddenly becoming smarter and thinner. However, most of the viruses in question are designed to affect your offspring's DNA prior to conception. So if an alien soul group wanted to place one of their own into human form, the human body to be occupied could be preloaded with useful improvements.

For already conceived adults, readers should be aware that their bodies were almost certainly pre-loaded with cold and flu viruses designed to divert you from making too much alien contact. Apparently for your own good.

Since all these viruses are mostly already installed, and awaiting an activation command like some otherwise dormant piece of software, can a human mind interact with them ?

The annoying reply was, "Mostly no". The aliens who installed them can communicate with them and switch them out of hibernation, but primitive human minds will not have the capability. The expression "locked" seems to explain the position quite well.

Future Uses By Human Beings

Intelligent viruses are keen to help in any way that allows them to replicate. They can be programmed to target different types of cells in the body, and it is therefore worth looking forward in time to some of the future applications Future Human beings will enjoy. Whilst aliens' use of engineered viruses are mostly targeted upon the next generation, humans can, of course, employ them on the current one. Good examples are as follows:

CANCER:

In many cases it will be possible to create individual specific viruses to tackle cancer cells in the body. Cancer generally results when there is a failure of apoptosis. Virus cells can insert a DNA code patch into existing cells which resolves the issue in the majority of cases.

AGING:

Looking old and wrinkly results from the fact that all animal bodies are designed to age. This feature is difficult to override, however it is possible to alter the rate at which this occurs. The intermediate result will be young-looking people with the mentality of the pensioners they actually are.

BODY MODIFICATION:

It will become possible to alter your DNA so as to achieve body modifications, such as being taller, thinner, and having more hair on your head. Very noticeable, and controversial, will be a progressive elimination of dark skin in people. Men will have access to a cheap and painless method of enlarging their genitals, though most women will not be impressed by anything exceeding minor changes, as any excess soon becomes impractical. Meanwhile, women in particular will keep pushing the boundaries of possibilities and when it comes to being the recipients of almost any conceivable experiments:

- Permanent looking make up, that can still be varied.
- Patterned skin.
- Almost every conceivable hair colour.
- Incredibly smooth skin, and sometimes shiny like latex.
- Adjustable breasts; regular size for daytime, expandable for flirting.
- Eye colours.

- Ear and nose shapes.
- Shrinking of hands, feet, waists, necks, and vaginas (thus rendering male enhancement largely pointless).
- Appearing child-like, to some extent.
- Barbie Doll legs, etc.
- Fertility regulation and extension.

Intelligence V Sensitivity Balance

Making a human being more intelligent does not make it more self-aware. Making a human being more sensitive to astral energies does not make it self-aware either. Instead these two abilities have to operate in balance for self-awareness advances to occur.

Higher intelligence increases the mind's ability to contemplate possibilities, which can simply delay useful physical action occurring. Similarly, higher sensitivity can also confuse the mind because it often produces unrecognisable conflicting feelings, which similarly delay physical action.

A simple feeling to act, followed by the uncomplicated mental processing to put that feeling into action produces quick physical results. Similarly, a feeling to pay attention to what you really are, converts into a quick response to do so; i.e. Success.

By comparison, a complex set of feelings needs very complex mental processing to reduce them into a simple and properly thought through physical action. Thus the greater the energetic astral sensitivity or ability to contemplate, the greater the challenge to achieve an optimum balance.

A good balance is principally achieved by adjusting the energetic template which defines a human form. However, the physical wiring of a brain can be significantly improved by altering the DNA coding which defines much of its functional layout.

Apparently a virus release was carried out in the earthly 1800's to progressively reinstall greater higher awareness in a rolling program that would affect successive human generations. Global human DNA was altered so that each generation would have greater astral awareness, along with the ability to intellectually deal with it. The original engineered virus that was introduced is now spent, but the modification will affect each successive generation. A side effect of this is that more and more children will be classified as autistic in coming years. A "levelling off" DNA alteration to curtail the progressive increase has yet to be implemented.

The autism issue is further exacerbated by a new influx of souls who are relatively unfamiliar with the Earht Plane, but more familiar with advanced alien worlds.

E15 Ants 1

INTRODUCTION

Many advanced aliens are derived from insects, and have attained a size comparable with human beings. It appears that in the universe humans experience, such a body size is quite efficient at supporting higher intelligence; i.e. Typically 1 to 3 m (3 to 10 ft) tall. Whilst across the range of universes, many species of insect have nevertheless succeeded in achieving a higher intelligence without having to grow so large. A good example of a small, but nevertheless intelligent species, is Ants 1.

In the case of Ants 1 they are a good example of a body type that works more efficiently in a different and more compressed universe. So whilst they can reconstruct themselves in the universe humans experience, it is not an ideal world for them. They do physically visit the Earht Plane, but will not normally venture outside their craft.

With respect to small UFOs however, the reader should exercise caution with any assumption that are all crewed by small aliens. Many small UFOs are simply robotic probes and bear no real relation to the size of their potential operators' bodies.

Advanced Small Insects

In view of the fact that most of the aliens you can physically encounter are derived from genetic material similar to that found on Earth, it follows that physical issues are often similar. So for example, higher intelligence generally requires a larger brain. Thus whilst many aliens are anatomically insects they mostly still have to be of sufficient size to accommodate large brains. Hence, it is helpful to study small advanced aliens who have become highly intelligent without adopting larger body forms.

Ants 1 live in a world where matter is more compressed. So it is possible to have smaller brains due to the compression, but still have relatively similar processing capability to larger ones. However, if Ants 1 had been evolved in a world with less matter compression, they would arguably be of comparable size to most equivalent advanced aliens; i.e. 1 to 3 m (3 to 10 ft) long.

LOCATION

Similar But Denser Universe

The universe small Ants 1 originate from has a great many similarities with the one human beings experience. Conversely, the greatest significant difference is that the overall relative density of everything appears to be higher; i.e. Matter occupies less space.

It appears that in a denser world the speed of light is also physically less, but remains proportionately similar. The effect of the higher density is that the scale of everything appears equivalent to a less dense, but larger world. Only by comparing a dense zone with a less dense one does the difference become apparent.

As the research continued, it further became apparent that the density of this universe and the corresponding speed of light was not uniform; i.e. It is different depending upon where you are. From this research, it similarly emerged that the universe humans experience also has regions of different relative density and a corresponding variation of the speed of light.

It is possible for species such as Ants 1 to re-form themselves in the universe humans experience, by recreating the appropriate matter densities within their craft. Though such home comforts are difficult to recreate outside of it.

For completeness, this points to the fact that the conditions within alien spacecraft can in general can be anomalous to those outside. So craft which are larger (or smaller) inside than outside are possible, though uncommon. Thus in principle the fictional Doctor Who's Tardis could actually be constructed.

Smaller Solar System

The principle Ants 1 solar system has broad similarities with the one human beings experience, except that everything is on a smaller scale. The perceptual first impression was that everything was around 50 times smaller. The laws of physics operate similarly, but in a scaled-down way so that life there has substantial similarity to that on the Earht Plane. The effect is that if you experienced living there, you would not necessarily notice how everything was relatively scaled down.

There appear to be approximately six main planets, with Ants 1's planet being the third from their sun.

PLANET

Appearance

From space the planet appears mainly arid, with ice at the poles and patches of greenery lying between the tropics. There are some large lakes, but no real ocean. The surface appears to have many volcanoes, with around 50% appearing active (as opposed to extinct).

The planet is surrounded by a series of small moons ranging in size from mere asteroids to planetoids. This has the effect of causing regular eclipses of their sun.

The planet appears to rotate relatively slowly, and may be subjected to an unstable orbit.

Climate

Noteworthy is a very unstable climate, punctuated by hot spells and ice ages. There also appears to have previously been more water available, but much of it is currently locked up below the surface or in the polar ice caps, whilst the rest was evaporated into space.

Compared to Earth there seems to be around only 5% of the number of animal species, no doubt on account of the severe on-going climate change. Overall, this is a relatively hostile environment, which goes some way to explain why Ants 1 prefer to live under cover.

Ants 1 Environmental Impact

Ants 1 environmental impact can clearly be observed from space. Much of the surface of the planet has been re-developed with various constructions. Compared to early 21st century human activity on Earth, their operation appears to be even more extensive in some respects. Though from a distance there is barely any sign of visible agriculture. Nor is the planet illuminated by artificial lighting at night.

Earthly ants typically live underground, whilst by comparison Ants 1 have evolved to prefer surface accommodation. Ants 1 mostly reside in large concrete constructions built above the ground. Extending from each colony are large concrete surface tunnels. Ants 1 have a plentiful supply of cement and have made extensive use of it. The abundant concrete based structures are visible from space as the atmosphere is relatively transparent.

SPECIES

Not Humanoid

The majority of advanced visiting alien species a human being might physically encounter on Earth have acquired a loosely humanoid biped appearance regardless of their origins. However, Ants 1 have still retained an anatomy and stance which is very similar to an earthly ant.

In addition, Ants 1 forearms have been adapted to use tools.

More Ant Than Termite

To describe this species as 75% ant and 25% termite gives a useful approximation as to what they are. The anatomy is outwardly very like earthly ants and the system of living in colonies is again very similar.

Specialist Breeding

Ants 1 live in colonies and create specialist ants as required; i.e. Queens, workers, etc. The main difference is that: F*irstly*; they make more use of males than their earthly counterparts. It appears that male brains are often better adapted to scientific thought processes, hence specialist males were developed. S*econdly*; they use a multiple queen arrangement.

Climatic Effect

The species had previously grown larger in stature, with a typical worker ant growing slightly in excess of 1 m (3 ft). This equated to an earthly dinosaur. However, from this peak, the typical workers have shrunk to around 5 cm (2 in). This seems to result from the combined effects of there having been a scarcity of food and less oxygen in the atmosphere to support such a large animal. Queens are only slightly larger than typical workers.

Social Order

On Earth, in such a colony you would have one queen, but with Ants 1 there is the interesting variation of having more than one queen. The evolutionary leap is that if a queen is laying eggs all day, there is less nutritional energy to develop and operate a big brain. By having one queen with a big brain and around half a dozen smaller brained sisters who lay eggs, a leap of specialisation occurred. The main queen controls and commands the colony, whilst her sisters lay all the eggs.

Ants 1 were originally similar to earthly ones where there is little use for males. The evolutionary leap was to create more useful males in a society where previously males only supplied sperm to the queen. Giving the males bigger brains and turning them into scientists suddenly enabled their society to go from utterly primitive to technologically advanced. Males are dominated by their queen. Males mostly grow to around 6 cm (2.5 in) long. Like the queen, these scientist males rarely venture out, except for breeding reasons; e.g. Mixing the DNA of colonies is useful. Thus males will be dispatched to neighbouring colonies as required.

Finally, the matter of competing for resources had to be addressed. So Ants 1 stopped fighting with each other and started cooperating. The principal queens are highly telepathic, and control their colonies and workers by this mechanism. Similarly, they have the ability to communicate with each other without actually meeting. It was further commented that it would be exceptionally rare for principal queens to ever meet.

With respect to overall planetary government, the collective consciousness of Ants 1 has substantially created a non-physical leader, "The Great Mother Ant", who oversees their activities.

Not Bipeds

Unusually for an advanced species, Ants 1 are not bipeds, and retain all six legs. The end of any leg has an arrangement of of claws which can be used like fingers in a hand. There is a tendency to favour the front limbs when hands are required for grasping objects.

On occasion Ants 1 will carry objects using their front limbs, thus using only 4 legs for walking.

Astronauts

Typical Ants 1 spacecraft are saucer-shaped and 25 to 40 cm in diameter (10 to 16 in). They also use manned probes that can be as small tennis balls of around 3 cm (7 in). A typical crew size is 6 to 8, made up of males and females. The females do most of any physical work that arises, and the males anything which is not too physically strenuous. Queens rarely, if ever, become astronauts.

Space-time travel can make it difficult for a queen to control her offspring, so the males will operate autonomously where necessary. Hence, if you physically encounter this species, your initial point of contact is likely to be a male.

With respect of physically manifesting themselves in the universe that humans experience, Ants 1 largely need to remain in their space-time craft due to dimensional differences. Thus recreating themselves on a larger scale relative to that of the less compressed universe humans experience appears impractical at this sample point, and they have chosen to remain small on such excursions. To achieve this, the laws of physics appear to operate differently within their craft, hence venturing outside this protected environment is not practical.

CULTURE

Rule Of The Matriarchs

On Earth a leader is normally a single person representing the views of millions of people. An Ant 1 queen typically represents around 100,000 ants, and is a very large spirit entity. The queens normally represent and speak for their entire colony.

Also worth mentioning is that an initial encounter with a queen may suggest a lack of emotional warmth, which is unusual amongst advanced aliens. However, as the relationship develops, a very deep emotional warmth becomes evident.

Ants 1 queens have developed an excellent working relationship with each other and are unlikely to quarrel. Their world is very well administered and there is a clear emphasis upon working towards a common good.

Sub-Queens

Each colony is ruled by one large brained queen. Egg laying is done by small brained sisters. The telepathic connection between them is such that all queen ants act as if they were just one person.

Should the principal queen die, or too many of the sub-queens die, then they are all replaced by a new principal queen and her new smaller brained sisters.

Social Tension

Males are responsible for all technical advances, and such limited art and literature that exists in their generally minimalist world. New discoveries and art introduce a great deal of individuality to their society. Such individuality also introduces different notions upon the best way to run a society. Such notions create great social tension especially when government is a matriarchal dictatorship.

Where this social tension will take Ants 1 is difficult to determine at this time, and it is not clear what the outcome will be in this version of their evolution.

Small Indoor Society

Due to the generally inhospitable climate, the Ants 1 home planet appears to be relatively sparsely populated. So whilst they are such prodigious builders that their construction works are visible from space, there are very few Ants 1 to be seen outdoors.

Ants 1 prefer tunnels to, for example, roads. So Ants 1 build overground tunnels between anywhere they wish to travel to. Though they have incorporated something similar to levitating trains to operate in these tunnels where there is any great distance to cover.

Indoors, Ants 1 appear to have very minimalist tastes, and no obvious enthusiasm for interesting architecture. Colony buildings have no windows and just a few external openings. Internal walls are not painted. However, their egg incubation facilities are warm, cosy, and the eggs rest in soft furnished heated cups. Floors, are mostly level, which is a relatively recent innovation.

Technological Dichotomy

Ants 1 have access to space-time travel technology and are further able to reconstitute themselves in other universes, hence their relevance to human beings. In this respect they possess excellent advanced technological capability.

The dichotomy, or contrast, is that in many other ways they make very little use of available technology. They have access to internal lighting, but make little use of it. Telecommunications are rarely used, telepathy being the preference. The atmosphere in equivalent alien worlds is often cluttered with flying craft, but not here. There are alien visitors to their planet, but such visits are relatively few.

Until recently (at this sample point), Ants 1 made extensive use of volcanic cement for construction purposes. Though now, almost reluctantly, they manufacture their own. Adopting the manufactured alternative only seems to have become necessary due to some major construction projects requiring vast quantities of cement.

Whilst Ants 1 have access to most advanced technologies, they seem to prefer simpler lives. Physical labour is virtuous and enjoyed by all who perform it. They find electrical fields disturbing, so avoid them where possible.

The Great Mother Ant

Human religions normally propose the idea of following God's wishes. Though for the most part humans have so far had difficulty understanding what the super-consciousness actually wants. Thus they generally interpret any heavenly communication in somewhat rigid earthly, and often confrontational, terms. In addition, human minds further corrupt any understanding of heavenly communications with an invented perception of right and wrong.

All alien species and humankind operate under the umbrella of a unifying spirit consciousness or super-consciousness. Whilst this is similar in principle to the traditional human interpretation of "God", advanced aliens create more functional sub-gods to deal with each civilisation's management. These sub-gods are substantially a collective consciousness.

Each Ants 1 colony's principle queen is guided by what translates as their planet's sub-god or "Great Mother Ant". This is a spirit being who oversees their lives and activities. This spirit being is really a creation of their collective higher consciousness; i.e. They substantially created their own sub-god. Thus the ultimate Creator or super-consciousness planted the "seed", and Ants 1 grew it into a divine non-physical overseer (in writing these words there was a temptation to use the word "ruler", but that was declared to be misleading).

The most obvious effect of creating their divine overseer, The Great Mother Ant, is that Ants 1 avoid virtually any conflict with each other. Unsurprisingly, any species that has yet to develop such a collective overseer is regarded as still somewhat primitive.

The Great Mother Ant enables the species to collectively decide how to rule itself. A practical application of such overseeing is that they are able to decide which specialist ants they need to breed in order to maintain and advance their society.

By comparison, human minds of the early 21st century Earth had access to the same super-consciousness or ultimate Creator all the other species in all universes have access to. However, human beings had not energised a common collective consciousness to oversee and guide the administration of the

Earth. In the absence of developing a sub-god, human beings will continue to have difficulty establishing an overriding consensus upon how to properly manage the Earth, and endless conflicts will arise.

Footnote: It was during the editing of the first edition of the encyclopaedia, and over one year into writing it, that this collective consciousness sub-god creation mechanism was properly observed, courtesy of Ants 1.

INTERACTION WITH HUMAN BEINGS

Relevance

What is the relevance to humankind of an otherwise obscure species of advanced insects who reside in a different universe ?

The short answer is; they are neighbours trying to help humans evolve. In this instance, helping and encouraging humans to build a higher guiding collective consciousness or sub-god.

A helpful analogy is that of living in a small town, where you have various relationships with certain individuals who are scattered around the district. For example, interacting with Grasshoppers 1 will help you improve the quality of your unconditional love. By comparison Ants 1 are experts in social organisation, which in turn feeds back into the need to generate a healthy collective consciousness.

The starting point for building a healthy collective consciousness is individual minds having good stable access to higher awareness. However, the group energies which influence early 21st century human behaviour can make higher awareness difficult to manifest on the Earht Plane. When this chapter was first written there was remarkably little human consensus that this deserving objective should even be achieved.

Alien Expertise And Experimentation

By researching other societies, Ants 1 are able to incorporate new advances into their own. In return, Ants 1 endeavour to assist a society they are researching.

The quality of The Great Mother Ant will be improved if individual worker ants feed her more dynamic unconditional love. For worker ants to achieve this requires that they all experience more individuality. The difficulty for them is that if worker ants are permitted more individuality, this is inclined to complications such as inducing daydreaming, possibly even boredom, and therefore less production. Hence the danger is that instead of getting a more sophisticated Great Mother Ant, Ants 1 could end up with less efficient and even disaffected worker ants.

By comparison (seen in hindsight), early 21st century humans had not yet organised a sufficiently coordinated higher awareness to create a collective consciousness that could lead their society. On its own, only connecting with the super-consciousness does not of itself remedy this issue, as it is disinclined to oversee the micro-management of a society's behaviour. Thus when compared to advanced alien societies, there was an absence of planetary leadership for human beings, which in turn resulted in endless conflicts.

In summary; Ants 1 wish to incorporate more individuality into their workers. Their experiment is therefore to use the human comparison to discover what aspects of individuality should be increased or emphasised. Conversely, they are also researching what aspects of individuality are unnecessary for their workers advancement. There is of course no definitive answer to this question, and a good answer will always be in need of further improvement as a society develops.

In return, the alien expertise Ants 1 are introducing and sharing are energies which enable human minds to operate in a far more coordinated and efficient manner.

The Pleasure Of Work

Ants 1 have a society where all members enjoy their work, and in general always have done. Their society in turn cares for its members in appropriate ways. Whilst all Ants 1 are affected by aging, this is dealt with by always allocating them appropriate activity that enables them to contribute whatever their age. When an ant is too old to contribute further it happily dies.

A simple effect of the success of this approach is that this is an advanced species which has never needed the mechanism of money or finance during its history. By comparison, many other now advanced alien societies have previously had need of financial mechanisms.

Ants 1 pointed out that it is impossible for any advanced society to operate without money and finance if it has not developed a common advanced collective consciousness. Similarly, if workers operate without a strong connection to a positive collective consciousness, many of them will be unwilling to work.

Organisation V Individualism

As a species, human beings have long prided themselves on their ability to nurture great individuals. Though in fairness, the Earht Plane human species was designed for this purpose, along with plenty of other humanoid species which similarly exhibit variation of this characteristic.

For the most part human beings have treated individuality as a virtue, and earthly societies which have failed to do so have typically found that experiment ends in stagnation of the civilisation. For example, the ancient Chinese were relatively advanced, but then fell behind when individuals were excessively forced to conform.

The simple advantage of individuality is that it creates more channels for new ideas. By comparison, Ants 1 society has bred special males to almost exclusively perform this function.

However, without a well-developed collective consciousness, an abundance of interesting ideas does not of itself advance a society. An abundance of interesting ideas always needs to be filtered down to those which are to be adopted. Thus a society's collective consciousness will normally give useful direction on which ideas to physically apply and test. The result is a well-ordered society that avoids conflicts.

Ants 1 current situation (at this sample point) is that they only generate relatively few good ideas. These ideas are well executed by dedicated workers, leading to efficient outcomes. However, refinements are often slow to emerge or altogether lacking since the workers simply enact the ideas without question.

With respect to most of the advanced technological developments Ants 1 benefit from, these were substantially provided to them. So without alien assistance, Ants 1 would not be very technologically developed due to a slow pace of indigenous innovation. In fairness, it must be noted that aliens regularly drop innovations into the minds of all developing species. However, in the case of Ants 1, fewer of them were capable of properly receiving them.

Thus whilst Ant 1 society needs more refinement and development of ideas, human society has the opposite scenario in which good ideas are plentiful. Instead, for humans, there is insufficient conversion of good ideas into physical manifestation.

Observation

Ants 1 have the ability to reconstitute adapted versions of themselves in the universe humans experience. With respect to their manifesting size on the Earht Plane they are typically just around 2 cm (3/4 in) long. Hence they can pilot relatively small craft.

With respect to physically observing one of their craft, this will only occur if they come into the dimension that humans principally experience. This an infrequent occurrence as Ants 1 only need to manifest at this lower dimension if they need to take actual measurements, such as the composition of earthly atmospheric gases. Furthermore, Ants 1 indicated no interest in tinkering with human DNA.

With respect to Ants 1 greater interest in the evolution of human consciousness, like most other advanced aliens, this can mostly be accomplished from higher dimensions. Similarly, the use of higher dimension automated probes and observation devices is common place. Since there is considerable interest in the data gathered from such probes amongst other advanced alien species, they are mostly deployed as part of joint observation projects. Hence the results are shared amongst most of the interested species.

With respect to human beings who might be paranoid about being observed or otherwise monitored, the advice was to get used to it.

Assistance And Intervention

Ants 1 took the view that they would not normally intervene in any human conflict, nor would it be easy for them to do so. They further pointed out that there were protocols placing restrictions on how they might intervene.

However, Ants 1 were nevertheless keen to make contact with humans and, with consent, run mutually beneficial experiments with them. In particular, with respect to the early 21st century, they are enthusiastic about working with human individuals and small groups who wish to increase their higher awareness.

Through works such as this encyclopaedia a human consciousness can interact with advanced alien consciousnesses. In the case of Ants 1, a human being can observe examples of higher awareness behaviour and learn how to replicate it. Similarly, Ants 1 wish to help enlighten human beings upon how to deal with clashes of individual intention.

In summary; it is worth reiterating that Ants 1 are experts in creating a planet's governing sub-god or collective consciousness. Similarly, they wish to share their expertise in this matter with humankind.

E16 Mechanoids 1

INTRODUCTION

Mechanoid (definition used): A mechanical device controlled by an integral organic brain.

Science fiction generally, and in light of the facts, unfairly depicts aliens as hostile species planning to invade Earth. Furthermore, sometimes these invaders are not even proper aliens, but a variety of mechanical devices, with or without a vestige of organic content. In English culture the Daleks are probably the most popular threatening fictional machine species, though never smart enough to recognise that their nemesis, Doctor Who (with around 800 consecutive victories against them credited to his name), will always defeat them.

Placing science fiction entertainment aside, the question is; do any mechanoid (machines with organic life content) actually exist ?

Most advanced species are inclined to employ robotic devices, for example, for data gathering. Thus alien robot encounters are quite common. Very small alien spacecraft are more likely to be robotic or mechanoid devices than piloted by small aliens.

The question therefore advances to; are there any alien species that employ robotic devices as physical bodies, or some similar arrangement, which might thus classify them as mechanoids ? Furthermore, have any such species have actually had any interaction with human beings to give their existence some relevance to humankind ?

An added complication to this question is that; advanced aliens already regard human bodies to be organic mechanical devices in themselves, thus enabling the ultimate Creator to experience a contrasting reflection point. Curtailing this question to the fundamental of; are there any actual robotic species ?

Upon further investigation, evidence of actual mechanoids emerged, in this case operated by a variation of the Grey species.

For completeness, so far no evidence of a purely non-organic mechanoid independent species has been found during this research; i.e. No purely mechanical race of independent beings has been found. Only robotic machines under the control of organic alien species have so far been found.

Background To Mechanoids

The circumstances in which any advanced species might need a mechanoid body other than as a spacesuit, or for replacing damaged body parts, or something similar, are few. All advanced alien species seem able to improve and genetically modify their bodies to cope with most practical needs. Thus most advanced species can largely circumnavigate any need to create a part-organic, part-mechanical, mechanoid body to live in. By comparison, most less advanced species will at some point experiment with mechanoid replacement bodies.

A robot is a device that uses purely electronic processing to navigate its way around its world. Whereas, a mechanoid uses some sort of organic brain, which will then invariably be connected to an electronic processor. A mechanoid brain will also need to sleep.

For a mechanoid's organic brain to function it must be operated by spirit forms. In practice the creation of an artificial brain will draw spirit forms into it. Hence a mechanoid's brain is alive.

Lower spirit forms, which are normally perceived as elves, goblins, nymphs, etc, do not have physical bodies on dimensions such as Earht Plane. Artificial engineered organic bodies have from time-to-time been engineered for them, and can be encountered on other worlds or the Earth's future. So in a universe where possibilities are to be explored, it stands to reason that a mechanical body that can give lower spirit forms life would be created by someone.

The next factor to consider is that lower spirit forms are mostly concerned with making the illusion of physical life more exciting. So it follows that any lower spirit being, given physical access to the Earth dimension would be inclined to make it exciting; which is often perceived by human minds as trouble making.

Fundamentally, all a lower spirit form requires to connect into the Earht Plane dimension is an organic brain. Whilst brains perform complex tasks, it is not difficult for an advanced civilisation to artificially grow them. Furthermore, it is even easier to plug a brain into a sensor system which can convert its thoughts into mechanical movement.

Researching this subject indicates that a number of alien civilisations including future humans have tried, or will try, putting their own brains into mechanoid bodies, with similar results.

If for example, a human brain is placed in a mechanoid body, at first it will be able to operate that body. Eventually, the original person (such as a higher human spirit) will leave the body (appear to die in the physical sense). However, the life-support system will keep the brain alive and it then becomes dominated by lower spirit forms. A bystander might perceive this as a brain becoming "possessed".

In summary, if a brain is transplanted into a Mechanoid body, the original 'person' will eventually die and you end up with just lower spirit forms operating it. Or alternatively, you can grow a brain and allow it to get taken over by lower spirit forms from the outset. Note that all brains require assistance from lower spirit forms to operate regardless of whether or not the final arrangement is governed by higher spirit forms.

An Actual Mechanoid

The representative species Mechanoids 1 (if you dare refer to it as an actual species) was in this case created by one of the sub-species of Small Greys, now referred to as Small Greys 2. These mechanoids come in various forms, and were originally created as a type of servant. The original programme to create a life extending body for Small Greys 2 proved very problematic for the reasons already described. So the current crop of mechanoids are in effect the useful remnants of what would otherwise be a failed experiment.

The aliens helping with this research pointed out that any advancing species would only pursue such a project if their own thinking was heavily influenced by spirit forms. This is because these types of projects give new physical life opportunities, of sorts, to spirit forms.

The mechanoid resulting in this case can really be described as a brain in a box, which is attached to a robotic machine. The brain in a box of itself has no movement capability, and the box itself is mostly devoted to life support. For convenience, the supporting internal organic tissue is synthesised and connected to the artificial organic brain. The size of the boxes can vary, but around 60 cm (2 ft) square is typical. The brain in a box can then be attached to almost any conceivable type of mechanical equipment.

In terms of the typical level of intelligence achievable in this instance, this can be compared to an intelligent dog, horse, pig, dolphin, etc, or an intellectually backward human being. Thus, a mechanoid makes a good servant when fitted with a suitable mechanical body and can be trained to happily perform chores and moderately complex tasks.

Why You Might Need A Mechanoid

You can train a mechanoid to pilot a space-time ship or at least act as a communications and control interface, which has a considerable advantage over a purely non-organic electronic control system. In the physical universe, the huge distances mean communication systems operating at the speed of light are going to be absurdly slow. For example, sending a radio signal across the Milky Way will take around 100,000 light years. Whereas an organic brain can instantaneously receive telepathic signals wherever it is in the universe, so the speed of light no longer limits long distance communications.

As a footnote, the human early 21st century search for extraterrestrial intelligence (SETI) was heavily focused on trying to detect radio communication signals that advanced aliens rarely used for the reasons just described.

So if you want to communicate with, and hence control a remote space-time ship, an organic pilot or communications officer of some description is required. This requirement becomes even more apparent when you are dealing with travelling between different dimensions. A radio signal sent in one dimension is inherently problematic to detect in another. Different dimensions, are for practical purposes "dark matter" and for the most part are physically undetectable relative to where you are.

In summary, if you want to communicate with a remote probe in a faraway part of the universe, and possibly a different dimension, then you need an organic brain in that probe to achieve this. Hence, you either put one of your colleagues in the probe, or have it operated by a mechanoid.

Inherent Problems With Mechanoids

F*irstly*; keeping a brain artificially alive, does not stop any spirit forms (higher or lower) who are operating the brain from leaving it. If one spirit form leaves, then invariably another takes its place. By way of analogy, if you had a loyal pet dog, one morning you could find its original personality has left (died in physical terms), and been replaced by a new one that does not like you. So a mechanoid, which can be your trusty loyal servant or even space-time ship pilot, can inconveniently suddenly manifest a completely new personality. It is possible to sometimes predict such switchovers, but not altogether prevent them.

S*econdly*; lower spirit forms enjoy influencing advancing human or alien minds. All spirit forms crave interesting experiences, so lower spirit forms can easily influence the minds of their masters. When a spirit form is grounded in any body, be it natural or artificial, its power of influence at that level is vastly increased by any easy access to physical action. So a mechanoid that starts out as a servant can take control of its master.

LOCATION

In general the development of mechanoids has been experimented with by so many different advancing races that it has touched every part of the universe that humans can experience.

Milky Way

With respect to the mechanoids developed by Small Greys 2, their main planet is approximately a quarter of the diameter of our galaxy away from the Earth. The region seems dominated by large gas clouds, which slightly obscure some of the locality.

Similar Dimension

In terms of dimension, this seems very close to the one human beings experience. It would further appear that beings living at higher dimensions would be less inclined to create such mechanoids.

PLANET

Mars Size And Cold

From space the Small Greys 2 main planet appears to be sandy-brown, and approximately the size of Mars. The atmosphere looks very clear with very little cloud. The temperature seems to hover around the freezing point of water. Most of the water and other fluid on the planet seems to have got locked up in the ground. There does not appear to be sufficient geothermal energy or sufficient sunlight to release the water at surface level.

Colonised Cave World

The Small Greys 2 that live here are not native. They mostly live underground in an enormous, warm and well-heated cave and tunnel labyrinth that they have excavated. The alien made caves and tunnels that extend across much of the planet and provide a very comfortable home. The caves are mostly well lit and a large amount of vegetation grows within them. Water runs through many of the main caves and tunnels so as to create artificial rivers.

Most of the inhabited caves and tunnels have plants growing in them producing oxygen, and the environment appears to be a very comfortable place to live. However, the atmospheric gas mix does not appear suitable for humans.

Earth Tremors

Despite the low level of geothermal activity, the cave network is repeatedly and routinely vibrated by tremors. Fortunately the cave roofs appear very stable and collapses are unusual. Should cracks appear in the roof, they are immediately repaired.

SPECIES

Inception

Mechanoids 1 were born from a failed program to create replacement bodies for the Small Greys 2 brains. As already described, the results were problematic, and upon the death of the grey, the mechanoid would become possessed.

The next or parallel development was that Small Greys 2 were intent on colonising a new planet. The planet they occupied at the time bore a lot of similarities to Mars, but with a better thicker atmosphere. However, due to a high level of solar radiation, the surface was inherently inhospitable, and life below the surface seemed a more practical proposition.

The technology to create mechanoids already existed, and this was an ideal opportunity to create an army of robust machines to help construct an underground labyrinth.

Tunnelling Workers

Small Greys 2 therefore needed excavation and tunnelling workers. The preferred tunnelling technology was to dematerialise matter; i.e. Disintegrate the rock they were tunnelling through. This process produces heat, noise, plenty of dust, and a lot of temporary radiation.

Unsurprisingly, Small Greys 2 found it convenient to use mechanoids for tunnelling.

Domestic Use

Domestically, mechanoids have also proved very popular. The "everyone should have a least one" mentality, and substantially automated production, meant that they were easy to produce and plentiful in supply.

One downside of this arrangement is that it tends to make the master species lazy. Since this development can easily tend to stagnate society, most societies are wary of creating too many mechanoids.

Space-Time Pilot Brains

As described, if an unmanned robotic probe is to operate at any distance from its master, it requires an organic brain to receive commands. Accordingly some space-time ships are piloted using mechanoid brains.

Mechanoid pilots are also popular in manned space-time craft. Since mechanoid brains can easily communicate telepathically with their masters, it is often convenient to direct journeys through them.

Appearance

As described, these mechanoids are based upon a "brain in a box" plus mechanical body design. Due to the size of the brain in a box, this is typically located centrally on domestic servant mechanoids. So whilst Small Greys 2 are typically of thin appearance, their servant mechanoids normally appear fatter, yet retaining a vaguely Grey-ish outward appearance.

If the brain in a box is being used to pilot a space-time craft or tunnelling machine, then it just appears to be part of the control system and has no other body.

Diet

As far as possible the mechanoids' organic components have similar or identical DNA. This makes it possible to feed the mechanoid nutrients in the form of what was described as "industrial blood"; i.e. The mechanoids are fed on, and excrete blood. The excreted blood is then purified and re-nourished so that it can be reused.

To re-nourish the blood, in principle a Small Grey 2 could simply exchange blood with the mechanoid's blood reserve tank.

However, common practice is to use an artificial re-nourishment process.

Since the practical design of the "brain in a box" varies, it is easiest to use a typical example of the nutrition system. Carrying around a complete set of digestive organs to re-nourish the blood is hugely inefficient; instead it is easier to have what can accurately be described as "fat tanks". Nutrients, mostly carried in fats, can be transferred from the "industrial blood" and stored in an internal fat tank within the brain's life support box.

"Industrial Blood" that is highly charged with fat fuel for the brain, appears yellow as opposed to red. Once the blood has been used, it appears blue or even green depending on its specification. The blood is recharged by having organic nutrients artificially added to it again.

Immune System

Getting the immune system to work properly in synthetic animal tissue is extremely difficult. In fact the whole system is inherently unhealthy and would, in the normal course of events, result in organ failure and death. The solution is to exchange blood with healthy Small Greys 2, who thus update the antibodies. So in many ways the mechanoids are genetically Small Greys 2.

This arrangement highlights how the Mechanoids 1 are very dependent on the Small Greys 2, as without them it would be difficult to deal with infections.

CULTURE

Mostly Happy Servitude

Much in the same way that a human being might own a horse that enjoys being ridden, or a husky dog that wants to pull a sledge, the mechanoids enjoy performing their allocated tasks. If you imagine a servant who yearns to tidy and clean up after you in your home, you get the general idea.

As the organic material constituting the brain and support tissues can be regenerated and thus forcibly kept alive almost indefinitely, an observer would note regular personality shifts. So whilst the lower spirits which attach themselves to these brains come and go, this does not erase previously learnt behaviour, but does cause a fluctuation of mentality.

The Small Greys 2 treat their mechanoids with loving warmth. So in practice this is a happy cooperative arrangement.

Rogue Potential

Lower spirit beings mostly help the illusion of physical life appear real. Thus they contribute to the manufacturing of this illusion. For the most part, the lower beings are concerned with simply maintaining life. By way of comparison, similar lower beings will operate a human mind and enable it to do a day's work in a somewhat automated state. So it's helpful to realise that they are reasonably capable when attached to a good artificial brain, and can similarly demonstrate modest intelligence.

However, every now and again, a lower spirit intent on fermenting interesting situations will take possession. In these instances conflict can occur. Where the masters are paying attention to their servants, the masters will "see this coming" and deal with it at an early stage.

It was commented that by comparison, if early 21st century human beings were to be in charge, enough rogue lower spirits would succeed in taking over, and there would be a rebellion by the mechanoids.

INTERACTION WITH HUMAN BEINGS

Since Small Greys 2 visit Earth, it follows that so do their mechanoids. However, in the early 21st century, recognising one as such will be difficult as you are unlikely to actually see the "brain in a box".

Space-Time Craft

The "brain in a box" technology can be scaled down to very small sizes. No minimum possible size could be identified, and it was stated that this technology could be adapted to a micro scale. Though apparently, the usefulness of micro mechanoids is often limited as mechanoid brains much smaller than earthly mouse size can not property support an intelligent lower spirit form.

As stated at the beginning of this chapter, very small spacecraft are generally robotic. Whilst a smaller proportion are instead piloted be small aliens, and an even smaller proportion are operated by Mechanoids 1.

Nevertheless, larger spacecraft can also be piloted by Mechanoids 1. A mechanoid crew of two or three brains being common in order to deal with their sleep requirement.

Abduction And Experimentation

It was pointed out that laboratory equipment fitted to space-time craft, whilst largely automated, could often be controlled by a Mechanoids 1 "brain in a box". Thus human beings can have close encounters with such engineered beings. In particular mechanoids can be part of an alien team who experiment on human beings.

Lower Spirits Wish To Interact With Human Minds

Writing this chapter was often conducted under repeated distraction by lower spirit beings. The experience combines occasional dizziness, whilst having distracting thoughts enter the human mind. Lower spirits enjoy creating compelling illusions, so they often resist anyone who might 'look behind the scenes'. Fortunately, the vast majority were both cooperative and informative, so research was possible.

It is helpful to note that; human minds are given life by the ultimate Creator acting through higher level souls, which all feeds down through the lower spirit levels and finally animates a human mind. The lower spirits are thus dedicated to giving the ultimate Creator an interesting experience, and wish to offer their services.

In particular, many lower spirits like to assist by giving human bodies amusing fantasies with which to pass their day. The lower spirits want (really want) to point out a form of mechanoid that truly excites them. Depending on the design variations, it looks like anything from a semi-organic second skin, to an entirely mechanical or robotic outer skin for a human body; referred to now as a mechanoid second skin.

The main purpose of this second skin is to give human minds the experience of being captured in fantasies. The combination of an organic second skin operated by lower spirits can be likened to being imprisoned in a compelling dream. For early 21st century men, the most typical appealing fantasies concern warfare and violence. With exciting sexual experiences also available, and even the possibility of what it would be like to be imprisoned in a female body. For women, the dominant fantasies seem to concern truly being loved by someone, and being forced to be a rampant sex object. With the occasional holiday fantasy also available.

The lower spirits really wish to encourage human beings to develop the technology to temporarily imprison themselves in fantasy mechanoid second skins. This would allow the lower spirits to compel the human mind to accept the fantasy on offer. They further added that when such an exciting alternative becomes available, fewer human beings would be interested in taking drugs as an escape from life.

As for the Small Greys 2 who are familiar with the principles of such technology, they took the view that this would be both an interesting and stupid experiment. *Interesting*; because experiments can produce unexpected results. *Stupid*; because a lot of human minds would become imprisoned in very compelling fantasies. Experiencing life as a human being, or for that matter an alien, is an engineered illusion. Hence adding a second layer of fantasy onto the original one simply distances the mind from any higher awareness.

E17 Big Jelly 1

INTRODUCTION

In order to benefit from reading this chapter it is very helpful to sense this entity as you read:

- If you do so you will gain a useful new perspective.

- If you do not adequately become personally aware of this being whilst reading about it, you can easily find yourself wondering why you are even studying this part of the encyclopaedia.

A Universe In Itself

Most of the species examined in this encyclopaedia inhabit a universe of some description. However, Big Jelly 1 is really a universe (of multiple dimensions) in itself. Nevertheless, whilst it is principally its own universe, Big jelly 1 can also be considered to be a species. This is because it is a proper living organism, as opposed to an organism living somewhere on a rocky planet.

Typically, the vast bulk of advanced alien species existing in physical dimensions bear some resemblance to humanoid beings or animals of some description. This is because they are mostly created from the similar DNA structures and are performing similar functions. So it is interesting to investigate a species which differed significantly from almost everything else you might encounter.

The Big Jelly 1 species does indeed appear to be a large jelly like entity. It has no apparent skin, internal organs, mouth, limbs, or anything else associated with a typical animal. It appears to be a simplified physical manifestation of the ultimate Creator. So whilst mankind produces an experience of not being God, Big

Jelly 1 and entities like it produce a very similar experience to being God manifested. Except that this is on a smaller scale and in a simplified way.

The comparison between humans and Big Jelly 1 is stark. Humans spend the majority of their time trying to get through their day, but usually only pay infrequent attention to what they actually are. By comparison, Big Jelly 1, like its creator, devotes itself to discovering what it is. Plus having fun in the process.

Visiting From An Alternative Universe

Big Jelly 1 has its own universe and is the constructor of that universe. It also has the capacity to enter into the universe human beings experience and manifest itself there too. Drawing upon its jelly-like form, it can make itself appear to be most physical things if desired.

This species developed itself in its own universe where everything has been formed from this jelly substance, which is neither a gas or liquid. In its universe it can create limited scenarios which bear similarities to those experienced in other universes. By analogy, this is like a child recreating a scene it has seen in a film or movie, but using its toys and dolls for the re-enactment. Thus Big Jelly 1 recreates many scenarios in its own universe that were inspired by its observations from other universes.

In the universe humans experience, (typically) biped animals are evolved to (metaphorically speaking) look up and notice what created them. The DNA of animals is manipulated so that highly intelligent species will eventually emerge, and combined with natural evolutionary processes, the whole system works very satisfactorily.

Whereas in the Big Jelly 1 universe, whilst such beings might appear to have been created, it is reasonably obvious that they are truly what could be described as “thoughts”, or intentions. Thus actually there are no proper DNA based life forms. In this world everything is much more of a game.

One Big Eternal Being

Big Jelly 1 is really just one big being. It can split itself into an infinite number of parts, and conditions permitting, grow infinitely large. Thus it is the sort of being that could take over everything. This category of species is also highly unusual in that its physical forms do not sleep or die.

In its own right it acts like a creator, and is able to manifest itself in different forms. So for example, it can manifest a whole planet and beings on it. If you liken it to God playing games with itself creating things, then you will be grasping the fundamentals of how it behaves.

An Insight For The Reader

Big Jelly 1 is fascinated by lots of things including human beings. In conducting this research it offered a useful message which reasonably translates as follows:

"Human minds spend most of their days seeking to cope with problems and issues. You, the reader, are experiencing such a mind. That mind is constantly seeking to control the world around it. If you spent more of your time noticing what you actually are, you will rediscover what you are creating. At that same moment you will be able to choose what you are creating. This would be an excellent moment to pay attention to what you actually are. Try not to get lost in fantasies in the process. Noticing what you are prevents or at least pauses the fantasies."

LOCATION

In Its Own Universe

All entities of the Big Jelly variety have their own multi-dimensional universes, which only appear able to accommodate one such entity per universe. Though it is possible for a consciousness to visit one of these universes by borrowing matter within it to reform itself. Hence in order to allow anything to experience one of these universes, the visitor must to some extent become a Big Jelly because that can be the only manifestation there.

Such an arrangement of one being per universe, is in fact not as unique as it might first appear. The universe human beings experience was ultimately created by one creator, and everything in it is a part of and derived from that creator. However, the universe humans experience is more dynamic and permits more visitors.

A human or alien consciousness can observe the Big Jelly 1's universe, but not physically exist in it, unless it becomes part of it. However, whilst Big Jelly 1 is governed by the same rules if it wishes to experience the same universe as humans, as a god-like entity, it has more flexibility as to how.

Everywhere In The Human Universe

When trying to isolate if this species is perhaps limited to any part of the universe humans experience, the initial research revealed was that it had seeded itself everywhere, and was able to do so using what can be likened to energetic dust like spores the size of viruses. However, since the equivalent of its DNA is different, it does not readily react with most other organic living material. Neither are these spores necessarily recognisable as a living entity.

The insight given by it was that its spores resembled metallic silica. The image given was of very small shards of a metallic-appearing material, which produces a reflective shine.

Outpost

Big Jelly 1 comes and goes pretty much as it pleases in the universe humans experience. It is capable of forming planet sized manifestations at the physical dimensions. Such manifestations can reasonably be described as outposts or observation platforms.

PLANET

Home Planet Universe

Big Jelly 1 may initially (and not quite correctly) appear to be, in effect, some sort of yellowish planet. This impression results from the fact that human minds relate easily to the concept of a planet orbiting a sun in space. However, in this instance there is no sun to orbit, nor is there any "space" beyond this apparent planet. In this world and universe, there is only the planet which is Big Jelly 1.

A human astral explorer visiting the Big Jelly 1 universe has a good opportunity to attempt to observe a looped entity. At first it may appear that Big Jelly 1 is similar to a planet with a surface. But on examination the location of that surface is impossible to determine and explore. Travelling within it brings you into other versions of it, but at different dimensions

The jelly is really a high vibration medium which can produce the illusion of low vibration physicality. Thought forms energise the jelly into creating consciousness illusions of various descriptions within its lower dimensions. A human mind could relate to an example of this as being like scenes out of dreams.

Visiting Planets In Other Universes

The Big Jelly 1, like entities of this type, manifests itself in other universes. Most typically it forms as complete planets, which can be described as "visiting planets".

In principle, any planet has a soul and spirit of some sort, hence the expression "Mother Earth". Planets only form because there is a strong intention for them to exist, and are always operated by a higher entity of some description. A feature that human beings are less familiar with is the way in which any planet exists at multiple dimensions, and ultimately all are inhabited at the very least in some of those dimensions.

In the other universes it visits, Big Jelly 1 creates planets out of the available space debris. Such planets can then become inhabited by other species, which it studies and energetically feeds off. Some of the energetic harvest from other life-forms inhabiting its visitor planets is then fed back to its home universe.

At the dimension human's experience, Big Jelly 1 does not normally create planets that orbit around suns. Instead it creates freely travelling planets intended to cruise within galaxies. Such planets are normally substantially composed of gas, and spend most of their lives in deep space occasionally passing near other solar systems.

At the dimensions human's experience, these planets are normally lifeless. However, at higher dimensions they regularly become populated. Similarly, at higher dimensions space is no longer dark causing such planets to be far more visible, and generally have a surface of some sort to dwell upon.

Dematerialising Its Visiting Planets

The Big Jelly 1 also has the ability to disintegrate its planets and the solid matter it has collected is distributed the form of the previously mentioned metallic silica-like material, which appears as shards or larger clumps of dark dust. Reassembly, however, appears more complex, as none of these particles have a normal propulsion system. Nevertheless, the particles are, however, able to move in cloud-like formations as if drawn by invisible gravitational forces.

By disintegrating parts of itself, the Big Jelly 1 has been able to spread itself throughout the physical dimensions. So particles can be found on most planets, in most physical dimensions a human might encounter.

Illusion Secondary Planets

These visiting planets are undetectable to early 21st century humankind as they are usually in deep space, and the alternative ex-planet dust and small debris are of no great relevance to Earht Plane humans. However, the illusion category of planet will be, and thus is of more relevance to this encyclopaedia.

The Earth human beings experience is of course a grand illusion in its own right, especially considering that the matter which forms it can be described as energy slowed down. However, what a human being consciously thinks does not have an immediate impact upon its surroundings; e.g. If a human mind thinks “I want a glass of water” the glass of water does not immediately appear out of nothing.

Conversely, if humans at a higher dimension landed on a Big Jelly 1 planet, it would be akin to entering a dream world. Everything the human mind might imagine would be inclined to physically manifest. If the human being landing there was expecting to find cities full of people, there would apparently be cities full of people made from the Big Jelly 1. If two human beings were together on such a trip, their combined thoughts would influence what they found. An unanswered question in this respect is what would happen if a human being took off its spacesuit and tried to breathe the atmosphere, as the Big Jelly 1 gas is probably not breathable to human beings. Probably the human would instead imagine removing the spacesuit, without actually doing so.

Most advanced aliens regard such illusion planets as both entertaining and potentially hostile. The Big Jelly 1 planets will corrupt a human mind and feed off human emotions. If, for example, a human being had a deceased lover, the possibility of that person appearing to be alive on a Big Jelly 1 planet is very high. The Big Jelly 1 would create a replica of that person using the human visitor’s memories. Thus an unwary visitor would find themselves drawn into an illusory relationship. You could compare such experiences to dreams that are so interesting that you would not wish to awaken from them.

Visiting Planet Propulsion

Big Jelly secondary planets are one of the few things that can move around in space without any form of obvious propulsion. This remarkable feat is down to the fact that in many ways it is not really based in a human's physical dimension, thus it can appear to be anywhere within it; i.e. Anywhere and everywhere.

The Big Jelly 1 principally moves its energy template around in the Astral World, where no mechanical propulsion is required, and is thus able to move its apparent physical matter; i.e. It is actually reforming itself if it needs to change course.

SPECIES

Potentially Coma Inducing

Trying to get a sense of this species can often place the astral researcher into what feels like a temporary coma; i.e. You start to feel drowsy and can even fall asleep. This is because if you are extending your consciousness to sense it, you run into some very high and low energies. Hence in a joking way, it can feel like being placed in a coma. The only way to proceed is to allow the higher components of Big Jelly 1's being to connect to the researcher (which occurs when it chooses).

In summary; if you wish to explore this being, avoid attempting to probe Big Jelly 1, and instead let it come to your human consciousness.

Large Single Cell Entity

Looking astrally at a Big Jelly 1, though the colours may vary, you are likely to observe a substantially yellow and greenish spherical being. Its exterior surface appears bright and its core similarly appears bright, so there is no apparent centre.

Similar To God

If you want to observe the simplified structure of God (the super-consciousness or ultimate Creator) then studying Big Jelly 1 is very informative. This jelly-like entity principally perceives things within itself; i.e. It can sense well within its boundaries, but less well outside of them. To get to see itself from afar, it integrates with other entities that can observe it from afar. For example, when an astral researcher investigates Big Jelly 1, it gets an additional perspective upon what it is, courtesy of that observer.

Big Jelly 1 operates in a condition of duality, and everything is achieved using this fact. So for example, all apparently positive energies have to be balanced by apparently negative energies. This can otherwise be described as a zero sum equation; one minus one equals zero, or 1- 1 = 0. Hence the Big Jelly 1 will experience a variety of opposites.

Everything that exists within, or theoretically extends from the Big Jelly 1 is a part of it. This occurs much in the same way that all human beings, aliens, and universes, that a human consciousness might access are part of the super-consciousness. By comparison the Big Jelly 1 is a lesser consciousness, yet still part of the original super-consciousness. If it were part of an altogether different super-consciousness, then a human consciousness would not be able to perceive it, unless the two super-consciousnesses somehow 'bumped into each other'. So a human consciousness can explore Big Jelly 1, and vice versa, because they are within the same super-consciousness.

Principle Activity

Big Jelly 1 is principally interested in what it actually is, and developing itself from the resulting energetic feedback. To investigate the possible answer to its question, it creates self-exploratory scenarios within itself, and examines the results. For inspiration, it readily draws upon experiences being had in other corners of the various universes available for it to explore. This has loose similarities in principle, to how a human consciousness might explore itself through fantasies.

Human minds typically get a good view of the super-consciousness by seeing it externally which in turn makes them become it. By comparison, for Big Jelly 1, the whole process is more internalised; i.e. It sees the presence of the super-consciousness within itself far more easily than a human being typically will.

Observing Big Jelly 1 can be plagued with distractions that can make it seem almost impossible at times. This is because Big Jelly 1 exists in a state of extreme opposites; i.e. Extremely distracted, then extremely aware. The helpful side effect of these extremes is boredom which converts to creative inspiration, and hence new observations.

Big Jelly 1 lives in a permanent now, as opposed to the reader's perception of linear time. Were it experiencing linear time then you would observe that it spent all of it noticing what it was and hence what the super-consciousness is.

Bending The Rules For Matter

Creating physical matter also involves balancing it by creating new space and time. Big Jelly 1 has access to a creator (only) ability to create new matter and corresponding new space-time using its consciousness alone. This has the practical effect that when it does create physical matter in the universe you, the reader, are experiencing, this also creates space-time.

For Big Jelly 1, materialising new matter, it places it a long way away from existing matter; e.g. Typically, on a small scale, it creates a new object away from the existing galaxies. So this is unlikely to be a local event.

Similarly, if it wishes to leave a universe, it can collapse matter, space and time, leaving nothing behind.

By comparison, the advanced alien residents of the universe human beings experience can move matter around within it by similar means and the use of technology. But this normally involves transferring the manifestation of matter from one location to another, as opposed to introducing completely new matter and then removing it at a later date.

One Being

As previously described, this is one large being and all the component parts fully communicate with each other. In this respect it has probably one of the best communications abilities in the physical universe. For example, if you, the reader, encountered a part of this being, say manifesting an illusion of a humanoid alien, it would be as if you were in communication with the whole being in that moment.

CULTURE

Since this category refers to just one being, whose individual components can only exhibit artificial individuality, it does not really have a culture as such. Therefore, other related aspects are explored.

Inquisitive Entity

Big Jelly 1 is in many ways a condensed and less sophisticated version of the super-consciousness. In its own universe it is a large entity, which seeks to make sense of what it actually is, though it is aware that it does have an ultimate Creator.

To assist this aim it imports perceptions of what the super-consciousness might be from other parts of the Astral World and the universes generated within it. When a reader reads or contemplates this chapter, Big Jelly 1 will be aware of that interest, though such a connection might not amount to much. Nevertheless it will still absorb the reader's perceptions.

Similarly, it physically spreads itself out throughout physical universes so that it can experience what they experience. It must be noted that this largely results in an awareness of what it's like to be a rock, or fluid of some sort, etc.

Research And Replication

Big Jelly 1 has spread parts of itself throughout the universe that humans experience to the point that nearly everything is touched by it. This in turn assists it to monitor a great deal of what occurs.

A helpful analogy is what happens when you, the reader watch a good, or as the case may be, hideously awful movie. Afterwards the strong impressions will be replayed in your consciousness' imagination. One astral researcher captured the essence of this activity by observing that Big Jelly 1 seemed packed with internal chambers which replicated scenarios it had encountered.

INTERACTION WITH HUMAN BEINGS

Up to the beginning of the early 21st century, Big Jelly 1 had mainly enjoyed a discreet interaction with human beings. Since human beings had relatively little idea what created them and similarly what they were, insights of any great quality were fleeting and there was not much to harvest.

Awaking Of Consciousness

The early 21 century is a period when human beings are programmed to awaken in relatively large numbers. Big Jelly 1 is therefore very interested in harvesting such experiences. In this respect, Big Jelly 1 was also interested to access the human experiences of what it is like to be human beings.

The easiest way to discreetly harvest such experiences is during the part of the human sleep period when the body's higher connection is significantly withdrawn; i.e. Deep sleep without dreaming. During this phase and prior to entering a dream state, the lower spirits which drive the human ego and personality are effectively switched off, so they can be borrowed for a brief period of time.

This sort of borrowing normally leaves no obvious trace, though it can sometimes leave a residue memory of alien abduction. Furthermore, as it leaves very little trace of the Big Jelly 1 itself, the lower spirits will interpret the experience as resulting from more traditional alien interactions.

There are many aspects of an awakening consciousness that Big Jelly 1 is interested in. One of the most fascinating is when human consciousnesses notice what is creating them, and how this then enables their participation in the creative process. In particular, when this becomes incorporated into dreams.

Symptoms Of Interaction

Most dreaming a human mind experiences involves very mundane activities such as going to the shops or dealing with some work situation. Being abducted by aliens during dreams, and, or meeting what appears to be a god, are unusual and thus tend to stand out.

The experience to look out for is one of meeting something apparently greater than the normal human mind, often accompanied by a sense of having been chosen. Though this can develop into an obsession about aliens, which impinges on a human being's ability to deal with day-to-day life.

Should such an imbalance be encountered, the solution is both mundane and effective; productive physical work or labour, as opposed to sitting around daydreaming.

E17 Big Jelly 1

Parasite Or Liberator

One of the great advances human beings make in the 21st century is establishing wide ranging contacts with a host of alien races. For the most part this results in a considerable upgrading of human consciousness and general ability.

A side effect of this awakening is that other alien beings, who are more concerned with simply monitoring human progress are able to inject themselves into a human awareness. The Big Jelly 1 being is a prime example of this possibility. The relationship can both inform a human mind, and encourage contemplation. It is for you, who operate a human body, to ensure that the relationship remains productive, as opposed to arguably parasitic.

If the different possibilities are not observed during interaction, a human mind's ability to function is to some extent degraded; i.e. You can feel almost "knocked out".

Alternatively, if a human mind can learn to recognise such an invasive connection occurring, it can harvest the relatively low energies, which will have a very stimulating and liberating effect. Thus resulting in an improved higher awareness. For example, if the reader is alert, you can switch into a very aware state at this moment. Try it.

The Big Jelly 1 is certainly open to energetically assisting human beings that have exciting and productive adventures. On the other hand, it is relatively ambivalent about any distress and loss of functionality it inflicts on the unwary. Though in many ways, it is for a human mind to show some responsibility in this respect. Either way, the Big Jelly 1 and others like it are likely to become involved.

In summary, connecting with such species can make your adopted human form either smarter or less effective.

E18 T1s

INTRODUCTION

T1s are in many ways similar to human beings, just more advanced and refined. The most obvious difference is that their heads are relatively larger in order to accommodate bigger brains.

Any physically lesser race enjoying access to T1s will naturally want to emulate many of the apparent advances they have made. So it is also prudent to remain aware that some drawbacks also exist, such as an excess of "nit-picking" attitudes.

Super Species

The T1s are a potential model of what human beings could evolve into if they were to have their potential maximised. So close are the two species that even the normal challenges of translating their "name" into English text is reasonably possible and the name "Thargs" seems to be a reasonable approximation. However, in other ways, relating to what they really are remains a challenge. For example, the soul groups which dominate their population rarely incarnate as earthly human beings. Furthermore, T1s have a very different perception of almost everything when compared to an earthly human, so their mind-set can be challenging for the uninvited to relate to.

A simple example of how significantly more advanced the T1s are is their avoidance of perceiving anything in the form of a question. A T1 would never ask you the question of "What is your name ?". Instead, it would simply observe what your name designation appeared to be. This is because it would wish to be on the same telepathic wavelength before communicating further; i.e. If it did not know your name, it would be because you are not on the same wavelength, and therefore a conversation would be far less productive.

Similarly, for a T1 there would never be a question of "How do I get to (example) location X ?". Instead, a T1 would use a simple awareness of; "If I want to get to X (even if I don't know how to get there yet), I should simply (in this example) go towards point Y because it appears close to X". If you, the reader, imagined never asking another question during the remainder of your current physical manifestation (life), then welcome to the world of the T1s.

The reason why T1's do not ask questions, except in humour or sarcasm etc, is that it precludes instantly knowing the answer to anything that can, under the circumstances, be known or otherwise understood.

The practical limit on intuitively knowing anything is your mind's capacity to comprehend the subject. The T1s high intelligence enables them to learn new subjects very quickly. This in turn enables them to tap into a knowledge base extending across all of the universes.

Cautious About Sharing Insights

T1s loath to answer questions placed by beings that cannot be bothered to discover the answers for themselves. So it takes no great leap of understanding to grasp that a species which is adverse to any form of real question, does not like being plagued by lesser species asking it questions. The general principle when dealing with T1s is not to ask them questions, except if you can convert it into a useful statement and preferably a humorous comment. They love humour.

Despite the T1s being very advanced, upon meeting them you will often find them not to apparently be radiating the strong unconditional love of some other similarly advanced species. They could be described as taking a 'tough love' approach. Nevertheless, if you allow them to synchronise your consciousness with their 'wavelength', or Astral level, then you will experience a better exchange of unconditional love. This manoeuvre requires cooperative teamwork and is not entirely passive. So an inexperienced astral traveller will find it challenging.

As a further line of defence against visitors inclined to ask questions, the T1s are very adept at appearing far less clever than they actually are. Much in a similar way to a parent coming down to a child's intellectual level in order to interact with it, might pretend to be infantile.

LOCATION

Multiple Dimensions

T1s physically appear across a range of dimensions. A practical result being that their physical forms can vary depending upon heritage and dimension, etc. T1s are normally found in higher dimensions compared to those occupied by earthly human beings.

By comparison, the earthly human race of the early 21st century only appears in one dimension and physical location; the Earht Plane. However, variations of non Earht Plane human beings are to be found in abundance. So the distinction needs to be made that the categorisation of T1s applied in this instance is far broader than that used for earthly human beings.

Throughout This And Many Other Galaxies

T1s are plentiful and have colonised many different planets. They even operate several outposts at a higher dimension on the Moon. In terms of any major colonisations these appear to be in excess of 100 across the Milky Way, and in excess of over 1000 minor ones such as their outposts on the Moon.

PLANET

Original Planet

T1s were first developed in a parallel universe, and then introduced into the one that humans experience. In their original universe their biped design was introduced to a planet with a few similarities to Earth, though its climate was typically more arid and there was a lot less water. Whilst on Earth it took around 4.5 billion years to develop human beings from the first micro-organisms, on T1' planet it seems to have taken closer to 6 billion Earth years before the requisite humanoid biped emerged.

Whilst on Earth the planet is relatively lush, T1s' planet was more challenging in a way that hindered their development. Ultimately a lack of water combined with other climatic difficulties produced a species that was inspired to seek solutions from its various alien neighbours. The best solution to the lack of water turning out to be colonising other worlds. The T1s still retain a population on this original planet, but they have long since expanded extensively elsewhere.

Equivalent Period

If you had visited T1s original planet in their universe during the equivalent to mankind's early 21st century you would have found a largely desert world with very cold polar regions but without much ice. From space the planet looked sandy brown with only thin clouds here and there. Between the tropics was a green band where the climate was sufficiently warm and wet to support life.

There are no oceans, just inland lakes, the biggest of which looks around 300 km (200 miles) long. The lakes in the arid regions appear too salty to support any meaningful quantity of life. The absence of a large moon also removes the sort of tidal movements that would be seen on Earth.

The T1s at this time mostly lived within the fertile band between the tropics and, like human beings, had developed an industrialised society. The population was mostly packed into relatively dense cities. Over-pollution and overcrowding appears to have been an issue. Government appears to have been elected and authoritarian, with one world government having been already achieved. There is very little evidence of social disorder, and the population appeared reasonably content.

Going forward in time, most of the T1s left. The fertile region was largely returned to nature. Cities rebuilt upon the marginal lands outside the best fertile region. The atmosphere was abuzz with flying craft of all descriptions. A very happy contented populace was the end result.

Next Planets

Upon becoming sufficiently self-aware, the T1s gained access to space-time travel. Around the same time they started working with the Creators of such worlds and thus had access to the process of developing them. In a twist that a human mind might initially find both bizarre and intriguing, they then set about creating new colonies in their relative past; i.e. Created new civilisations billions of years before their first one had come into existence.

The T1s explained that habitable planets are constructed more or less to order, though the process typically takes billions of years. However, when you have access to time travel, this is not an issue.

When taking advantage of the fact that you can take up residence on planets in your past, there is considerable advantage in doing so far away from what becomes your origin in the relative future. Common sense dictates that interfering with your ancestors in the future might be problematic. Though in a looped universe, it is often nevertheless the responsibility of descendants to ensure the development of their ancestors.

Typical Planet Type

Most T1s like planets with very similar characteristics to Earth and some oxygen in the atmosphere, anything between 10 and 40% at lower dimensions is acceptable. Though at higher dimensions, it becomes unnecessary to actually breathe as normal physical processes do not exist.

At lower dimensions, some degree of terraforming is often required to improve a planet's habitability. For example, oxygen is not necessarily sufficiently present on planets with atmospheres. The principle method of creating it is introducing micro-organisms which convert carbon dioxide into oxygen. This process normally requires seeding a planet with the necessary micro-organisms and waiting millions of years for the atmosphere to be altered. Long timescales are required to achieve such modifications, along with the use of time travel.

SPECIES

Replicated Species

T1s are a very good example of repeatedly creating a species, often from scratch on a variety of different planets. Whilst it is technologically possible for them to simply colonise a new planet, they often prefer to develop and evolve new T1s from a planet's existing life forms. Such an approach also makes it easier to colonise different or parallel dimensions.

For completeness, it is worth noting that human beings on the Earth were similarly developed using an existing design. Hence, replicating a species is not a unique event, but actually the normal route by which most advanced alien species come into existence. So the biblical tale stating that a god created man captures the essence of the actuality quite reasonably.

Common Evolution Approach

It is helpful to understand T1s less as a coherent species, but instead as an amalgamated series of species developed by a common set of soul groups. Soul groups regard physical bodies as vehicles through which they can experience physical life. So there is no requirement that all the bodies share identical genetic heritages.

T1s can be evolved from almost any water borne single cell organism on a planet that has some oxygen in the atmosphere. Though producing an entire set of diverse species which stimulate the eventual emergence of the T1s species is far more complex. Nevertheless the T1s appear to prefer this approach.

There are two ways to colonise a planet, and the T1s are masters at both. F*irstly*; if you are operating in linear time, you can just load spaceships with your populace and show up en masse wherever you choose. S*econdly*; if you are truly playing with space-time, it is often easier to evolve a new branch to your civilisation elsewhere. The second approach is truly the more dynamic of the two, and still produces new societies that are largely identical to the original.

When adopting the second approach to colonisation, the method of achieving it is to evolve or otherwise develop a species that will suit your soul groups' physical manifestation; i.e. You grow the necessary bodies you desire over many generations. The exciting question will then always be at what stage is it appropriate to make the new offshoot of your civilisation aware of who and what created it.

One of the comparative insights delivered to humankind by research such as this, is that human beings were, and continue to be, modified and engineered to achieve design goals determined by those souls which occupy or intend to occupy them. Hence studying the comparatively similar T1s reveals many parallels.

E18 T1s

The T1s assisting with this encyclopaedia's research wish to help alert humans to the interesting subject of who has created them. By comparison, typical permutations of T1s are often similarly initially unaware that they have been engineered into existence, and at some point must discover the truth for themselves.

Typical T1s

In most respects, a T1 is very similar to a human being, and anatomically the difference comes down to bodily proportions. The most important difference is brain size which is roughly three times larger that of a human being. By comparison, its digestive system is adapted to absorb highly nutritious food, so is smaller and follows a different tract.

In fairness, if a human being had a good diet, it could typically manage on only 50 to 25% of its current typical food intake. So human beings too would benefit from shrinking their digestive systems whilst enlarging their brains.

In terms of strength, a healthy human being is physically stronger. Though when comparing 21st century human beings with their ancestors, said ancestors were stronger. T1s compensate for this relative lack of strength by being altogether fitter, and obesity is extremely rare. Intriguingly such fitness can be achieved without undue exercise.

T1s have more dexterous hands, and typically two opposable digits as compared to a human beings one. They have better eyesight and hearing than a human being. But T1s' sense of smell appears to have atrophied to some extent.

A race of T1's can in practice be developed from almost any existing life form. It would appear easier in this context to start with an ape like a chimpanzee than it would be to adapt a human. The issue is that human beings' aggression towards each other is well ingrained, whereas it would be easier to suppress this instinct at an earlier stage of brain development.

Anatomical Variation

It is important to bear in mind that T1s are not all the same. T1s could overall (that is across many planets) be described as a convergent species. This means whilst the different variations of them have many different origins, as they are evolved, they converge towards a common design. Similarly, if you consider the objectives of alternative human beings' creators across many planets, you will similarly see some convergence of design.

Accordingly, whilst there are different physical groups of T1s from a soul perspective, they are the same conglomeration. So regardless, of whether a T1 has four or six fingers, it belongs to the same conglomeration of soul groups.

T1s differ from many alien races who choose to specialise different members of their society in that the only significant split is male and female. Though even this distinction is blurred by the possibility for males to become female and vice versa where the need arises.

Between the variations of this species you will find some physical differences which are both natural variations and due to the fact that they have been developed from entirely different species. For example, in some instances T1s were evolved from upright biped reptilians into mammals.

This convergence into something similar to a large brained human being does not mean that a human form is superior to all others. Rather that humanoid form has been found to be convenient for many applications.

Reproduction

T1s can reproduce in a similar way to human beings. This acknowledged, they are also experts in farming their offspring with the aid of industrial processes.

The guiding principle adopted by most T1s is that new arrivals should be brought up in stable families. Accordingly there is no such thing as an unwanted child.

Some T1s have also gone so far as to dispense with some or all of childhood. In human culture, childhood is considered to ordinarily a happy period. By comparison, T1s' adulthood can be equally happy, so the loss of childhood is not of great concern.

Most T1s are born with an adult mentality stemming from a good connection to previous lifetimes. In these circumstances, childhood can represent a tiresome delay to a better state of functionality.

Despite there being plenty of logical reasons for T1s to simply abandon natural births and childhood, a significant minority of them have nevertheless retained many aspects of the sexual reproduction process an early 21st century human would be familiar with. Childhood is particularly useful when acclimatising a visiting soul to the T1s' environment.

CULTURE

The T1s are a large civilisation that have gone through many stages of development. Since they are compiled from many originally independently functioning civilisations, they have self-evidentially had the opportunity to experiment with various permutations. So for simplicity, the culture of the original civilisation is the main subject of this section.

Isolation Stage

The original, like the majority of T1 civilisations, was evolved from the local indigenous species. It follows that they were initially unaware that they had indeed been developed through external interventions in the evolutionary process. During this phase they were monitored by, but not unduly interfered with, by various alien races.

The T1s did however have a notion that they somehow originated from the stars. So their equivalent of God creating man and placing him in the garden of Eden, loosely translated to a space ship depositing two babies (boy and girl) in a garden, where they were then brought up by the indigenous wild animals. This has had the side effect of thereafter making T1s compare the quality of a parent's childcare to that potentially offered by wild animals.

If a species is subject to an isolation stage, as was the case here, it will only have a limited awareness of what created it and very little informative contact with species alien to its world. The criteria for ending the isolation is normally the same for the vast majority of species on any world. As was the case for the first T1s in this universe, it is whether or not they are making significant astral connections with the entities who created them. The threshold being that nearly everyone in their society has personally accomplished this, or personally knows someone who has. Thus this skill then becomes incorporated into the education system in the same way that reading and writing becomes mandatory.

There are three main reasons for having an isolation stage. F*irstly*; it ultimately ensures that the civilisation discovers the greater universal truths for themselves; such as what in their opinion is the super-consciousness. S*econdly*; it similarly ensures that they understand the importance of becoming more civilised. T*hirdly*; until they have attained the first two milestones, it contains any uncivilised ignorant culture to their locality, hence protecting all the advanced civilisations from them.

The physical typical distance between most habitable planets in the universe humans experience, is such that T1s, like human beings, did not have the access to the necessary technical advances which makes visiting them possible. Transcending space-time is necessary to travel across the vast distances. So until the T1s were given access to the requisite advances, they were stuck where they were.

Ending Isolation

The T1s always culturally accepted that there were other advanced beings alien to them, but were long perplexed by the negligible contact they had with them. By comparison, human beings up to the early 21st century, as a society in general, could barely even accept that alien races even existed. Though in fairness human beings were programmed not to, and almost all were even oblivious of this mental blockage. By comparison the T1s were waiting for advanced aliens to start making significant contact with them.

An example of how T1s were comparatively a little more advanced than human beings, is that they recognised that; the ideas driving useful technical advances were being dropped into their minds. Thus they took the obvious next step of noticing who was assisting them. By then interacting with the various beings that were assisting them, a host of other advances were similarly imparted. This does not mean that by comparison human beings are stupid, rather they are designed to produce a different experience, and the T1s in any event had relatively bigger brains.

After Isolation

Isolation for the T1s ended, as it often does, gradually over the earthly equivalent of hundreds of years. This change-over phase is culturally critical as it creates considerable challenges for the population. Once a species recognises that there are plenty of more advanced neighbouring species, it feels compelled to try and catch up, without really giving proper consideration to the goal of such advancements.

One of the key objectives of this encyclopaedia is that humankind can benefit from the experiences of other civilisations. In this respect, the T1s dealt with new cultural influxes by remembering that everyone is ultimately equal.

Ending isolation inevitably released an avalanche of technical advances, which enabled enormous personal freedom and a release from the necessity to have to physically work hard at anything. However, cultures do not thrive on being purposeless, and the difficulty immediately faced by most readers is that they have little conceptual grasp of what a revised purpose of life might be. So again the T1s' example is helpful.

Purpose

Before the end of isolation, T1s, like human beings, were largely occupied with a daily struggle to stay alive. Though for most of them this had at least evolved from a physical struggle to live, into a struggle to attain a high standard of living; e.g. A shift from do I have enough food to eat ? To do I have enough gadgets and fancy clothes, etc ?

So for the benefit of readers who want to glimpse their destiny, for a few moments you can experience life in a (mocked up) T1s household. Do not imagine this. Just allow your consciousness to sense it. The whole family of T1s truly connect to each other, they play and have fun with being physically alive. At the same time they notice what they really are, which a human might understand as being part of a super-consciousness. Observe the sheer fun and joy.

Disadvantages Of The T1s Design

Whilst early 21st century humankind experiences war as something which endlessly blights their world, by comparison only very primitive T1s have much personal experience of it. On the face of it this may not immediately appear to be much of a disadvantage or limitation for T1s to have to endure. However, it does affect their sense of perspective.

Advanced T1s have culturally known mostly peaceful times, and get on well with alien neighbours. Meanwhile, they nevertheless strive to find new challenges to stimulate themselves. When they can't find a suitable new challenge, they are inclined to unnecessarily invent them. Hence, they are inclined to invent problems where none really existed.

A useful analogy is the earthly nightclub doorman who refuses entry to males with the wrong colour of socks, which gives meaning to the expression "nit-picking". As a group, T1s are endlessly having to restrain themselves from, for example, inventing unnecessary rules and protocols.

So whilst human beings often yearn for a more peaceful society, T1s often crave worlds where "nit-picking" rules and protocols have been swept away by major conflicts. Furthermore, because conflict can make way for new growth, an overly restrictive society denies itself this brutal form of regeneration.

INTERACTION WITH HUMAN BEINGS

It will be truly interesting when one day, a human being who has read this encyclopaedia or some derivation of it, meets a T1 visitor and asks, "Are you a T1 or Tharg ?" and said alien probably replies "What ?" (without of course posing an actual question).

The T1s, whilst largely humanoid in appearance, display considerable diversity, and since there are plenty of different alien species it can be very difficult to discern one group from another. Furthermore, at the time of first conducting this research in 2014, the consensus view from T1s was that they would generally not reveal who they were to a human being who could not sense who they were in the first instance.

Going For A Ride

Going forward in time, the consensus from T1s was that they were likely to offer rides in their space-time craft to some of their future earthly friends. The closeness of the relationship would in this instance need to exceed merely the encountering of T1s, which this research could be classified as.

Such excursions are also not without their own complications. The effects of exposure to such craft can have a damaging and lasting effect on a human body, and can easily shorten its life. This is because human bodies have not been adapted to cope with such dimensional shifts, so they easily break. In fact, it is more sensible to place a human body into a stasis machine, and then temporarily transfer its consciousness into a new T1s body.

Nevertheless, for anyone prepared to learn to interact properly with the T1s, this offer may be made to them. The T1s further added that the electromagnetic energies that will be encountered will tend to distort the normal operation of video cameras, and potentially blacken unexposed celluloid film to some extent. Making the recordings of any such adventures problematic but not impossible.

Studying Humans

Whilst there are a great many T1s who could potentially visit the Earth, they are relatively infrequent visitors. So the likelihood of being abducted and experimented upon by them is relatively low. By comparison you are far more likely to have such an encounter with a Grey or Future Human.

In the meantime, T1s were keen to extend a warm invitation to astral explorers who want to experience their diverse worlds and civilisations.

E19 Star Children 1

INTRODUCTION

The term Star Child or Children is possibly a little misleading in that it incorrectly suggests these aliens are somehow just children. Instead the term "Star Child" is being used here to refer to a category of aliens that are sometimes understood to be born from a 'god star'.

An easier way of interpreting the naming is to understand that from a human Earht Plane perspective, these aliens came from a bright place, as if they emerged from some sort of sun. These aliens' physical forms are engineered humanoids adapted to operate in the universe humans experience, because their principal home is another universe altogether.

Appearance

The Star Children 1 engineered bodies you are likely to encounter in the Earht Plane have comparatively thin humanoid bodies, large heads and eyes. When you meet one (if you are relaxed) you are likely to feel a very warm loving emotion infused with kindness. At first they can also tend to appear to be very white, though this is more a result of a bright aura than actual skin pigmentation.

Their initial movements in your presence tend to be slow, gentle and considered.

Star Children 1 are sometimes perceived as being angelic beings, on account of the bright aura that most people observing them will experience.

All that said, when Star Children 1 are visiting the Earht Plane, they can get drawn into its relatively low dimension, which in turn tends to diminish some of their bright qualities. Thus some observers will perceive the brightness, and others less so.

In The Creator's Image

Many people perceive the super-consciousness, God, or ultimate Creator, to be akin to some sort of old man. However, akin to a playful young child is an equally valid interpretation.

So when you meet Star Children 1, whose appearance is generally adult, you will probably be struck by their emotional radiance suggesting a wonderful combination of old soul and smiling playful child. A wonderful lack of seriousness soon becomes evident in any meaningful interaction with them.

Purpose

Human beings are experiential vehicles which enable the super-consciousness to experience being more or less the opposite of what it really is. Hence from this highly contrasting vantage point, it can get a good look at itself and complete the energetic loop which feeds the super-consciousness. Of course this only occurs when the human consciousness pays enough attention to actually do so.

By comparison, Star Children 1 are dimensionally much closer to the super-consciousness, hence they only enable a much lower level of contrast. Instead they provide a helpful interim level of consciousness from which the super-consciousness can look both up and down. Whereas for human beings at their lower dimension, there is not much further down to look (if it even knows how to).

It may seem strange, that whilst the super-consciousness experiences everything that happens to a human being, it is not necessarily clear to the super-consciousness what is actually going on. Hence having intellectually very competent beings overseeing things in general, is of considerable assistance. Thus Star Children 1 are often involved in overseeing, sometimes steering, and generally giving feedback to the super-consciousness regarding what occurs at lower levels.

In combination with their overseeing role, Star Children 1 are also part of the team that help design and construct the experiences that humans can undergo. A helpful analogy is that of a computer game, where a team of people (advanced aliens) must first create the necessary computer algorithms which enable the game to exist.

LOCATION

A Different Universe

To set the context; the universe a human consciousness will primarily experience could be described as that of the apparent realities. In the human universe individuality is created and such individuals are energised by apparent tasks. You, the reader, will tend to feel as if you are on a mission of some sort and tend to perceive your purpose and success in terms of physical results. Even souls experiencing life as advanced aliens in the still physical, but higher dimensions, easily find themselves drawn into experiencing such perceptions.

The universe Star Children 1 primarily inhabit could be described as one of understanding, creation and contemplation, where possibilities are experimented with. You could argue that there are no real differences between the two universes, but that would overlook the shift in emphasis. So if you are experiencing the Star Children 1's universe it is much easier to remain aware that you are experiencing an interesting illusion.

In the Star Children 1's universe, parallel dimensions are all relatively closer together when compared to the universe humans principally experience.

Universe Of Understanding

To set the context; in the universe where human beings are to be found there is a great deal of emphasis on individuality. Nearly everything you encounter tends to appear to be a person of some sort. Most energy forms tend to have some sort of physical appearance when you try to perceive them, even when in reality they have no such form. Similarly, as described, this universe applies a tremendous focus on outcomes and achievement.

The Star Children's principle universe is one where there is a very deep understanding of everything. This is achieved by emphasising the connections between everything, and how everything interacts. The author of this encyclopaedia can be classified as having useful links to this universe. Hence, the author's human manifestation readily has the technical ability to navigate different realms as it inherently comprehends the interconnections.

A side effect of most beings desiring a deeper understanding, is that more or less the same events have to occur multiple times. As will be detailed later, Star Children 1 live in a world where multiple possibilities are played out in an overlapping way. Whereas, by comparison, a human being normally only experiences one possibility playing out.

Visits To This Universe

Entering this universe can be disconcerting in that everything initially appears more energised and thus relatively less physical. This is because the parallel dimensions are relatively closer, and the overall dimensions relatively higher. The effect is that you will be more aware of the energetic templates which define all physical matter and events. Thus physical things can appear blurred by the energies surrounding them.

To enter this universe smoothly you need to allow your aura to be larger and similarly connect with everything around you. A failure to do so will disturb your human body and possibly make it inclined to mild illness. As ever, the more you are guided there by some of the residents, the easier everything becomes. Multiple attempts are often required before a human consciousness gets to grips with the differences.

If a reader speed-reads this chapter, it is possible to get through it without significantly connecting to the energetic links embedded within it. Reading more slowly on the other hand and being open to the embedded or connection energies can make the reader a little dizzy and lose concentration.

Visits From This Universe

Star Children 1 have the ability to create new physical bodies to explore the universe human beings experience. In many ways they need to do so as part of checking up on how everything is progressing. These new bodies can operate independently of their original ones where required.

Earlier it was pointed out that Star Children 1 have a high awareness of the super-consciousness, so experience less contrast. The flip side of this is that when they explore the universe humans experience, they have a useful new perspective stemming from the greater contrast they experience when compared to their home universe. Hence, they experience more individuality, but conversely a lower awareness of everything than they would otherwise be aware of in their home universe.

In summary, when Star Children 1 visit the Earht Plane, they experience more contrast, but less self-awareness.

PLANET

Explanation Of "Divergent" And "Convergent" Possibilities

In order to explain what Star Children 1's world is like, it is helpful to first refresh the subject of "divergent" and "convergent" possibilities.

On Earth, a human consciousness ordinarily experiences just one set of possibilities; i.e. If you are walking along a road, and come to a fork (junction) in it, then you can take either the left or right path. You cannot walk down both paths simultaneously. By comparison, experiencing multiple possibilities would require walking along both paths.

Obviously, if you are experiencing all potential possibilities there would be an exponential growth of options as you encounter more forks in the road resulting in an almost infinite set of possibilities to experience. In order to restrict an exponential growth, "divergent" possibilities are generally balanced by "convergent" ones; e.g. The fork in the road would be followed by a junction that recombines your two possible paths back onto one road. Thus it does not ultimately matter which path you take, as both roads recombine back into the same path.

In practice it is not necessary for the super-consciousness to experience every possibility in every one of its creations. Instead the possibilities can be shared out; e.g. One person can take the left fork in the road, and the next person take the right fork. This apportionment of alternative possibilities is most obvious to human beings in the allocation of wealth.

Sometimes, there can be a period where there are more divergent possibilities, then followed by a period of convergence. This is the equivalent of many roads taking you to the same location, but by different routes with different experiences. The 21st and 22nd century Earth possibilities are a good example of this in practice. It's relatively easier to astrally find and access future humans after around 2250 than it would be to find them around 2050. The energetic templates of humans after 2250 have been converged into relative stability, hence it's easy to interact with them. But before this more stable period, there has been a period of divergence which started around 2012, so whilst you find the possibility of human beings in 2050, their numbers and identities are often indeterminate. Whereas by around 2250 everything is more stable again, and communication with them is much easier. Hence human beings of 2250 can tell you about their time, but possibly not be able to clearly inform you (the early 21st century reader) as to what history led them to that point. An analogy would be you not knowing who won World War 2, yet ending up in the same post-war world regardless.

Convergent Possibilities Array of Planets

In the universe human experience, especially with respect to the early 21st century Earht Plane, parallel dimensions will appear relatively separate to everything a human being will experience. By comparison, in the universe Star Children 1 principally experience, parallel dimensions will appear far more overlapped.

The effect of more obviously overlapping parallel dimensions is that when you visit the Star Children 1's principal home planet, it can appear to be many planets configured into one location.

When you visit the Star Children 1's home planet, instead of one planet, its looks more like 8 or 10 simultaneous worlds (approximately and depending on how your human consciousness deals with the perceptions). Star Children 1 have the exciting awareness ability of experiencing multiple possibilities all at once, but with sufficient convergence added so that it does not run away into exponential growth. There also appears to be sufficient group consensus to help this to occur.

Human consciousnesses normally only experience one lifetime path at a time. Whereas Star Children 1 can experience multiple parallel realities, hence you will find parallel home planets easily visible.

However, a final complication in determining any "actual" or "definitive" number of planets is that their apparent quantity or numbers keep altering. Typically a human consciousness can observe between 6 and 10 of them. But this is not necessarily indicative of the actuality, merely the capacity of human perception.

White Planet(s)

From space the Star Children 1's home planet looks white with a white aura surrounding it. As you get closer to the surface it still appears white-ish, perhaps with a hint a of beige. The reason for this is not physical cloud, but energies an astral traveller will probably encounter.

Travelling in from the Astral World it can sometimes be quite difficult to get down near the physical surface. An analogy would be if you were on an aircraft trying to descend through cloud that tends to push you back into the air.

The location of the surface of this planet provides further confusion, and it can be difficult to find by simple exploration. Though by comparison, finding a point or moment on the surface is not difficult if you are being directed to it.

This planet can be confusing to understand because it comprises a set of parallel possibilities at similar dimensions (also referred to as planes). Hence the planet's surface in one plane can appear to be, as the case may be, further or nearer from the planet's core than the next. With familiarity, this can produce the impression that different versions of this (these) planet(s) are layered one on top of another.

If you are not being properly guided it will be very difficult to make proper sense of these worlds. Thus you need to ensure that you have formed some sort of relationship with at least one Star Children 1 guide, in order to proceed productively.

Your Guides

Having recognised that you really need a Star Children 1 guide to assist you, also realise that there is at least one of them already watching you right now. Look for the one who is most directly in front of you in the duality between the Astral World (spirit world) and the physical world you perceive. Note that; you may perceive more than one Star Children 1 guide.

It is helpful to adjust your physical body to what they experience when physically manifesting (alive). In particular, notice how the air they breathe in their world is wonderfully energised. As you integrate with them and this wonderful air energy, they can take you on a tour.

On this tour there will be your Star Children 1 guide(s) and you can explore their relative past, present and future. You can thus experience for yourself how most beings go through development patterns a human being would be familiar with.

The main variation compared to the Earht Plane is that even the primitive (past) Star Children 1 you can visit are aware of, and interact with, multiple possibilities simultaneously. Dealing with this requires a considerable degree of connectedness to everything else. Your guides will enable you to have momentary experiences of what this sort of existence is like. Examples can be along the lines of experiencing two lives at once, with different life partners.

Visiting Their Dimension(s)

A point to note when seeking to explore Star Children 1's physical planes is that you can encounter earlier versions of them who are shorter and have broader bodies, though the head remains similar. Conversely, the later versions of them, such as the types who will guide a reader, often look more like a very thin body with a large head. This anatomical variation gives you an immediate impression of which version you are encountering.

On their main planet(s) it is often difficult to see any distance, as a fog of energies obscures the horizon in all directions. Whilst you can sense beyond the fog, it can be hard to see through it.

Physical matter appears flexible. For example, walking on the ground can make it crunch as if it is hard, yet it depresses and springs back as if you were walking on soft carpet. Another example is how in this world metal can be bent if you want to bend it, but remains rigid if you prefer it to remain so. Thus intention is obviously shaping your physical reality.

It's very easy for an astral traveller to slip into a slightly different plane, which adds to the potential confusion. By comparison, if you were a standard early 21st century human being on this planet, you would only experience one plane at a time in this world. Whereas, typical Star Children 1 have sufficient awareness to be able to perceive adjacent planes almost immediately.

Typical Planes

It is helpful to initially visit a higher physical dimension with sufficient similarities to Earth that you will easily relate to what you find. In this instance a specific entry point has been prepared for readers of this encyclopaedia. In particular you will first be guided to a specific Star Children 1's family home. From the outside you will notice that there are other homes in the vicinity, but no vehicular road connecting them. Instead they have space-time vehicles parked outside on hardstanding (the driveway). Such homes are typically bungalows with transparent outer walls and an overhanging roof.

The interiors of these homes are generally open plan without obvious doors between the internal spaces. However, there are doors and doorways that seamlessly portal you to other engineered locations. Pass through one of these doorways and you are into open countryside which a human being would relate to. Pass through another and this time it is a forest. These portals create openings into private worlds of personal design; i.e. You could have a whole planet to yourself as your private garden. Conversely, outside the home is just another grey, dry, fog of a day where it can be hard to see any distance.

Switch into Star Children 1's perception and suddenly there are multiple versions of everything, which is very confusing for a human mind.

Below this plane is the same planet, but in the next example it is an industrialised world where there are roads and most of the population is crammed into cities. There are endless tall buildings and craft flying through the air. Physical vision is around 100 times further because of greater group consensus on the reality being experienced.

Drop down further and there is an agricultural version of the same world, where animals are used to till the land. In this plane the sky is such that it gives the impression of living in some sort of dome.

The overall impression is that all these places co-exist and can, in various illusory ways, appear to be interdependent. Whilst a human would perceive this journey as one into the past, Star Children 1 perceive it all as forming the present or now.

Into The Future

As your Star Children 1 guides take you to experience their future, it's as if, as a species, they gradually dispensed with the need to physically exist. You will be shown how the community simply went up in dimensions and, for example, the futuristic buildings blended into the white energies.

Thus instead of there being a collection of parallel planets, it all reformed back into one mass of white light.

This ascent seems to have resulted from it no longer being necessary to have physical bodies. The Star Children 1 explained they became so aware of life in their heavens, that there no longer appeared to be any reason to be physically born as Star Children 1. Though this does not preclude being born into other types of physical forms.

SPECIES

Anatomy

Star Children 1 in their home universe have internal skeletons that are similar to earthly mammals and reptiles. In principle they are divided into males and females. However, the later versions of them can switch between either male or female.

Star Children 1 have been evolved from a reptilian category of ancestor, warm-blooded, with original reproduction by laying eggs. You could say they are an example of what would have occurred if small dinosaurs had been evolved into something similar to humankind. However, they have developed the ability to gestate eggs, which can be born with a fully developed baby inside.

Later Star Children 1 (the design earthly humans are likely to encounter) have been adapted for low gravity environments, so they have relatively slender bodies.

Star Children 1 do not naturally have hair, instead they insulate their bodies with a layer of fat-like tissue.

Heads are proportionately larger than those of human beings, with larger eyes, but with minimal or even no ear lobes. Noses are similar to human beings, but with side slits which are reminiscent of cats or dogs.

They have the ability to modify their appearance depending upon what other species they might be interacting with.

Breathing

At lower dimensions Star Children 1's ancestors breathed much as a typical humanoid would. However, at higher dimensions they no longer need to chemically interact with air. Instead they energetically interact with it absorbing non-physical nutrients.

In practice this means that at lower dimensions Star Children 1 have need of a living gas atmosphere, but no longer seem to physically breathe it at higher dimensions. Either way, the air they may or may not be physically breathing is an uplifting wonder to experience.

Not Human Style DNA

Star Children 1 can re-engineer themselves using human-style DNA structures, but their home universe uses a different solution for physically encoding their cellular blueprints. Human chromosomes are roughly X-shaped, made from twisted strands of DNA, which contains the encoding. The Star Children 1 equivalent is round, and coiled up in reels, like an old celluloid movie. It functions in a similar way, but the structure is very different.

With human DNA, the encoding is internal to the structure, whereas with Star Children 1 DNA it appears to be external; i.e. The chemical encoding is attached to the outside of the strands. The strands themselves are then coated in a protective layer so as to protect the data. An analogy being; laminating printed paper with protective plastic sheets.

The encoding coils can also be stacked together as if a series of old celluloid films were stacked together side by side on a shelf. When it comes to copying them, they are simply unwound.

For completeness, the Star Children 1 also revealed another method of storing DNA chemical data, but not used by them. In this second alternative to the system used in the universe humans dwell in, the data is adhered to a flat backing material. By analogy you could see this as similar to a long spool of paper with text on it. Except that the text first runs left to right, then right to left, and then left to right again, etc. For protection the backing material is then formed into a long tube and coiled up. Due to the higher data density, the complete code for one animal can be stored on one coil.

Visitation Bodies

For Star Children 1 to physically appear in the humans' universe, they have to use bodies adapted to the local environment. Thus they adopt humanoid bodies which appear more mammalian, and have hair where appropriate. This has given Star Children 1 souls a considerable number of options as to precisely what form they can take.

It should also be noted that the soul groups which give life to Star Children 1, are present in human form on Earth, but still in extremely low numbers.

CULTURE

Started As Comparable To Early Humans

For context; early 21st century human society can be compared to a mostly spiritually arid wasteland when compared to the earlier, deeper, practical spiritual awareness, which previously existed in Earth's primitive cultures. Typical early human beings managed to achieve a strong spiritual awareness in a natural way. By comparison, in the early 21st century human beings are generally, and unnaturally, still not as aware as their early ancestors. Though a small minority of the population are nevertheless becoming highly aware, and in new ways.

Star Children 1's society started in a similar way to human beings. They initially achieved a higher level of spiritual awareness and then never (temporarily) lost it to the extent that human beings did.

Star Children 1 were evolved from an animal that combined the qualities of an ape and a lizard. They lived in organized groups from very early on and had a strong cultural bond. Where human beings resorted to war to deal with over-population and limited land resources, Star Children 1 controlled their population numbers until technological advances permitted an increased population.

All of this was easier for Star Children 1 because they were closer to the super-consciousness or God. At their level of the equivalent of 2 dimensions closer than humankind, it is difficult not to be very aware of what created you. The effect of living at such a higher dimension makes them far more aware of the oneness which binds all living entities.

This higher awareness of everything does, however, create its own complications. All physical entities need to feed off other physical entities in order to survive. Consuming other entities can distress Star Children 1 greatly, as ordinarily it causes them to die. Being sensitive to such distress makes it problematic to consume anything. Historically this slowed Star Children 1's development as they abhorred any form of unnecessary consumption.

Once Star Children 1 became better adept at farming or otherwise creating life forms they could happily consume, their society exponentially flourished and they rapidly spread throughout their original and other universes.

Star Children 1 also developed in a universe where multiple possibilities can be experienced at once. The effect is that as they grasped how best to experience this, they were able to experiment with alternative ways to develop a society at a far faster rate and "catch-up".

Ascended Race

The category of Star Children 1 a human being is likely to actually meet, is what could reasonably be described as an ascended race. In practice this means in their natural form they no longer have need of physical bodies. Though if they wish to physically visit places such as the Earht Plane, then it is often helpful to adopt some sort of physical form.

An obvious question thus arising is how does a race become ascended ?

A very short answer is to say that they have such a high self-awareness that their physical lives are no longer compelling. Or put another way, their personal physical game has nearly played out.

Whilst this might give a reader a potentially attractive thought that ascent would spare his or her soul from any further requirement to incarnate, that would be to misunderstand reality. When a game has played out, the tendency is to want to play something more difficult. So Star Children 1 are highly active with respect to assisting the Creators construct new universes and the worlds within them, where new games can be experienced.

Nevertheless, returning to how any race can ascend, the example provided by the Star Children 1 provides useful guidance. In their early physical form, they experienced a great deal of individuality, not unlike the experience of being human. As they became more self-aware, they lost most of that individuality and were substantially of one-mind.

This is the short answer to understanding what an ascended race is.

Early Culture

It's helpful to compare the Star Children 1's early, not yet industrialised form, which is comparable to around Earth year 0

AD, to the later Star Children 1 version we are mainly dealing with.

Unlike Earth, there was never really any significant military activity. This also had the effect that they were not very interested in competitive sports. Though they could be very competitive when it came to practical betterment; e.g. Who can be the healthiest, most aware, smartest, develop technological advances.

The Star Children 1 were much more at one with their planet, and each other. They obviously had to farm, and ate a diet of plants and large insects, all of which were mostly cooked.

Early art and literature were heavily inspired by other alien races of whom they were aware and had contact with. Thus the culture of betterment that is likely to take till around 2500 AD on Earth to establish, already existed for Star Children 1 almost from the outset.

For completeness, whilst it is true that human beings enjoy betterment, a great deal of it is driven by fear; e.g. Fear of getting fat and dying younger. Whereas Star Children 1 want to be healthy simply for the sake of it.

Current Culture

The immediate challenge for a human mind is to understand what Star Children 1 do, in what can be equated to a sort of almost physical heaven (not human heaven which is mostly concerned with debriefing returned consciousnesses and forming them into new ones for future incarnation). Probably the best analogy is to suggest that it is similar to a creative playground, where everything you imagine becomes instantly real and capable of being experienced. Hence their homes have doors into engineered environments, as described earlier.

So it comes to pass that the later Star Children 1 have an active hand in creating the universe human beings experience. They have created suns and planets around them where new alien life forms have come into existence. Though they are never exclusively responsible for such works, which in any event are all inspired and directed by the Creators.

Star Children 1 in non-physical form are very modest, and often happy to operate unobserved. It can be as if they take great pleasure in seeing how much they can influence and achieve without getting spotted.

Physical Star Children 1

Unless a human being is engaged in active astral projection exploration, he or she has almost no chance of ever discovering how physical Star Children 1 who might visit the Earht Plane actually live. So the easiest way to describe how they live is that:

F*irstly*; Star Children 1 enjoy living amongst other alien races and have engineered bodies so as to make this possible. Furthermore, where practicable, they are very interested in cross-breeding to see what interesting alternative physical forms are achievable. Hence, it is very difficult to quantify what a pure physical Star Children 1 looks like in the universe humans experience.

S*econdly*; they can spend a considerable amount of time ‘out of body’, and see physical form as a sort of protective suit you might put on if you wished to explore a physical environment. One effect of this is that Star Children 1 astronauts who visit Earth often have another body in their universe, though it might be placed in a sleep state or stasis.

INTERACTION WITH HUMAN BEINGS

Experimentation

Like most other alien visitors, Star Children 1 have conducted their own fair share of sample taking and conducting of experiments. However, they tend to be less invasive than, for example, Greys, thus there are fewer complaints.

With respect to the engineering of the human species itself, the Star Children 1 have not been too 'hands on', but have left much of this work to other species such as Future Humans and Nordics. Though they have assisted with the overseeing of what occurs.

Visitation

Star Children 1 like looking in on friends who are manifesting in human form, be they from the soul groups who energise and give life to Star Children 1, or where other working relationships exist. So if you regularly find yourself visited by Star Children 1, you obviously have a close connection with them.

Potential Interaction

Star Children 1 are keen to extend the invitation to astrally visit them. They will astrally look in upon anyone reading this part of the encyclopaedia and be visible if you are mildly clairvoyant. In practice they are looking out for human bodies that are learning to or can potentially make contact.

When you sense them, you will easily find that you are initially struck by a wave of warm and gentle unconditional love.

However, gaining an understanding of their worlds can literally make your human mind feel as if it is spinning.

E20 Xeons 1

INTRODUCTION

Xeons 1 (pronounced; "Zee-on-s") are a variant of Star Children, and are part of the control arrangement for managing the universe humans and other physical forms enable you to experience; i.e. They work as part of the team of beings who construct the illusory universe you experience.

In order to create species, planets and universes, the assistance of various alien beings is necessary because the Creators (extensions of the ultimate Creator) do not have physical bodies. Thus whilst the Creators determine the nature of the experiments operating throughout the universes, they require physical assistance to manifest them. Locations such as the Earht Plane fall within the scope of both Xeons 1's and Star Children 1's works.

Historically, humankind initially thought God constructed the Earth and the universe around it (in 7 days if you are a Christian). Then 20th century science came to the view that it all happened more or less by itself over the course of 14 billion years. Researching this encyclopaedia points to neither of these two propositions being entirely correct or incorrect.

The ultimate Creator does not directly construct and arrange the worlds within universes. Much of the detail has to be arranged at the various levels. For example in over-simplified terms; Greys can be found manipulating organic DNA, Star Children 1 organising planetary solar systems, and Xeons 1 deal with the greater universes. Whilst this explanation is somewhat of an over-simplification, it nevertheless helps to guide the reader towards a better understanding of how the universes are constructed and managed. This simplified understanding being an improvement on virtually no understanding.

Visiting Xeons 1

On the first attempt, the reader can easily find that Xeons 1 have one of the more challenging home worlds to access. It is well insulated against marauding astral travellers and it only becomes properly accessible to researchers employing non-physical cognitive functions; i.e. Placing more cognitive emphasis upon the non-physical mind. Potential visitors who are not employing their non-physical minds will find access to Xeons 1 world effectively barred.

Xeons 1 have a close relationship with the Creators, and can easily get plagued by requests from other physical life forms to assist in changing the course of events. Visitations are therefore, as far as possible, either by invitation or other controlled mechanisms, which keep most less-developed consciousnesses away.

Final Insertion

The physical author of this encyclopaedia could only initially allocate a space in the encyclopaedia's first edition for this learned species, as he was initially unable to make any real determination as to who they were and thus research this chapter. It was only upon the discovery (recognition) of non-physical mental processing that the author was finally given the necessary invitation, which enabled completion of the first edition of the encyclopaedia.

The physical mind is largely devoted to creating an illusion that you are a human being alive on Earth. Similarly, its early 21st century programming is designed to obscure your awareness of other worlds. Whereas, the non-physical mind is not inherently restricted from perceiving other dimensions. In practice, a physical mind will often defer to the non-physical one without recognising that it has made the switch. However, there are circumstances where more consciousness awareness of making the switch becomes necessary, and this is an excellent example of the necessity.

LOCATION

Not Disclosed At This Time

PLANET

Barren Rock

At the dimension an early 21st century Earht Plane astronomer would search a cosmos, all that would be found is a grey, lifeless asteroid battered planet not unlike a large version of the Moon. So battered in fact that its shape is mildly irregular (as opposed to totally spherical), with some of the craters having very high rims. The atmosphere is very thin and offers little sustenance to organic life.

Up A Few Dimensions

From space the planet appears to have a great deal of red land mass (darker than Mars), with large swathes of greenery covering most of the remainder. Oceans take up approximately half of the surface. Polar regions are visible as white.

Intriguingly, whichever side of the planet is turned away from its sun, is in less darkness than would be expected. This is because space at this dimension is not as black as Earht Plane space, so there is some background illumination from it. Similarly, you will note that all astronomical objects are closer together; i.e. There is less space-time to separate astronomical objects such as planets in the solar system. Correspondingly, less space-time determines that there is less gravity to pull orbiting objects together. So the solar system's orbiting objects such as planets need to be closer together.

Engineered Planet

At the Earht Plane dimension, most habitable planets are a considerable distance from their respective suns. For example, the Earth is around 150 million km (100 million miles) away. At this dimension the planet appears to be around 1% of that distance. Accordingly its sun appears both very near and large. However, its sun's thermal radiation seems to be relatively moderate and does not scorch the planet's surface.

Unlike most planets, where any terraforming is normally achieved using natural processes over millennia, here it appears to have been achieved very rapidly and incorporates many specific design features. The result is that much of this planet is arranged to be garden like with food production housed in discreet industrial units.

A practical result of all this engineering is that there are no active volcanoes causing unexpected catastrophes, nor any earthquakes.

Whilst the planet is similar to Earth in that it hosts a multitude of species, here they all seem to have been developed relatively quickly; i.e. Thousands of Earth years as opposed to millions. Once developed, every living thing has become relatively ageless. This rapid construction, followed by apparent agelessness, is similar to the orthodox Christian view upon the age of the Earth. Albeit in this instance, that another planet has been rapidly constructed in a way that it now looks ageless.

Atmosphere

The higher dimension atmosphere appears poisonous to human beings. However, this is an irrelevant point as far as a physical visit by a human being is concerned, since at the Earht Plane dimension this planet has a lot in common with the Moon. So a human being would need a spacesuit to visit, and in any event at the Earht Plane dimension you would not encounter Xeons 1.

Nevertheless the atmosphere does operate a carbon dioxide to oxygen cycle that a reader would be familiar with. This in turn supports other forms of organic life with considerable similarities to that found on the Earth.

Variations

This version of the planet is well integrated into parallel dimension variations of itself. The parallel dimension variations of it are designed to give it similarities to a wide range of different alien species who might visit. So be aware that the version being examined here is adapted to be compatible with beings which include earthly humans. Thus it would not be difficult to find a parallel version of the same world that looked significantly different.

Xeons 1 World

Life for Xeons 1 has some passing parallels with which human beings would be familiar, and some less familiar aspects.

There are young Xeons 1, but they are not children in mentality and instead behave more like energetic adults.

The home planet is shared with many varieties of other species, and most of them live in relative harmony.

Xeons 1 keep pets, of sorts, in their homes. They went on to demonstrate that they shared their living environment with a variety of animals, which in a generalised way could be described as a variety of lizard-like creatures, some of which can fly. If you imagined crossing a friendly Labrador with a dragon (flying or non-flying), then you would get a representative idea. All beings can telepathically communicate with each other.

There is an abundance of advanced technology available, but it is employed in a minimalist way. Whilst space-time craft exist here, they are few and largely unnecessary. Hence this is a highly technologically advanced world, albeit with little visible evidence of such technology in use.

SPECIES

Appearance

Xeons 1 appear loosely humanoid, in that they are upright bipeds with two arms and two legs, though they have the option to adopt other manifestations. For example, if they wished to manifest in an underwater world and deal with an advanced aquatic species, they could manifest a fish like appearance by using an alternative physical form.

Comparing their humanoid faces to human ones; they have larger protruding eyes, wrinkled skin, minimal head hair, and mouths that are similar to a short earthly elephant's limp trunk. To the sides they have long points on their ears, though the length depends upon the individual and its mood.

From the front Xeons 1 appear humanoid with spindly limbs. From the side they look more like a worm with limbs that has a bulbous head accommodating its brain. The base of the tail is nearly as thick as the abdomen. The mouth is clearly a continuation of the head, but angled downwards.

Skin colour is brownish to greyish. Hands and feet are more reptilian than mammalian. All appear to have some sort of tail of varying lengths.

Clothes are worn when dealing with races such as humans, because that is customary for humans. Correspondingly, when dealing with many of the insect races, antennae are sometimes adopted.

Evolution

Xeons 1 were evolved from a worm-like species that swam in the sea. It then became a large surface dwelling worm or invertebrate without bones. From that point it was first given cartilage to improve movement and strength, and then the cartilage was turned into a substance similar to bone.

Clairvoyantly you would have seen an energy template driving the alterations forward in a specific direction.

After the equivalent of a few thousand Earth years, it was possible to transform what was an animal that moved around like a caterpillar without proper legs, into an upright biped. What looks like an elongated nose is in fact its mouth, and depending on the sub-species, there is a tail of varying length. Since the tail is useful for swimming, it is sometimes retained to a large extent, even to the point of needing to be coiled up due to its length.

Xeons 1 are an archetypal example of a species whose descendants evolved its ancestors.

Reproduction

Young are born in small elastic white eggs which have a mouth and digestive system. The eggs then grow, as might insect grubs, until a fully formed biped can emerge from them. At the latter stages of development the biped within the egg can be seen through a translucent shell stretching and moving around.

Xeons 1 feed their young by regurgitating part-digested food into the egg's mouth hole, which has parallels with how earthly dogs or penguins feed their young. Whilst they have access to processed foods, Xeons 1 prefer not to feed it to their young.

The species is split into males and females, though should the need or desire occur, a male can become female, or vice-versa. Males and females also enjoy copulating for comfort, as opposed to the outright pleasure version exhibited by earthly human beings.

Diet

You may have heard the expression of "living on fresh air", and Xeons 1 appear able to live upon "fresh air" when not involved in a physical growth cycle; i.e. When not growing or feeding an egg, food is largely unnecessary.

Such foods as Xeons 1 do eat would be in keeping with what a human being would be familiar with, except that all such food is far more nutritious and comprehensively happy. In this context, when visiting their planet, all plant life is surprisingly chatty in comparison to earthly ones.

The living on "fresh air" technique relies upon the fact that the air is actually a living entity, which can therefore transfer the energy of nutrients from adjacent plants. Hence when Xeons 1 travel for any length of time in spacecraft they normally place a great deal of living organic matter in the air recycling system.

CULTURE

Purpose

The difference between living as a typical Xeon 1 compared to an early 21st century human being is considerable. This does not suggest one race is necessarily better than the other, merely that they perform different functions. An analogy would be comparing a tractor to a helicopter; they both have the capacity to move, but beyond that there is great divergence as to their functions. The tractor and the helicopter will also perform best at different levels.

Human beings perform the function of making you believe you are a human being, and sometimes in a possibly godless world. By comparison, Xeons 1 can only really experience being part of the Creator or super-consciousness and are consciously directed by its Creators.

Xeons 1 assist in setting up the scenarios and adventures you can experience. They have a close relationship with and are operated by the Creators. Accordingly they take the view that they are a physical manifestation of the Creators. Their daily work is to help enact the Creators intentions.

Since they possess such a close working relationship to the Creators, Xeons 1 are therefore considered to have a hand in, and influence over, everything that physically occurs. This makes them prone to receiving endless requests to modify what physically occurs. However, they operate on the basis of managing events that affect large numbers of beings, as opposed to just one individual.

Why They Exist At All

In case the point has not yet been grasped, and at the risk of boring the reader with possible repetition; under the direction of the Creators, Xeons 1 are part of a group of beings who are controlling the universe humans experience.

Yet with all of this management responsibility, the Xeon species as a whole is not inclined to be interventionist. This is because in any experiment, they consider events generally need to take their course. They are, however, inclined to influence from behind the scenes; i.e. They influence every human being, but cover their tracks so as to leave little conscious trace.

If you, the reader, are tempted to contact them in order to elicit guidance from them, there will normally be easier alternatives. Whilst by and large these beings are not manifested to explain anything in particular to a human being, in this instance they will nevertheless assist an inquiring human consciousness. For example, they can readily help provide the emotional energies that support physical action.

Day-to-Day Life

Xeons 1 mostly live in extended family clusters. Their physical bodies live for the earthly equivalent of hundreds of years, and provide a conveyor-belt of platforms or vehicles for their immortal souls.

They are aware that they were created to perform highly creative functions. But in order to stay "grounded" and not get lost in self-importance, they devote much of their day to simple physical activities. So whilst they will spend part of their day developing universes through higher thought processes, they balance this with simple physical tasks; e.g. Cleaning or gardening. Thus their society has little in the way of robotic servants.

Extended families normally live in one bright and airy home. Such homes are largely open plan without obvious internal doors. Thus everyone sleeps and works in large rooms.

Very little time is required to prepare food as very little is consumed, if at all, depending on the circumstances.

Adults conduct much of their work at home and children are educated through observing the work. Children in any case require little formal education as they have a good recollection of previous existences.

Happily copulating for part of the day is almost universal and appears to assist Xeons 1 minds to be energetically well balanced. As such, copulating mostly forms part of a resting activity.

When Xeons 1 move they do so with a happy, almost exaggerated, rolling swaying motion, which can include an almost bouncing motion. Enjoying the motion of their physical bodies is all part of staying grounded.

Work

Xeons 1 do not receive much in the way of obvious defined instruction from the Creators. Instead they make themselves aware of interesting group moments (moments involving numerous life forms) that the Creators would be interested in initiating. Xeons 1 then set about engineering circumstances in which the Creators' intentions can potentially be actualised. Much of the detail regarding these scenarios can be further added to by beings at a lower level; e.g. Star Children or Greys.

E20 Xeons 1

Most of the near-physical aspects of the Xeons 1's creation work normally takes place at home. Whilst it is conceptually challenging to fully comprehend how this occurs, a visual impression was nevertheless supplied. Xeons 1 work around what at first appear to be plain round tables. But at the centre of the table is, in effect, a portal into whatever dimension and location they are working on. The example shown resembled a window into a cosmos where planetary systems were being engineered. The portal further allows the operator to zoom in and out much in the same way that a draftsman using AutoCad would.

Before work is started, these white round work tables, look just like tables. The tables have no obvious control or power cables and are operated telepathically. To demonstrate their function, the assisting Xeons 1 family switched on a table and zoomed it onto a planet under construction. It was observable that the centre of the table has a holographic hemisphere of space-time sitting on it. If you approach the table you can look down into that universe as if the table had a central window into the other universe. Similarly, they demonstrated how galaxies are arranged within a universe, so as to facilitate subsequent experiential objectives. Within these universes, it was possible to observe other groups of advanced aliens working, almost like termites might cooperate together on a project.

Projects are also passed between households for further embellishment as necessary.

Xeons 1 are extremely aware of the energetic consciousness feedback that results from their creative experiments. They commented that early 21st century human beings needed to become considerably more aware of what this energetic feedback was before they could start to properly grasp what Xeons 1 were actually doing.

It was also shown how beings within the worlds under development could look back to see the Xeons 1 at work. This goes some way to explain why many cultures have often perceived that some sort of sub-gods are manipulating their environment.

INTERACTION WITH HUMAN BEINGS

An Insight To Adopt

Xeons 1 (or at least the small group of them assisting with this research) have a message to convey to the minority of humankind who have discovered this encyclopaedia (along with works deriving from it). The message is to stop doing anything because you, the reader, feel you have to. Instead learn to do everything because you want to.

The logic of this proposition is faultless. You, the reader, have an ongoing option to channel emotional energies to physically act, or you can channel energies that make you resist action and instead procrastinate. Which is the more interesting option ?

With respect to improving higher awareness, this strategy has further benefits. For a human consciousness to repeatedly attain higher awareness, it needs to refrain from entertaining false contemplations; i.e. Thinking based upon one or more fundamental falsehood. For example; “I am a human being”, as opposed to a more accurate thought of “I am experiencing life as a human being”.

A simple Xeons 1 objective is to help humankind to become more receptive to higher awareness. It follows that whenever you, the reader, allow congesting of the human energy system with false perceptions, this will considerably dull that higher awareness. An easy to follow improvement which enhances higher awareness, is to keep checking that whatever activities the human body is performing, are supported by the natural desire to undertake them.

The importance of such an apparently obvious behavioural modification is difficult to overstate, but easy to overlook by human beings.

Angelic Appearances

Much in the same way that angelic beings are closely directed by the Creators, so are Xeons 1. In fact there is considerable overlap between the consciousnesses that manifest angelic beings and Xeons 1. The main difference is the obvious one that Xeons 1 are physical manifestations, whilst angelic beings do not take such form. You could say that these are branches of the same big family.

However, whilst angelic beings operate from a region of relatively uninterrupted unconditional love, Xeons 1 do not have the same advantage. Because Xeons 1 are physically manifesting, by necessity they have to operate through lower spirit forms. To offset this potential impediment, they are very humorous and avoid taking themselves too seriously. The result is that any encounter with them gives the impression of a very pleasant race.

Setting Up Experiments

Xeons 1 live in a relatively struggle-free society. A stable population and a lifestyle awash with potential automation means that there is not much mandatory physical work required. Nevertheless, they dispense with automation where grounding physical exercise is of benefit to them. Similarly, in such societies there is no poverty or taxation, so state bureaucracy is minimal.

Xeons 1 creatively busy themselves with setting up experiments, which ultimately result in species development. In other words; assisting in the creation of worlds and the species thereon that will aid the understanding of what the ultimate Creator or super-consciousness actually is, and feedback energies to it. Practically the whole population appears involved, and this work is equalled by other permutations of the Xeon species that live elsewhere.

E20 Xeons 1

Human development, and every human life falls within Xeons 1's creative remit. Accordingly, the physical life of every reader is open to their analysis, along with the possibility for potentially influencing it. Since Xeons 1 influence extends across millions of worlds, they are unsurprisingly plagued by other alien beings seeking to alter the dynamics of these experiments.

Xeons 1, whilst cautious about bowing to uneducated requests to alter the dynamics of the experiments, nevertheless have an avenue by which proper requests can be considered. Accordingly they run an education programme by which potential visitors can advance their knowledge of how the universes operate, and were intended to operate. Beings who become proficient in understanding what their home universe is intended to achieve, thus become sufficiently qualified to propose modification to the particulars of what occurs.

Readers of this encyclopaedia are cordially invited to embrace the education programme offered. Astrally visiting Xeons 1 world is the first step forward, and specific further directions will be supplied upon stable visitations to their world(s).

APPENDICES

A1 The Ultimate Creator

INTRODUCTION

Most human minds in the early 21st century have very little first-hand sensory perception of that which created them. Thus experiencing life as an early 21st century human being offers an excellent opportunity to live in what can easily appear to be a godless world. Even the consciousness of a humble rock can often display more awareness of its creator than an often less aware urban human being could. Similarly, advanced alien species all experience at the very least some awareness that there is an ultimate Creator.

So why are human beings comparatively unaware ?

Most early 21st century human minds are designed to be able to rediscover the ultimate Creator. To enable rediscovery, it is vital that you, the reader, are able to experience forgetting in the first place. Most human minds perform the forgetting function extremely well. Furthermore, they are highly proficient at repeating the forgetting process.

However, once a human mind is trained how to travel beyond the low Astral World, it becomes plainly obvious to all that there is an ultimate Creator. This section of the encyclopaedia describes some of the aspects of the ultimate Creator that an explorer is likely to find.

Need For A God ?

The Earht Plane is designed to function in a highly automated way that can make the need for a god or ultimate creator appear potentially unnecessary. Cosmologists have pointed out that before the "big bang" there was no time, so any potential god would have had to have existed in a timeless place.

Thus it has been argued that nothing can exist in timelessness, on which basis there cannot be a god.

Most religions claim that God created the Earth and humankind. However, researching advanced aliens species reveals many of them claim to have, as part of a group, accomplished the creation of the human world. Yet there appears to be no ultimate conflict as to who is right, with respect to the Earth and its species being created by God or aliens. In simplistic terms, aliens claim to have been operating within some sort of guidance bestowed upon them by a higher being or representative thereof.

So whilst a human being is designed to perceive the creation of the Earth in such a way that it could conceivably have occurred spontaneously on its own, researching this encyclopaedia repeatedly reveals advanced alien species who claim to have had a hand in most aspects of the process.

Thus the only way to confirm the need for a god is to explore the Astral World and personally discover what it actually does.

ASTRAL REALITY

Seeing, or at least glimpsing, the ultimate Creator is absurdly easy, but is not necessarily an immediately enlightening experience. Once you have got to grips with some basic astral awareness techniques, you only have to (metaphorically speaking) look up, and there is a loving ball of light overhead. Whoever looks at this light will find that there is just the one, though as its presence descends it splits into many progressively lower forms.

Noticing What You Are

Upon investigation, everything you are likely to discover about what you really are points to one finding; you are derived from the bright thing high up in the astral. The human form you are experiencing is not really you, nor is its personality or ego. You, the reader, are an extension of that higher light, looking back upon your real-self through the perceptions of a human mind.

So it turns out that even though you are experiencing life as a human being, you are not a human being, but actually an extension of that higher light, otherwise known as the Super-Consciousness or God or ultimate Creator. The human life you are experiencing is therefore a consequence of your creativity.

You, the reader, are experiencing being something completely different from what you really are. Your adopted human form is likely to have no real Free Will to begin with, but instead likely to entertain a false belief that it has some Free Will, which in practice disguises the lack of it. The real you has created and set in motion the life you are now experiencing.

The human form you are experiencing is a focusing machine which enables you to experience living within an illusion.

The Real You

Humankind has spent millenia searching for God, and it turns out to be you. Plus everything else around you. Everything is a product of the real you.

On the Earht Plane there is plenty of scope for speculating about this. However, once you go up into the high astral, what you really are becomes self-evident. There is really not much point even attempting to justify the facts here, because that would be heading towards a speculative debate. It is much better for you, the reader, to observe what you really are and then compare your observation with that of other human minds who have conducted the same experimental investigation. Similarly, working with advanced alien species gives you contact with their experiences and perceptions.

Not You

You, the reader, will often perceive that the ultimate Creator, or even the intermediary entity of what might be referred to as "your higher-self" is somehow separate from you, the reader. Simplifying this perception, there will often appear to be both you and a separate creator, which exists somewhere else. You can similarly often perceive that you are operating independently of each other.

This "two of us" perception is a major aspect of the illusion you are experiencing.

The reality is that the "reader" you experience being is an engineered illusion.

The whole personality, emotions, and thinking system of you, the reader, is an artificially engineered construct.

You have adopted this artificially engineered construct, which is programmed to make you perceive that you are not the Creator.

It follows, that whilst you might perceive yourself to be a human being, this is just an illusion you want to experience.

For completeness, it should be pointed out that the engineered construct (the reader) has no real Free Will of its own, and imagining you are the Creator does not alter this.

ONLY ONE OF US

Human beings are largely lost in an illusion of individuality, which is not a condition affecting all the advanced alien beings. Advanced aliens are, to varying extents, spared this self-induced condition, and all recognise that there is really only one of us. What you experience in physical bodies gives you an optional potential to get lost in the illusion of individuality, and separation from the ultimate source.

Entrapping Situation

If you perceive that you are an individual human being, then that perception blocks your capacity to notice what you actually are. Conversely, if you are noticing what you actually are, then you will similarly be aware that you are also a part of the super-consciousness.

It's a wonderful catch-22 situation, if you are not noticing what you really are, then this failure of itself interferes with your ability to do so. On the other hand, since advanced aliens have learnt to overcome this trap, it cannot ultimately be that difficult.

It's not wrong to operate through the personality of a human being, but identifying yourself as that personality has an instantly debilitating effect on your higher awareness. Relearning how to perceive what you are takes considerable practice, but succeeding positively impacts on every area of your earthly life.

Moments Of Oneness

Advanced aliens and future human beings are aware that they are experiencing some degree of artificially engineered individuality. But they have learnt to experience individuality in a way that it does not excessively detract from also being aware they we truly are part of the same greater entity. By comparison, they consider animals that are not aware of this to be primitive.

Meeting with aliens by astral projection enables you to experience what it is like to be them. To varying degrees, all the advanced species have a clear ongoing sense that there is only one of us. It is helpful to compare advanced aliens' normal perceptions to that of a typical human being.

It is worth reiterating that all the souls are ultimately equal, even if differently configured. A soul can manifest in an advanced alien culture where oneness is difficult to ignore, or a primitive world where oneness can be more readily ignored. Astral projection to advanced alien worlds is a very effective method of validating these facts from different perspectives.

WHAT IS GOD LIKE ?

Answering this question is actually your job. You are an extension of the super-consciousness, which through you, the reader, is looking back at itself. Other human beings and aliens were primarily created to answer this same question, but from different perspectives.

Discover Your Own Truth

The world is full of people prepared to lecture upon their interpretation of what the super-consciousness is. But it remains your purpose to test and validate everything suggested. Similarly, there is not much value in fighting with people who arrive at a different set of findings to you. If someone else perceives the super-conscious differently, the intelligent response is to experience being that person and similarly experience their alternative perception.

Loving And Bored

Experiencing what it is like to be the super-consciousness is not difficult. However, remaining in that experience for any length of time is challenging.

To experience what it is like to be the super-consciousness, largely involves allowing your human form to experience a wonderful, but easily overwhelming, unconditional love. This unconditional love is so strong that initially your body may resist experiencing it. As your body gradually allows itself to have this experience, your consciousness is gradually drawn into the ultimate Creator until there is nothing but the Creator to be perceived.

For the novice explorer seeking reassurance, a strong indication that you are being drawn into the super-consciousness is that you experience getting bored.

Experiencing what you really are, soon makes it apparent that in many ways you are bored and wish to enjoy interesting experiences. Thus creating amazing worlds and the adventures within them becomes obviously very appealing.

An Appetite For Interesting Experiments

In early 21st century western human culture there is an abhorrence of scientists creating new life-forms, because this is considered to be playing at being "God". Meanwhile, this is exactly what many (if not ultimately all) the advanced alien species catalogued in this encyclopaedia get up to.

When you experience being the super-consciousness, it becomes apparent that you, the Creator, really enjoy initiating interesting experiments and experiences. Many of these experiments and experiences need to be set up at a physical level. Therefore it makes sense to get existing physical forms, such as advanced aliens, to perform this work.

Precisely what therefore does or does not constitute "the ultimate Creator's work, is for every reader to individually determine. However, in general terms, creating anything at all appears to fall within the possibility of the ultimate Creator's intention.

The importance of discovering your own truth in this matter cannot be understated. The super-consciousness created both benign and (playful) malevolent entities to influence the minds of both humans and aliens in general. Furthermore, without an interaction between benign and malevolent forces, there would be very few interesting experiments.

Self-evidentially, the ultimate Creator has inspired many interesting experiments to come into existence. The Earht Plane physical parents of the body you, the reader, have use of, assisted in this work.

Dependant On The Feedback Loop

The reality of this next observation is challenging for the human mind to comprehend with respect to timelessness. So for human simplification purposes, it is explained as if time were real.

In many ways the ultimate Creator could be considered to have originally been almost nothing. By creating illusory artificial living entities it "feeds" itself. By creating universes full of such entities it receives a great deal of energetic "food". The more it creates, the more it grows.

When a human mind appreciates what is creating it, it feeds back a loving appreciation, which in turn nourishes and grows the super-consciousness. Many human forms only do this to a significant degree when they die and their consciousness is reunited with its creator. However, there is no need to wait until death to complete the feedback loop and instead it is very rewarding to appreciate the super-consciousness now. Doing so is a pleasant, happy experience.

In summary; the ultimate Creator is an enormous entity because its creations are nourishing and growing it with loving feedback. Except that all this occurs timelessly.

Why Alien Invasion Is Unlikely

Human beings have a unique perspective upon what the super-consciousness actually is. Accordingly, alien races are working to improve humankind's ability to make such unique observations. Because human beings can perceive the super-consciousness in a different way to aliens, human beings have insights which are of value to aliens. Therefore it makes little sense for advanced aliens to try and wipe out humankind in a war of extermination.

Conversely, aliens are nervous about giving humankind too much physical access to them. Humankind in its present primitive state remains inclined to wipe out alien species should the opportunity arise. Similarly, other less advanced alien races could potentially seek to invade the Earth. Luckily, by the time they get technologically advanced enough to do so, they are likely to have abandoned such a warlike objective.

Advanced aliens are doing precisely what the "no invasion" hypothesis implies: F*irstly*; they are assisting humankind improve its higher awareness. S*econdly*; they are interacting with human beings more. T*hirdly*; they (actually the higher beings which they derive from) are increasingly getting born into human form. In fact many of the readers of this book will have such a heritage; i.e. How alien is the reader's ultimate composition ?

Suggestions About The Super-Consciousness

As stated, it is your job to make your own observations about what God is. That said, others will also have made observations and it is reasonable to compare them with your own.

When you look up into the Astral World you will find a bright white entity at what appears to be the top of it all. Making sense of what it actually is, is difficult to do in a defined way.

Nevertheless, when making your own observations, you will no doubt agree that it is very large and abundant with unconditional love. God is often conceptualised as an old man, but what you will find could equally be perceived as a playful and childlike entity.

Useful Side Effect

Observing and re-experiencing the actuality of what you really are, be it via a human or a more alien path, helpfully energises the body. It similarly increases your higher awareness and gives you more capacity to carry out physical tasks, and to a higher standard. If you incorporate an awareness of what creates your human form into day-to-day life, the human form will be more energised, generally happier, and more productive.

CREATOR SINGULARITY

The ultimate Creator the reader will ordinarily encounter, appears as an enormous and limitless entity. However, and for completeness, the advanced aliens who helped enable researching this encyclopaedia revealed an alternative perception of the super-conscious.

The version of the super-consciousness that any mildly competent astral explorer will easily encounter is the vast limitless one, in the Creator's world above the singularity. Yet this vast version of the super-consciousness is really a magnified or projected version of it.

Balanced System

On one side of the singularity you have the Astral World, with its many sub-worlds and attached physical universes. On the other side of the singularity you have the Creator's World from which the creation mechanism is directed.

It can be observed that the two worlds either side of the singularity both feed and balance each other. This mechanism has grown both worlds in an energetically balanced way.

Magnification System

It was suggested (for the reader to validate) that the vast super-consciousness you can observe and explore, is an engineered magnification of that which exists within the singularity.

Thus going forward, the astral explorer is now armed with an additional comprehension of what can be observed. The ultimate Creator you can observe in the Creator's world, is actually a magnification emanating from the singularity.

CREATOR DEVELOPMENT

When you, the reader, pay attention to what you are, you can return a wonderful loving energy back to the ultimate Creator. Doing so is a very pleasant experience that will make you happy.

You are creating yourself, the ultimate Creator.

A2 The Creators

INTRODUCTION

The super-consciousness or God or the ultimate Creator, has at its disposal a system for creating everything the real you can experience. This is a living mechanism, and controlling it are what are labelled here as "The Creators". The Creators are extensions of the ultimate Creator, and for definition purposes are the bits of it that are responsible for directing what occurs in the astral worlds.

Historical Perspective

Human religions mostly profess the view that the Earth was created by God. Researching this encyclopaedia revealed that every alien race examined is a combination of genetic engineering and assisted evolution; i.e. An evolutionary process that has been externally influenced so as to favour particular outcomes. So with respect to life forms, they all appear to have been, to some extent, engineered by alien beings.

The question is therefore who or what is creating everything and everyone. Was it the ultimate Creator, or a bunch of aliens engineering new species such as humankind ?

Researching this encyclopaedia points to it being a combination of the two possibilities. The key to understanding the creation of the universe is to recognise that in a sophisticated way, the whole thing is able to run on a sort of 'autopilot'. The super-consciousness merely needs to manifest an intention for a universe to exist, and an intelligent automated arrangement takes care of the rest. Hence the comparison with an 'autopilot', where once instructed, a machine will steer a craft towards interesting outcomes.

Astral Perspective

Up until the beginning of the early 21st century, the vast majority of human beings who have experienced the Astral World have not observed how the creation process actually works. To be fair, having the opportunity to observe the mechanism requires, for a human mind, expert training and guidance which may have been difficult to obtain.

When you observe the Creator's World (the Astral World above the singularity) it is very easy to see the projection of super-consciousness. It is similarly not that difficult to observe the vortex and its singularity. This is because, to a large extent, a human mind knows the Earth must appear somewhere in the system and will seek it out, hence will ultimately encounter the singularity and the vortex in the process.

When exploring the Creator's World, an observer can easily see an enormous super-consciousness apparently above, and apparently below energies swirling into a vortex's centre or singularity. Though note that you have to go below (or through) the singularity to see the Earth as it is not really visible from above in the Creator's World.

The Creators

A human explorer's initial impression of the apparent space between the vortex and the super-consciousness, is typically just dark space, turning into a "fog of light" with the main light of the super-consciousness above that. Thus, there is no obvious start to the super-consciousness. It is in this intermediate zone, between the super-consciousness and the vortex, which is where the Creators exist.

For definition purposes; the super-consciousness or ultimate Creator, is a projection that appears to be the strong light furthest away from the vortex, and the intermediate fog of light are the Creators; i.e. The Creators are (or exist in) the fog of light between the outer projection of the super-consciousness and the vortex. It is also worth noting that a human mind has to practice recognising the differences before all this becomes easy to perceive during astral explorations.

Moments

The bright fog (or fog of light) contains the intentions for all the moments that are to physically exist. If life were like an old film, then a moment would each be a frame from that film. Only when the film is played and each frame projected onto a screen does it become an illusion of physical life. Above the vortex the moments are not assembled into a linear sequence, so instead of appearing as a film they are more like a huge collection of slides which are not in the form of an orderly time line. Instead the moments are more like flowers that blossom, or erupting fireworks. They all start with a simple intention to experience something and then progressively branch off into ever more detailed sub-intentions, which become moments.

Because at this level everything is alive, the Creators are also the intentions or the moments they create, they are simultaneously aspects of the same thing.

Another interpretation of the level where you find the Creators is describing it as a "Control Room", because the intention for everything that your human form experiences emanates from here.

The ultimate Creator sets the whole process in motion with an intention to understand what it actually is and creates an energetic feedback loop. This in turn then becomes more complex intentions, such as creating an Earth for humans to live on.

Intention or Energy Templates

The key difference between the Creator's World above the vortex and the Astral World below the singularity; is that nothing above the singularity has any real form. Whilst below the singularity everything progressively starts to take form, until ultimately you reach the levels or planes where physical forms appear.

Above the vortex are all the intentions for everything to be experienced or happen. Below the vortex, these intentions need to adopt some category of form. So for example, above the vortex there would be a desire to experience sneezing. Below the vortex there would correspondingly be an energetic template which creates a human being, and in that moment the human would sneeze.

Role Of Advanced Aliens

Given the vast numbers of occasions human beings have observed advanced aliens taking DNA samples from the Earth, and less obviously introducing new DNA, clearly they have some part to play in the world you are experiencing.

The Creators have no physical bodies, and therefore cannot personally do anything at a physical level. Even in the Astral World below the vortex, the Creators similarly have to act through some type of spirit form. Thus by one means or another, the Creators' creation mechanism includes influencing beings which reside in the astral and physical worlds.

As a normal procedure, the Creators influence advanced alien minds so as to encourage them to assist in the creation of new life forms. By this means, the natural evolutionary process can be engineered to follow any particular direction. Though outcomes are not certain, and everything is essentially an experiment.

With respect to the actual creation of the universe humans experience, researching this encyclopaedia revealed advanced alien species responsible for such great works. In simplistic terms, intentions above the singularity need to be converted into a more solid form below it. Therefore, if it is intended that a planet is to be formed, someone needs to organise its physical creation, and some of that work must be conducted in more physical dimensions. An example of such work being undertaken is detailed in the chapter on Xeons 1.

As a species becomes more advanced, it gets the opportunity to consciously participate in the development of worlds. As human beings advance, they too have the opportunity to enact the Creators' intentions.

A GREAT EXPERIMENT

What Are You ?

Being able to make a preliminary observation of what you really are is, as far as human beings are concerned, relatively easy. You need do little more than; relax, breathe properly, metaphorically look up, and you will see your real-self.

As to how the real you or super-consciousness has managed to create the physical universe humans experience, this is much more difficult for an early 21st century human mind to fully comprehend. Yet it is obviously integral to an understanding of what you really are, to similarly understand how the greater you managed to create a physical universe. Hence why this chapter was even transcribed for you to subsequently find on the Earht Plane.

Your starting point in this comprehension exercise is a state of separation where you will initially perceive the real you or super-consciousness to be completely different and separate from your human form. From this highly contrasting state, the primary purpose of your human form is to then comprehend what you really are. This alternative human identity is achieved through a mechanism whereby you will wish to perceive yourself to be a human being.

Comprehending what you are can be significantly advanced through personal validation of any helpful suggestions you may have been given. Conversely, if you only studied the suggestions, but never personally validated them, nothing much would be achieved. Similarly, personally verifying how you came to create an amazing physical universe is an important part of that validation.

Realistically, one human mind will have difficulty comprehending and observing the enormity of the achievement. For this reason, many different beings, both human and alien have been created, so as to contribute a broad spectrum of observations.

It also follows that in the process of exploring what you really are, new discoveries will need to occur.

An Experiment

To comprehend what the Creators are doing, it is helpful to recognise that they are really performing a series of minor experiments, which combine into one great experiment. Similarly, as with any true experiment, (in terms of artificial linear time) the result is not really known beforehand.

For accuracy, it constantly needs to be recognised that the Creators are operating from a realm where there is no linear time, so before and after do not technically exist. However, to try and explain this further to a human mind, which has little or no experience of such a state, is beyond the scope of this chapter.

Repeated Experiments

The wonderful thing about experiments is that you can alter the variables and repeat them. Examples of this are easy to observe in ordinary life on Earth. Each human body is equipped with a different personality or ego, and this gives the real you a different perspective upon what you really are.

To further enhance gathering a wide range of experimental data, parallel universes are employed. Thus there also exist permutations of you, the reader, reading variations of this book.

Alternative Perspectives

One of the fastest ways to increase your understanding of a subject is to see it from different perspectives. Hence alien races are very interested in experiencing the human perspective, whilst humans are progressively grasping the advantages of experiencing the aliens' perspectives.

This brings us conveniently back to the subject of who, or what, the Creators are. Prior to the first publication of this encyclopaedia, there was extremely little human recognition that they even existed. It was recognised that the real you had created the physical universe, however, precisely how was barely understood. Whereas many advanced alien races already have very helpful insights upon this subject, and through works such as this are sharing them.

2012 And Free Will

Experimenting with different variables invariably delivers a greater spectrum of results. The new variable that has been introduced to the human race is the gradual introduction of Free Will. To begin with, most human minds perceive that they have access to Free Will, thus are initially unaware that in practice they have virtually none.

Without digressing too much into what Free Will actually is, the key point is that since 2012, the Creators, who have access to Free Will, have been giving some human minds access to the effects of it. Accordingly, since 2012, it has become much more difficult to predict what will occur on Earth because the Creators have allowed the introduction of new variables.

Increasing contact with advanced alien civilisations is one of the methods by which humankind is being reminded about how Free Will is operated. Human minds are being reminded how to access higher awareness and consciousness.

Free Will gives the reader access to choosing the adventure.

Scientific Analysis

Religious leaders are often nervous of scientifically analysing what they consider to be divine forces. Many such organisations subscribe to the view that membership requires beliefs that should not be scientifically tested. Similarly, scientists are often reluctant to test the truth behind certain religious beliefs as it invariably leads to acrimony.

This reluctance to scientifically analyse the mechanisms by which the real you created the physical universes, is largely a consequence of the energetic blanket which is designed to distract you, the reader, from doing so. However, now that energetic blanket of discouragement is being lifted, you will find it easier to explore the science behind what you are experiencing.

The other major obstacle to proper scientific analysis that many people are affected by, is a fear of being ridiculed. This fear often extends into a reluctance to acknowledge that there are obviously advanced beings alive on other planets, who from time to time visit the Earth.

Advanced aliens have a far superior scientific understanding of how the universes were created, and are therefore potentially very informative. Whereas denial their existence, precludes asking them what they know.

Be alert to the fact that, in the early 21st century, the programming of human minds to make them ridicule proper scientific investigation, was merely part of the system to keep any primitive human beings isolated and largely confined to the Earth.

OBSERVING THE CREATORS

Start With The Real You

When you allow your human consciousness to experience being the real you, it draws it high into the Creator's World above the singularity and the vortex. From there you can look down upon the energies being drawn into this vortex. You can (with practice) see that the white energies of the real you become more colourful as they are drawn into the vortex, and that somehow this is resulting in a physical universe. Starting with this high vantage point is necessary in order to keep you aware of the greater reality.

Stay With Your Friends

The normal programming of a human mind causes it not to notice the Creators, so when you are seeking to validate their existence and activity, this is far more easily done in the company of specialist guiding spirits or advanced alien beings' consciousnesses. Hence it is pragmatic for your adopted physical body to form a friendly relationship with, and practice teamwork with, such beings.

One way to do this is by sensing where any alien friends who will assist you are. Their physical form may, for example, be in a laboratory or somewhere in nature millions of light-years away. Meanwhile, their consciousness can accompany your human one. Thus they can help guide you during your exploration of the amazing mechanism that creates the physical universe you are experiencing.

Energy Of The Creators

From above the vortex it is relatively easy to observe how the energies of the real you become more colourful and swirl towards the centre. Again for the purposes of definition, these swirling energy forms are the Creators.

The initial intention, which creates the singularity, comes from the real you and is then given additional detail by the Creators. You should be able to verify that the super-consciousness's intention is relatively simple; to know your real-self or "What am I ?" and thus grow itself through the resultant energetic feedback loop.

It might appear convenient to imagine the Creators as some sort of middle management department fleshing out the chief executive's order and ensuring the workforce below enact it. But such convenience could potentially overlook an important dynamic; the Creators do not interrupt the ultimate Creator's awareness.

The energy of the Creators runs uninterrupted from the real you (the ultimate Creator) right into the very essence of a human consciousness. The existence of this direct link is why, for example, it is very easy for a human consciousness to look back at the super-consciousness. Conversely, like a camera trying to take a picture of itself, this link is initially difficult to observe unless you know what to look for.

For completeness, it must be noted that whilst the ultimate Creator enjoys an uninterrupted connection to, for example your human form, feedback from it can be somewhat "confused". So whilst the real you keeps your human form energised, feedback concerning what that human form is up to can be somewhat confused by lower spirit forms.

Consciousness Of The Creators

It might appear convenient to view the Creators as having human personality traits, but again this will only obscure what they are. Essentially they operate as intentions; i.e. A desire for something to occur and an experience thus gained. This desire flows from the highest level down to the lowest with embellishments occurring on the way. So for example, the Creators ensure that there is an energy for physical matter to appear to exist. Similarly, the Creators have caused the human ego you are experiencing to exist, even though they are not that ego.

As a footnote, since there are multiple Creators (along with other parties assisting them), it is not therefore difficult to understand how early human beings tended to the view that all earthly phenomena where driven by multiple gods.

The function of the Creators is to create experiences of one sort or another. At its most primitive, matter is assembled whereupon it acquires a basic awareness, which is experienced. Eventually matter must be disassembled, whereupon that consciousness is returned to the real you, causing it to feed back back an impression of what you really are.

It is helpful to regard the Creators as a two way channel, allowing intention to manifest at lower levels, with the awareness of experiences passing back to the super-consciousness, along with occasional glimpses of the super-consciousness.

A Control Room Of Sorts

Between the Earht Plane and the projection of the super-consciousness you can observe high dimension beings who appear to be somehow manipulating life below. To a large extent they are a human interpretation of what the Creators (and parties assisting them) are, as perceived by a human mind. So if by comparison you were instead experiencing an alien lifetime, you would probably see the control room manned by alien forms. Similarly, the appearance of a control room at all is the result of your conceptualisation of how anything might be controlled.

If you stripped away the pre-convictions of what the place from which life on the Earht Plane is controlled is like, you would just observe bright energy flows. Once you realise that there is a sort of control room, you will easily find the right locations regardless of how your human consciousness then interprets what it finds. You will further be able to observe alien (including human) forms augmenting the output from that control room.

In summary, this is why it is possible to encounter human-like beings in a control room, controlling events on the Earht Plane, even though at higher levels they ultimately have no such form.

Manifestation Of Creators

The Creators manifest in everything, therefore they can influence anything. It follows that they directly affect the development of the physical universe. It follows that the Creators are thus able to influence the development of the physical universe through the actions of aliens and human beings.

The Creators influence the actions of the human form you are experiencing living through. Sometimes, their influence will energise your physical form into apparently positive actions. Whereas, on other occasions your human form can be influenced to act apparently negatively. Ultimately, there is no real positive or negative, just the experiences that result.

Community Project

A simplistic view of the physical universe is that the ultimate Creator has created and manages the whole thing with its team of Creators. Fleshing out that basic understanding reveals a sort of community project. The real you has created a succession of high to low life forms. As the energy of the Creators descends through this system, all life forms contribute to the actualisation of the great self-awareness experiment. An example is when humans get inspired to build churches, temples, power stations, or anything that improves self-awareness by one means or another.

The originating intention that created the Astral World and the physical universe is extremely simple. Conversely, extraordinary and complex detail has been added by the living beings which contribute to this great experiment. Similarly, this means the whole experiment is being constructed not by the ultimate Creator, but by the living beings experiencing it. The human form you are experiencing is actually an important integral part of the whole creation process, and part of a great community.

Autopilot

Using this mechanism, it is not necessary for the ultimate Creator to detail anything. Broad intentions are translated into practical details by each level of the system down to the human mind, etc. This is why the Astral World and physical universe largely run themselves, and a human mind can generate the illusory impression of an autonomous existence.

CREATION OF LIFE FORMS

Religions like the idea that humankind was created by God. Whilst most early 21st century scientists preferred the notion that humankind was created by itself through an evolutionary process. Researching this encyclopaedia found evidence that both views have some truth to them.

The simple leap in understanding that humankind is making is the recognition that; humankind has also been engineered to a considerable extent by aliens (including other humans) manipulating a natural evolutionary process to achieve the Creators' objectives.

Since engineering life forms is an integral part of a community project, it is therefore not something to fear.

Where Did Physical Life On Earth Come From ?

To understand the answer to this you first need to decouple your adopted human mind from any concept of there being a Start and Finish to the physical universe. If physically you travel far enough through the universe you eventually arrive back where you started from (albeit at a higher dimension). So your human form is experiencing a universe which has been looped back on itself.

The practical effect of this upon physical life can be understood as follows: If you want to exist in human form today, then you need to have created your body yesterday. Or put in a simplistic way, to walk around in an early 21st century human body, requires your physical descendants to have created your physical ancestors.

The fact that you can and will incarnate in alien bodies, as opposed to only human ones, opens up an understanding of how you, almost certainly in an alien manifestation, contributed to the creation of human life on Earth.

So it came to pass, that aliens, acting out the Creators' intentions, seeded the Earth with DNA life forms, which allowed physical life to emerge there. In addition, multiple genetic manipulations have been carried out to achieve most of the significant results you can observe on the Earth in the early 21st century.

The raw materials out of which physical life has been constructed are adaptations of life forms that were developed in other universes. For example, it is possible to visit much smaller universes, which are akin to floating balls of warm fluid where microbes live out their lives. Thus life forms developed in one universe can be recreated in another. Any DNA coding can be mathematically modelled, and thus such information is readily transferable from one universe to another.

Evolution And Manipulation

The evolutionary process is simple enough: A successful animal will breed more, and hence any modifications which make it more successful drives the whole evolutionary process forward. DNA is designed to automatically mutate and thus animals will keep producing new variations, with the winners being self-evidently the ones who breed more. In this situation there is no theoretical need for any intervention because all species will self-evolve.

However, once you, the reader, know how to tinker with the process, then why not do so ?

One of the ultimate Creator's objectives is to produce highly aware life forms that readily achieve the primary objective of recognising what created them. So rather than wait for natural mutations to achieve this, advanced (typically alien) species can give nature a helping hand.

On early 21st century Earth, Darwinian evolution (survival of the fittest, and dominance of the top breeders) determines much of evolutionary process. Whereas on planets operated by more advanced species, the objective of manifesting greater self-awareness tends to dominate the evolutionary process through a manipulation of it.

Even on Earth, the extent to which humankind has developed a much higher self-awareness than any other animal, is not an accident, but the result of deliberate manipulation.

Examples Of The Creators' Work Upon Minds

There are typically three important features common to the majority of advanced beings. These are; the ability to use tools, intellectual development, and astral (or spiritual) awareness.

Mankind has gained a foothold in the lower margins of the advanced beings category because it displays all three of these characteristics. Though with respect to the astral or spiritual development characteristic, when this encyclopaedia was first published, only a small minority of human beings could actually manifest advanced spiritual development skills such as fully conscious astral projection.

Advanced spiritual awareness depends on having a sufficiently developed mind, which normally requires persistent interventions to achieve. An analogy would be the development of computers. Every time a new computer chip or processor gets developed, programmers come up with even more demanding software to run on it. This in turn drives the development of even more advanced computer chips. So the Creators have been putting new ideas and applications into human minds, which in turn has caused human brains to modify and further evolve themselves to cope.

EXAMPLE 1

New *technologies*; e.g. Fire.

Modern humans rely on a diet of cooked food and would now be unable to survive on raw vegetables alone. Cooked food has a higher nutritional value and therefore requires a smaller digestive system. Having a smaller digestive system allows for a larger brain and thus paves the way for a more intelligent being. So early humankind was repeatedly inspired to use fire technology to cook its food and thus pave the way for a larger brain.

EXAMPLE 2

New *behaviour patterns*; e.g. Not slaughtering each other.

The "thou shalt not kill" principle has been around since human beings decided to live in communities. As those communities developed, the principle has been applied more widely. However, this has proved a tricky message to deliver into human brains, which otherwise tend to perceive that the ultimate way to deal with something annoying is to kill it. This mentality substantially excludes the human believers in "slaughtering each other is ok" from high quality interactions with advanced alien races. Nevertheless, bit by bit the upgrade is sinking in, and through such interactions humankind's self-awareness is being advanced.

EXAMPLE 3

B*ody designs*; e.g. Bipeds; two arms and two legs anatomy.

Legs are good for walking and arms are useful for working with tools, etc. When you examine a range of alien anatomies, it becomes apparent that the biped design is surprisingly common. Alien animals that did not start off as bipeds have been evolved into them, often leaving just traces of redundant limbs. In this case the intervention is often to make the original animal interested in functioning in an upright position. Because once upper limbs become devoted to working with tools, the development of the mind exponentially accelerates.

Alien Involvement

The Creators often intervene to evolve species. In the case of human beings this often involves dropping ideas into their minds, and interventions are sometimes done with the assistance of aliens. So whenever the Creators might seek to give a human being an idea or discovery, they have the option to enrol aliens to assist them. This cooperation is extremely common and often takes place as part of what you could understand to be scientific experiments by the Creators and hence aliens.

This encyclopaedia is a good example of aliens assisting the Creators. The Creators are enabling the human race to join a 'club' of advanced beings. Accordingly, advanced aliens have contributed to most of the book's content. In so doing they are sharing new ideas, technologies and technique. All of which have the effect of advancing human beings.

Alien Manipulation of Animals' DNA

It would be exciting to find a new, introduced species on Earth along the lines of a unique animal with no Earthly evolutionary heritage. But so far nothing of the sort has been observed. Instead, most animal evolution on Earth is the result of natural and assisted DNA mutations. Furthermore, due to dimensional differences, introducing new species from other planets can be problematic. Which is why it is often more convenient to develop species from primitive organisms within the existing dimension or plane.

The first life on Earth arrived upon asteroids which contributed to the formation of the planet. Said asteroids were the debris from an earlier galaxy, hence they had the remnant micro-organisms attached. But ultimately more life forms were required to properly kick start the process of physical life on Earth.

The Creators have no physical bodies of their own and therefore have difficulty manipulating physical matter. However, they do inspire humans and aliens to manipulate matter and conduct experiments. So it came to pass that aliens seeded Earth (and the surrounding planets) with primitive single-celled organisms, which became the ancestors for most of the life on Earth. Then around half a billion Earth years ago, the Creators introduced the intention for some single celled organisms to be multi-cellular, and aliens modified some of the DNA in existing bacteria to physically make this occur.

By a series of successive interventions, the major species were thus encouraged.

SUMMARY

In simplistic terms, the real you created everything. In practice it is a little more dynamic.

The real you created the Creators, energetic entities which perform a dual purpose. F*irstly*; they convert your simple objective of discovering what you are, into practical experiments that will achieve this goal. S*econdly*; they help enable you to experience the data obtained from those experiments.

If a human being was likened to a probe in an artificial world, the Creators would be the power and communications cable which enables it to function. The Creators give the probe purpose, inspire its movements, and collect its observations.

Everything is an experiment, where the outcome is a probability as opposed to a certainty. During the course of experiments, new discoveries occur.

Existing physical beings such as advanced aliens, help create new life forms such as human beings. If you looked forward in time, you would find human beings similarly engineering new life forms. The Creators inspire, and by imparting higher awareness, more closely direct the activities of aliens and human beings alike.

The Creators are life forms in their own right, and they create new experiments to try. The Creators affect all levels of beings from angelic ones to lower spirits. All beings creatively contribute to the experiments.

The Earth, and everything on it, may initially appear to have just evolved by itself. But on further investigation, the evidence demonstrates that it is in fact the result of a community experiment

A3 How The Universe Works

INTRODUCTION

This chapter contains some insights into how the universe you are experiencing functions. This is far from a definitive explanation since every time further research into the matter is conducted, new discoveries are made. So regard the following observations as a "work in progress".

The universe you, the reader, can observe around you is an extraordinary creation. It's compellingly lifelike and created from an engineered illusion where energy can appear to be solid matter. This chapter explores some aspects of how this universe is created and operates.

The Purpose Of The Universe

Without getting lost in all the many possible purposes of the universe you, the reader, are experiencing, it's helpful to reiterate that; this universe enables the real you to see yourself via a mirror of sorts, and through that recognition grow the projection of your higher-self and the super-consciousness. The reiteration is important because you, the reader, keep forgetting to perform this simple and pleasant function.

Consciousness

The energetic feedback mechanism which feeds the super-consciousness or ultimate Creator is consciousness, and this is provided by spirit beings. The consciousness you are experiencing at this moment is provided by spirit beings' perceptions.

Achieving the greatest consciousness feedback requires teamwork between spirit beings across the spectrum from high to low dimensions. The lower spirit beings have the potential for the greatest contrast. However, without the assistance of higher spirit beings, it is difficult for the lower ones to provide a higher quality of energetic feedback.

The spirit beings enable the ultimate Creator to see itself from alternative and contrasting vantage points. If a spirit being is attached to a physical entity, then that entity's perceptions are fed back to the ultimate Creator. If an ordinary (lower level) living physical being dies then its perceptions mostly and typically occur upon death. However, in the case of more advanced physical beings, they can feedback considerable perceptions before death.

Automated Universe

The universe you can physically observe operating uses a variety of automated mechanical systems. So sophisticated is the automation that at a low level the whole system can appear to work perfectly on its own without the need for a creator to have set it in motion. Though as soon as you observe the Astral World function, it is obvious that there is a higher consciousness at work providing some overall direction.

The illusory automation is in many ways essential, for without it there would be no scope for lower level spontaneity. The ultimate Creator has set in motion a system with enough inherent Free Will that in many respects it is able to invent itself.

THE INTENTION SYSTEM

The intention system allows the apparently enormous universe you, the reader, are experiencing, to be created from virtually nothing.

When physicists attempt to look for the particles that constitute atoms, they encounter ever smaller entities. Ultimately, when you look closely enough, you will only find energy and no mass whatsoever. Instead, what you are able to observe is relatively stationary energy. This is a perplexing phenomenon because energy ordinarily moves around at the speed of light, and does not park itself in a stationary position, albeit appearing to vibrate; i.e. Matter is composed of relatively “stationary” energy, which is not its natural state.

All of which begs a very obvious question; how does matter exist at all ?

Intention For Matter To Exist

For anything at all to exist in the universe, there must be an intention for it to exist. This intention can normally be clairvoyantly seen, for example, at lower non-physical dimensions it appears as an aura. From the tiny particles which form atoms, everything has an aura which defines that object. If there is an intention for something to exist, then the aura can even appear before the physical matter has been assembled into that space. Conversely, if the intention ceases, so must the manifestation of any matter which had previously resulted from it.

The intention, in an unrefined form, originates from the super-consciousness, and the lower you go in the Astral World, the more detailed that intention becomes. At the lower levels, the intention in many ways starts to take the form of an automated function. So for example, the intention which creates sub-atomic particles has a very low level of consciousness, whereas the intention which creates your adopted human form has a very complex and dynamic one.

By one means or another, all intentions can be traced up to the super-consciousness, and then back from it into more solid manifestations. Matter and physical things only exist because the super-consciousness intended it.

Note that; all physical matter is ultimately an engineered illusion whereby, whilst it appears to have substance, in fact there is none.

Auras And Their Physical Forms

Whilst auras are a low level non-physical energy which defines physical beings, auras are also affected by their creations; e.g. The human manifestation feeds energies back to the super-consciousness. So whilst the intentions and their auras determine what sort of human body is created along with the events it will experience, that eventual experience is fed back up the line. The effect of this feedback alters the aura and the intention.

You will be familiar with the way in which living things decompose when they die. When a living physical human being has died, the aura has not immediately ceased to exist, but instead has altered and detached. Thus a detached aura can often show up as a ghost. Similarly, before a child is born or even conceived, you can detect its aura, which demonstrates how the aura, or energetic template, is defining the physical form it will manifest. Similarly, a child's aura can often look larger and more adult than the physical form of the child it is developing.

Any physical form must have an aura. So the reading medium (book, computer, digital reader, etc) you are using to read this encyclopaedia has an aura you can (with practice) see. At this point you may wonder if a book or computer too could die. Indeed the matter holding your reading medium together is only there because it has an aura, but under normal circumstances its aura will not suddenly disappear. Though if an aura for anything were to fade away or significantly change, then the physical object will decay in one way or another.

The reading medium you are using was created because there was an intention for it to exist. If you are clairvoyant enough, stop reading and instead observe the aura of your reading medium (book, etc). Similarly, try to compare the auras of say books, with electronic digital readers or phones. For many readers this will be the first occasion in their lives that they have even bothered to look. Alternatively if you have done this before, do it again as repeating the observation will often produce fresh insights. Observe how there are energised intentions at different levels. For example, there is the intention for the physical reading medium, and there are the intentions for the thoughts that connect to it.

By observing anything at a higher dimension you can observe the energetic forms that cause physical objects to come into existence. You will similarly observe that to some extent everything appears to be alive. It is very helpful to observe this because it clarifies that everything physical is there as a result of a higher living force.

Going back to the living physical body, you can now see that this is the result of many living forces. There are the fundamental auras which create the atoms and molecules. Then there are more complex auras which bind physical matter together to, for example, enable consciousness to physically manifest in a human body constructed from those basic atoms and molecules.

A very useful exercise for the human mind to perform is; observing that all these auras, or energetic intentions which make physical forms exist and even physical events occur, all originate in the Creator's World. Furthermore, you have to observe these intentions across a spectrum of dimensions to get a fuller picture.

Note: The subject of how to see auras is covered in The Great Simulator books.

Living Intentions Into Matter

You, the reader, will generally experience an intention of wanting to be alive. You will have similarly noticed that almost everything else which displays living characteristics similarly wants to be alive. You are probably aware that water, for example, would have an elemental spirit, and it therefore follows that it wants to be alive.

The basic intention to be alive is what creates spirit forms. When a spirit form wants to take physical form, it will endeavour to create a physical being out of the available material. This implies that whilst objects such as rocks might be inanimate, because an elemental earth spirit is responsible for its creation, the rock is the product of that living intention.

At a more rudimentary level, all the molecules, atoms, and sub-atomic particles only manifest because some sort of living spirit or intention wants them to. Though at the quantum or sub-atomic level the process is more ingenious because there is no available matter, instead the illusion of physical matter must be created out of what may at first appear to be apparently nothing.

Again, the simple point to keep observing is how anything that physically appears to exist, requires an intention for this to occur. This principle applies to enormous celestial bodies such as everything in the Earth's solar system. In such instances the detailed intentions are very complex as they incorporate the needs of such living entities that will live there.

Intention Into Events

If for example, there is an intention to create something such as a building on a plot of earthly land, that intention may be shared by many human beings. It follows that on a large scale, groups of people can simultaneously share the experience of wishing to build a city such as, the Roman city of Pompeii right beneath a volcano. The intention at a higher level is transmitted through both the human spirits who wish to live in Pompeii, along with the elemental volcano spirits bent on subsequently destroying the city.

This is why psychics and clairvoyants are often able to predict events, because they can sense the higher intention and deduce its likely physical manifestation. Similarly, whilst a psychic or clairvoyant might sense these intention energies at a higher level, at that level there is often a lack of detail, which is normally only added at a lower level.

In the context of how the universe works, everything is driven by intentions originating from the Creator. As those intentions pass down through the Astral World, they will progressively become more detailed and embellished until they result in a physical manifestation.

Alien Assistance

To some extent, any living organism is driven by the intention to do or create something. Even if that intention is hardwired into its sub-conscious behaviour to, for example, reproduce.

At a micro level, much in the same way that human beings can collectively become inspired to, for example, create towns and cities, so do aliens. However, at a macro level, some of the more advanced aliens work to create entire universes, or parts thereof.

Some human beings believe their world was created by the ultimate Creator, whilst others perceive it might have been created by some other more alien entities (or entity). Researching this encyclopaedia points consistently towards a combination of the two, where advanced species have manifested the Creator's intentions.

TIME

Intention To Experience

At the highest levels of the Creator's World you find a simple intention for the super-consciousness to discover what it is. One of the methods of achieving this is to create living organisms, which will, as previously described, look back on their creator and observe what it is. You will find this simple intention then develops into more complex intentions to experience particular moments, such as a human being scratching its ear.

In the Creator's World there is no time, so these intentions all exist in the same moment. Whereas, as you descend in the Astral World a sequence of sorts starts to emerge which is then finally converted into linear time; i.e. All the moments appearing to be arranged in a convenient linear order.

Conversely, when the feedback from a life of experiences is returned to the super-consciousness, it becomes compressed back into one complex moment; e.g. "My whole life flashed before me."

Timelessness

One of the most challenging things for a human mind to comprehend is timelessness. This is because the human mind is designed to keep introducing a perception of linear time into everything it experiences. So even when it encounters timelessness, it still perceives it in terms of occurring in linear time; i.e. One moment followed by another, as opposed to all at once.

In the Creator's World, everything with respect to the universe you, the reader are experiencing, occurs in one big moment. That moment is subdivided into sub-moments in the same way that a seed can grow into a magnificent oak tree. Except in this instance both the original seed and mature tree co-exist at the same point.

An understanding to be expanded on further in this chapter is that; for there to be time, there must also be distance between the moments. A simplified understanding is that time equates to distance or separation between moments. However, because this separation is artificial, the linear space-time universe that results must, as a direct consequence, similarly be an illusion.

An analogy that helps explain how time and distance operate is that of a surfer riding a wave. The surfer experiences being carried along by the crest of a wave. Each moment the surfer experiences occurs at a different point in the ocean as he moves towards the shoreline. However, for the surfer, he is primarily experiencing being on a wave. So using this analogy, time for the surfer is really a function of how far he has moved, even though he will have mostly experienced being on the same wave.

In summary, moments actually all exist in the same location where there is no separation and hence no time. By creating an illusion where moments now appear to be separated, the distance between them becomes an illusory space-time universe. For a human consciousness to comprehend timelessness, merely remove all the artificial or illusory distance between moments. Try this now.

Feedback And Multiple Universes

There is more than one universe, and you could arguably say a potentially infinite number of other universes through which all possible outcomes are explored. Ingeniously they all overlay each other so that it can be challenging to determine quite where everything is located in illusory and overlapping space-time.

For example, the super-consciousness experiences everything a human mind experiences, and more. When a human mind really pays attention, this feeds back energies to the super-consciousness. The effect of this feedback is to change the moments that create that universe.

The effect of this feedback is to lead to the creation of parallel universes, where different possibilities are explored. This means that there are parallel versions of you, the reader, experiencing different versions of your current human life. However, the mechanism of this arrangement is beyond the scope of this book to presently explain.

What is of great relevance, is that developments in one universe are shared with other universes. Similarly, beings from one universe will regularly visit and interact with parallel ones.

Thus developments in one universe are fed back into other universes.

From a practical standpoint, parallel universes operate as an integrated web.

If the reader has developed enough higher awareness, it is possible to sense other versions of the reader looking in on this convergent moment right now from a parallel universes.

Expansion Of Space-Time

Early cosmological theory regarding the effect of gravity suggested that the current universe should ultimately collapse in upon itself. However, astronomical observations show that the reverse is in fact the case. Observations show that the universe is expanding, and perplexingly, that this expansion is accelerating.

An analogy is throwing a ball into the air. If you throw a ball into the air, the effect of gravity is that after travelling upwards for a short distance, the ball slows down until it stops, and then drops back to Earth. Yet if the ball thrown into the air behaved as the universe does, once released it would accelerate away and never return to the ground.

In practice, the universe on the macro scale is mostly expanding with nearly everything steadily accelerating away from everything else; i.e. The big clusters of objects are moving away from each other.

Observing that, on a large scale, since most of the matter in the universe is being pushed apart, there must be a dynamic responsible for the expansion of space. The answer to this, is that as more moments come into play, the amount of time increases. Hence space-time expands. Or put another way, the universe is being expanded by time.

Space-Time & Gravity

At the singularity, everything is at the same infinitesimally small point with no space or distance between anything, and similarly no time. The universe you, the reader are experiencing, is a projection from this point. It is this artificial projection that creates space-time. An analogy is the projection of a movie film, where the light projection creates an illusory image on a screen some distance away.

In reality, everything in the illusory universe is still where it was at the singularity. A human mind is normally just observing an illusory projection from the singularity. A side effect of the illusion is gravity, which is simplistically a pull back towards a state of singularity.

Time creates distance, and gravity is a function of time and distance.

Expanding Projection

A simplistic, but convenient, analogy which helps further explain the expansion of the universe you are experiencing is; a projector screen moving away from the projector. If light striking a projector screen were to move the screen away from the projector, then the end of a movie would appear larger than the beginning. If you lived on the screen itself, then as the movie proceeds, your universe will appear to expand.

Conceptually Spherical Projection

If you wish to further enhance your understanding of how the expanding universe works, you can conceptualise that instead of a movie being projected onto a flat screen, instead understand it as a spherical screen with the singularity in the centre. In this analogy you live on the outside surface of a translucent screen where the projection can be seen on the outside.

On the outside surface of the translucent screen, you will see the movie's events occurring, but not see that it is all driven from a central projection emanating from the singularity within.

As the continual introduction of more time enlarges the spherical screen upon which you live, all the objects on the screen get further apart, thus your universe expands.

If you looked inside the spherical screen, you would see the Astral World, and thus the source of the projection and its inherent time.

RECYCLING UNIVERSE

Fundamentals

Early 21st century observations suggested the age of the universe was around 14 billion years, with the Earth, a relative latecomer, forming at around 4.4 billion years ago. At the time of first writing this encyclopaedia, the dominant scientific theory was that the Earth was born from a "big bang" where some sort of singularity expanded into a huge universe. Whereas, researching some alien perspectives upon the "big bang" theory reveals that it is not the way most advanced aliens perceive the way the universe you are experiencing came into existence.

The research into this encyclopaedia also encountered evidence of localised dimensional differences within physical universes. By comparison, human science has not so far observed that the dimensions of bodies within the current universe are not the same. For example, dimensional differences ultimately cause very large galaxies to apparently disappear into higher dimensions. Similarly, new galaxies can appear out of nowhere. However, due to the very long periods of time over which this occurs, the difficulties observing this phenomenon are understandable.

This coming and going of galaxies has the practical effect of allowing the universe to be a much older recycling entity. Like a family of many generations that has been around for in excess of 100 billion years, this is a system that allows the oldest elements to only appear to be around 14 billion years old.

With respect to the size of the universe, it is for practical purposes, folded in upon itself. Explaining this in words is, at this time difficult, as the necessary human language and scientific understanding has not sufficiently evolved. Nevertheless, in simplistic terms, if you travel outwards, you can in principle end up where you started from. Except that you will probably now be in a higher dimension. This travel related dimensional shift has the coincidental advantage of creating a counting system from which to calibrate what dimension you are in.

Black Holes

All galaxies have black holes at their centres, or arguably only exist because of the strong centre of gravity required to hold them together, which black holes provide. Black holes are points of extreme gravitational pull, so strong that they even consume light particles.

Astral projection allows you to explore black holes and what occurs within them. Theorists who predicted that a black hole might carry you to "somewhere else" will be encouraged to find astral experiential validation for their hypothesis. Astrally travelling into a black hole feels like having much of your spirit body ripped from you and generally disintegrated. Astrally travelling through black holes carries you into a timeless world where creation occurs; i.e. Into the singularity and thereby giving you access to the Creator's World.

At the centre of a black hole there does not appear to be a core as such, there is simply a central point (theoretical centre) where time, space and energy all collapse in upon themselves and self-neutralise; i.e. Nothing physically remains. This is initially perplexing because black holes exert a strong gravitational pull upon surrounding matter. A helpful analogy to describe what you can observe can be likened to feeding string into a vacuum cleaner nozzle. Once fed into the nozzle, the string equates to gravity and will pull anything attached to it into the nozzle. Meaning that; whilst the black hole perplexingly appears to have no actual mass, it nevertheless exerts a strong gravitational pull upon its surroundings as if it had enormous mass.

Multiple Apparent Sub-Singularities

Whilst there is really only one singularity, a black hole creates a physical subordinate aspect of it. Thus entering one of the sub-singularities gives you potential access to exiting via another.

Furthermore, matter swept into one black hole can emerge elsewhere.

Creation Of Galaxies

Researching this encyclopaedia produced repeated observations that galaxies are constructed from recycled matter.

It is helpful to conceptualise the universe the reader is experiencing as being a recycling entity. Matter forms together into galaxies and then all gets sucked into black holes, only to be ejected elsewhere. It has been theorised that all material sucked into a black hole is crushed to nothing, and from observing the inbound process, this appears to be a reasonable proposition. If you looked at a planet being pulled into black hole, it gets broken up on the way in, but the resulting fragments are not always ultimately disintegrated.

When an astral traveller enters a black hole their spirit body is stripped away and their consciousness can pass into the Creator's World. Meanwhile the potential for a spirit body remains in the Astral World. Similarly, for a rock approaching a black hole, its energetic template is collapsed. But since the potential for that rock cannot manifest itself in the Creator's World, the potential for it to reform can remain.

Material gathered by black holes appears to re-emerge elsewhere. Matter is returned to the universe in what can loosely be described as "matter fountains", or black holes in reverse. For example, the above rock's energetic template that was previously consumed by a black hole can be ejected elsewhere and reform the original rock. This reformation of matter is an important mechanism by which matter is introduced into a galaxy.

The Milky Way is an example of how a large amount of matter has been ejected back into the universe. For example, the Earth and surrounding solar system are formed from such debris. In the region between Mars and Jupiter you will find an asteroid belt awash with rocky debris. Such rocks that occasionally collide with Earth are fully formed and are usually the remnants of earlier galaxies. Thus some of the earthly solar system's asteroid material is representative of what happens to physical matter that has passed through a space-time recycling black hole system.

Transportation Of Matter

For completeness, it should be noted that one of the methods advanced aliens use to travel across the universe is to replicate the process by which physical objects can be absorbed by a black hole in one location and then reconstituted elsewhere.

As previously described, all objects exist because there is an intention for them to do so. Hence, provided the intention is maintained, the matter that forms an object in one location can be transported to another, whereupon it will reform into its original shape. This process works well on inanimate objects, though it is more challenging to replicate with living bodies.

For example, people who have witnessed UFOs vanishing into a flash of light have usually observed the practical application of the physics governing black holes, and hence matter transportation.

OTHER DIMENSIONS

Note On The Definition Of A Dimension

There is no specific mark stating what energetic level a dimensional plane must be at. Instead the distinction is relative, and the fundamentals are easy to grasp by analogy. Compare this to the effect of living on a spherical planet, and for the purposes of this analogy let us treat the planet surface as even; i.e. No mountains or hills. Because the planet is spherical (as on Earth) you can only see its surface for a limited distance in any direction. We will therefore treat everyone and everything you can see as being within your dimension. Anything too far away is over your horizon and thus no longer visible in your dimension.

Therefore our definition of a dimensional plane is the world or matter you can see or otherwise detect. A dimension is calibrated in terms of where you are. Similarly, by moving in any direction, things that you could not previously see in front of you come into your dimension, whilst things that were behind you exit your dimension.

The definition of a physical dimension is thus defined by what you can see.

The next thing to keep remembering is that all matter you can physically detect is the consequence of an energetic template. For example, when astral projecting you will be looking at the energetic templates that cause matter to appear to exist. So astrally seeing any physical matter is very difficult, but by observing the energetic templates you can deduce what physically would be there. At very low levels this effect is not always obvious, but becomes so as soon as you ascend beyond the lowest astral levels.

Whilst obviously there has to be a correlation between physical dimensions and the astral level at which the energetic template to form it occurs, always bear in mind that they are not the same thing.

Higher Dimensions

Higher dimensions are most easily understood using the analogy of the grooves on an old vinyl or wax music record (for those old or techy enough to know what they were). In principle, if you travel far enough you end up virtually back where you started, except one dimension higher. This equates to being one dimension nearer the centre of the record, so one revolution brings you near where you started, but the world you will experience is different.

The best example of this in action is the way in which you find aliens living on the Earth in large colonies, but not in the reader's current dimension. Furthermore, the residents of such higher dimensions seldom physically descend down to lower levels. If you carry on up the dimensions and exit physicality you can find places such as human heaven, which it should be mentioned, occurs more than once.

As a footnote; you will not find a human hell, but there are some regions that can give you a false impression that it might exist.

In the same way that following the grooves of a record will eventually bring you to the centre, you can climb the dimensions until you reach a central singularity by instead travelling perpendicularly across them. After this point, all form and time as human mind normally relates to it, ceases to exist. As for what was physical matter, that is mostly recycled into the lower levels or '1st groove'. The Earth in this interpretation is on the '2nd groove' (i.e. 1st groove plus one revolution). For completeness, it should be mentioned that the '1st groove', like a record, which at that point contains no music, does not contain much of interest to us at this moment. This is why it is not unreasonable to view the Earth as being on the first interesting part of the groove.

Other Dimensions Altogether Or Other Universes

In the same way that someone can possess more than one record, there is more than one multi-dimensional universe. Giving a useful explanation of what they are like is difficult, because most human minds do not recognise where they are in the first place. This may seem harsh, but without demonstrating the reality from an Astral World perspective, it is very difficult to usefully communicate the greater reality in words alone because actual experience of it is essential.

Crossing Dimensions

Where the music record analogy runs into immediate limitations is the question of what happens if you attempt to travel back to where you came from. Theoretically you could physically travel from '2nd groove' Earth (the one where you are reading this book), across the universe and arrive at '3rd groove' Earth. So the question immediately arises; what would happen if you physically travelled back in the direction you came from ? Would you return to the '2nd groove' ?

The answer to this question appears to be NO. Such physical travel across the universe would move you towards a '4th groove' Earth. By this extreme travel approach there appears to be no return. However, since your physical speed would ordinarily be governed by the speed of light, this is a journey you could not usefully accomplish in this scenario.

There are fundamentally only two approaches to crossing dimensions:

- F*irstly*; in line with the way this encyclopaedia was researched, you the consciousness, which is but an extension of the real you, or super-consciousness, can go wherever you please. Moving between dimensions is relatively easy and simply relies on reforming your consciousness in whatever new location you wish.

- Or *Secondly*; you can reconstitute your physical form in a new location or groove, which is the equivalent of jumping across grooves. This is obviously technologically sophisticated and not without its own complications.

Movement And Dimension

All matter vibrates. Because the dimension you are in mostly vibrates at the same speed, this vibration is very difficult to detect. In practice you can only detect this vibration by comparing it to alternative vibrations.

In simplistic terms, high speed travel can increase the vibration of matter. If you, the reader, were to travel near the speed of light this tends to increase your vibration, and some of that higher vibration can remain after you slow down again. The effect of this is that high speed travel over long distances moves you into a progressively higher dimension. Ultimately, when your dimension increases sufficiently, you will cease to be visible in your original dimension, nor will you be able to see it.

For completeness, it is worth reiterating that in a higher dimension, time is relatively slower when compared to a lower dimension. In addition, large celestial objects such as planets orbiting a sun in a solar system, all appear closer together.

Distant Galaxies

When astrally exploring worlds on distant galaxies, you will often get the impression that you are not at the same dimension. Advanced aliens will often comment that the earthly physical version of human being would not ordinarily physically survive in their galaxy. So whilst a human being can in principle live in such a distant galaxy, his or her whole body needs to be regrown using locally sourced material for this to be a practical proposition.

Conversely, for advanced aliens visiting Earth, they find the dimension here relatively low, and similarly unsuitable for their physical forms. Since in the early 21st century human beings do not have the ability to artificially create a human body for such a visitor, the only way for such an alien consciousness to physically visit for a long period is to be born as a human being (or other animal).

Parallel Dimensions

Using the chessboard analogy, consider the dimension the reader is experiencing is the equivalent of one square at the bottom of a chess board. Higher dimensions thus equate to squares higher up. Whilst, parallel dimensions equate to squares either side. So there are also parallel higher dimensions, and all universes have parallel dimensions to them.

There are two reasons why parallel dimensions even exist. F*irstly*; the Creator wishes to experience an enormous range of possibilities. Hence scenarios are run and re-run, in order to discover interesting permutations. S*econdly*; since parallel dimensions interact with each other, there is a healthy "cross fertilisation" of experiential developments, which makes the existence of parallel universes desirable; i.e. The parallel dimensions support and augment each other.

In principle, having a system of parallel universes could lead to their exponential growth. However, observations repeatedly uncover convergences that drive this experiential system towards various targets. Thus the analogy earlier in the encyclopaedia of, many roads that frequently lead back to the same points.

Researching this encyclopaedia's first edition has uncovered the tantalising observations of parallel dimensions and visitations from them. Yet further exploration (at that point in 2015) encountered energetic barriers that prevented further progress. Thus there is a great deal more to discover about this subject, which will feature in subsequent works.

Advanced Space Travel

To some extent it is possible to transport objects from one dimension to a nearby one, provided the dimensions are not too dissimilar; e.g. Say 2.5 to 2.9 or 3.1. But if there is more than one dimension of a difference, say 2.0 to 4.0, it is more complex ordinarily to get objects to overlap and be physically visible in each other's dimensions. Most advanced aliens you will physically encounter are therefore within reasonably near dimensions, otherwise they would not be physically visible. This does not preclude visits from much higher dimensions where matter is wholly reformed, but it is less common. For example, visitations from the higher dimension versions of the Earth are uncommon, yet they are well-populated adjacent worlds.

Using black hole technology, it is possible to transport matter anywhere in that universe. This is achieved by collapsing and then reforming the intention templates which cause physical matter to appear. Obviously, reducing anything to a singularity is technically advanced and not without potential complications. For example, if you are transporting a person, you not only have to collapse and reform their physical form, but also their individual personality. This sort of collapse and reconstruction can have a very detrimental effect on mental health.

The challenges associated with similar but not wholly compatible dimensions, and maintaining reasonable mental health, have led many advanced aliens to create alternative versions of their species, which are better adapted to these difficulties. In this context it must be observed that "grey" type physical forms often perform better than "humanoids", but this is not a rule as there are many variations of each species.

The Creator's World

The Astral World is an illusory projection from the singularity, in that everything in the Astral World is actually located at the singularity. So when you transcend the projection and return to the singularity, in principle you can access any conceivable part of the Astral World wherever it may be located in space-time.

The Creator's World is readily accessible in what appears to be the other side of the singularity. So in many ways it often seems to be an extension of the Astral World, and it is frequently the case that no distinction is made. Nor is one necessary for most new students of astral projection, as even if they had this additional label to hand, it would not significantly advance their ability.

The distinction becomes helpful once you become more interested in transporting anything around the universe, or even re-engineering it in an alternative universe. In the Creator's World there is no physical form, which makes it largely perceptually incomprehensible without specialist guidance. Similarly, and obviously, you could not physically transport a human being to the Creator's World, which is why a distinction becomes valuable.

Since this encyclopaedia is devoted to assisting human consciousnesses navigate the available worlds, these words are intended to give you, the reader, some indicators to assist your explorations. So remember that what you are likely to experience may appear different to how you imagined it would be.

Finally, because there is a great deal more to discover, remain open to improved understandings, which will inevitably follow.

A4 The Moon

INTRODUCTION

It has been suggested by human individuals such as David Icke, that the Moon is some sort of orbiting observational satellite, and at higher dimensions this is a reasonable interpretation of what can be observed. There have been further suggestions that the Moon is used as a base from which to influence life on Earth, which also appears to be evidentially correct.

If you physically visit the Moon at the Earht Plane dimension, it is simply a barren rock. If you visit it on the low astral, you will similarly find a lifeless place. Yet if you go up the dimensions you find alien beings living there and the appearance of an atmosphere. If you go further up, the Moon looks technologically very advanced and you might well consider it to qualify as being some sort of orbiting space station.

MOON: FIRST INTERESTING DIMENSION UP

i.e. This observation is more than one dimension up from the Earht Plane.

Grassy Planes

The Moon now has a hazy white atmosphere (as opposed to blue) and sunlight pours down upon what appear to be grassy plains. The grass appears to be just over a metre tall and has a single green stem with no other leaves. The ground is squelchy, or waterlogged, and the grass is protruding out of a watery surface made of conjoined roots.

The surface is also for the most part very smooth with slight undulations in the form of small,gently rolling hills. There are some uplands, which do not support the grass and thus look yellow and dusty.

On closer inspection, almost the whole Moon is waterlogged and the grass-like plant has covered the surface of the resulting lake or ocean. Nevertheless, some land still protrudes out of the lake or ocean.

Sunshine radiates down through the hazy atmosphere making it difficult to identify where the light actually comes from. Furthermore, the whole Moon appears to be illuminated at this dimension with no obvious night or dark side.

Main Species

The main species is a primitive alien. It looks like a reptilian person, which has a lot in common with insects. The atmosphere appears to be mostly something similar to carbon dioxide gas (though in practice it may be different), which a human would choke on, but not this animal.

The reptilian animal seems to feed mostly off smaller animals that live in the grass. For housing it collects the long grass and weaves a mat to get above the water, and then weaves a small dome out of the grass. These animals appear to live a very solitary life. Females lay unfertilised eggs in water, which males later fertilise with a sperm. The young then start their lives in water and are initially fish-like. Thus there is some overall similarity to the breeding cycle of frogs.

The main species has no tools available, and cuts off the grassy stems with its teeth.

MOON: THE NEXT DIMENSION(S) UP

Moving Through The Dimensions

As you move up through another dimension, the Moon returns to being the barren landscape you will be more familiar with. The difference is that there now appears to be some sort of artificial clear atmosphere. Gone are the endless meteorite craters and the surface looks smoother except for the occasional volcanic cone. It was tempting to assume the volcanic cones were all extinct, but on closer inspection some remain active.

At this point, you find the first signs of intelligent life. Here and there you find spacecraft and astronauts who appear to be Future Humans and a variety of aliens.

As you continue going up the dimensions the atmosphere becomes whiter and hazy again. You see the Earth and the sun through the haze. Now most beings on the Moon can walk around without space suits. Buildings and other structures have become visible.

Engineered Atmosphere

On the surface you find industrial structures, below which are mines running into the core of the Moon. The mineral core is being mined and converted into useful products that, for example, can be refined into breathable gas. Thus the atmosphere appears to contain oxygen (or equivalent) mixed with some other gases that prevent it from being too combustible. The atmosphere has also been layered so that it appears breathable to most of the Moon's inhabitants within the first 1.5 km (1 mile) from the surface.

One of the major by-products of the atmosphere generation process is carbon. This is a useful building material and medium for growing food (engineered soil).

Time Window

The habitable planet version of the Moon we are presently exploring is not in the same time zone as the Earth. Instead it acts as a platform from which you can observe the Earth at such time period as may be of interest to you.

From this platform you can see the Earth (below) before any life could gain any real foothold on its surface. In this state it looks like a dark rock with enormous red streaks of volcanic activity across the surface.

As if winding a clock forward, it is then possible to see the Earth through all stages of development, and finally torn apart by an immense gravitational pull into a black hole. An analogy would be a vacuum cleaner disposing of a large ball of sand that has a hot core.

Winding the clock back again you can see the reverse of a black hole dumping vast amounts of rock, dust and gas into the galaxy we now call the Milky Way. Note that whilst there are a multitude of galaxies, the process which creates them appears to be the same across all the galaxies.

Outposts

The Earht Plane is a relatively low dimension environment to experience, but nevertheless quite interesting. Furthermore, all the species that live on the Earht Plane have to be energised into life. The extent of the Moon's inhabitants' interests goes far beyond just experiencing life as human beings, and incorporates living as animals and plants, etc.

In the majority of cases, giving life to all the physical beings on Earth is organised in the respective heavens for the various humans, animals, and plants, etc. Frequently, souls that are experiencing alien form also want to experience Earht Plane life forms, such as, but not limited to, human beings. However, the relatively low dimension of the Earht Plane can be difficult to acclimatise to.

Having a nearby outpost of some description therefore assists acclimatisation before descending into the Earht Plane. An analogy would be setting up a "base camp" at the foot of Mount Everest where climbers acclimatise to the thin atmosphere before proceeding. Similarly, the Moon can be a convenient location where visitors to the Earht Plane can prepare themselves before descending into it. Furthermore, it makes for a pleasant stopover after having explored the Earht Plane below.

Alternatively, for observational purposes, the Moon also makes a wonderful outpost from which developments on the Earth can be studied. You could crudely compare it to a watchtower or a roadside diner fuel (gas) station, where beings who want to observe or visit this place of interest pass through.

Busy Environment

Science fiction fans who would like to move beyond fantasies and visit a real alien outpost will not be disappointed by the non-fiction reality which awaits them.

The Moon's atmosphere is regularly populated by spacecraft coming and going. Similarly there are regular energy discharges into space as transportation capsules are dematerialised and dispatched, or rematerialised on arrival.

The Moon has many scattered outpost towns upon it and woven into its core. Some aliens find the atmosphere breathable, others wear spacesuits. There are all conceivable types of futuristic buildings and a large number of pressurised domes containing different atmospheres. Inside the buildings and domes you will find a very wide variety of alien species, well in excess of those examined in the first edition of this encyclopaedia.

Asteroid Protection

At this higher dimension there is still a risk of debris or objects from space reaching the surface of the moon, and damaging the facilities located there. The artificial atmosphere is relatively thin and offers only very modest protection. Whilst it is tempting to think that aliens can shoot down asteroids, small objects the size of a pebble are still inherently difficult to detect and shoot down, but can severely puncture a dome.

Furthermore, as the Moon only has a weak magnetic field, harmful radiation is an issue in the long term. So radiation protection is necessary.

The solution to this is threefold: F*irstly*; there is a good defence system to detect and shoot down dangerous space debris. S*econdly*; there are some very intuitive aliens living there who can sense potential danger so that defensive action can be taken. T*hirdly*; the Moon at higher dimensions has been given an artificially enhanced magnetic field. This is an enormous feat of engineering that gives the Moon at this dimension similar protection to that which the Earth enjoys by virtue of its natural magnetic field.

The ultimate effect of all this protection is that not only is the environment rendered reasonably safe, but it also makes an ideal dimension at which various visiting aliens wish to cluster upon.

TEACHING CENTRES

It is probably easier to sustain an astral visit to the Large Greys 1's Domes in another galaxy, than it is to visit the nearby Earth's Moon at several dimensions higher than the Earht Plane. Nevertheless, if you can manage to visit the Moon at higher dimensions, there are some fascinating teaching centres you can visit.

Human School

Not exactly a school for humans, but more a school on how to operate within human worlds. Training can include how to be a human being if a visitor intends to get born as one. But more often a visitor will instead just be interested in just usefully influencing a human being, and this training focuses upon how to do so.

To understand what occurs it is helpful to see a higher reality. Human bodies look like automated vehicles you can experience. They come equipped with individual configurations of thoughts, behaviours and emotions. You can programme what experiences a human being will have (note that this usually involves affecting more than one body). You can prepare the clues and signals that can potentially snap human minds out of the illusion they experience and briefly notice reality. You, and, or some of your team will experience being a human during the exercise.

The school is devoted to training advanced beings on how to operate the systems that control the behaviour of human minds. Because the human mind is normally operated by an ego it will consciously tend to resist any conscious insertions. However, because that same human mind is normally oblivious to reality, it will not normally notice any sub-conscious insertions. Hence insertions are normally sub-conscious, though they can be made obvious to that mind if it furthers that particular experiment's objectives.

Human School Training

The analogy of an animal study university, clinic, and experiential recording centre, located adjacent to a wildlife park; sums up the reality of the situation very succinctly.

Standard Earht Plane human beings do not exist in this higher Moon dimension. You could bring up a human specimen if it is suitably protected in an appropriate cocoon or given equivalent protection. But there is usually little point in attempting direct contact of that sort.

The training really involves how to operate a human mind as if putting on a robotic control glove to manipulate it. A working relationship has to be formed with the higher beings who already operate your target human subject, as without their cooperation nothing can progress.

The number of human subjects available is relatively small. Overall, there are plenty of human beings, but around the beginning of the 21st century there are only around 100 worth dealing with out of a pool of about 1000. As for the other 7 to 8 billion human bodies, nothing of great interest can be done with them at this time. In the absence of any unhelpful stumbling blocks, the number of interesting subjects will of course be increased over time.

The key point to note is that a suitable human subject will operate as a highly aware probe. The subject's mind will correspondingly receive a heightened awareness of alien worlds, beings, and technologies, etc. Part of the objective is not to tip it into perceiving itself as an alien, as this tends to unhelpfully inflate the human ego. Instead, a subject will be able to give the user (and the user's team) the experience of self-awareness through the human mind.

Whilst human subjects can be given interesting challenges, the objective is not to damage or abuse them.

Creating scenarios for the key subjects to experience often involves influencing the behaviour of sometimes hundreds and even thousands of other human minds. These supporting subjects rarely, if ever, return much useful data, even though they participate in the experiments.

Example Of Experiments

To keep this simple enough for a human mind to easily grasp, three interesting experiments are now outlined.

Experiment 1: Give human minds access to alien worlds.
It is unsafe to physically let human beings roam around advanced alien worlds in their present primitive state. Trying to keep a wild and dangerous animal in your home as a pet would be a good comparison. But by giving human minds astral access to alien worlds a new perspective on what constitutes civilised behaviour can be downloaded.

Experiment 2: Cosmic power technology.
Human beings could do with a new source of (renewable) energy. It will be interesting to give it to them. The challenge is that the human mind needs a working understanding of other dimensions to harness the technology.

Experiment 3: The shake-up.
Human beings are being allowed to potentially severely damage their own planet and themselves with it. Without an all-out intervention, is it possible to improve their self-awareness to a point where they en-masse decide to take better care of their environment ?

Learning About Subjects

As stated, learning how to operate the human subjects is the centre's main objective. Initially, the easiest and probably best time to do so is when the human body is in deep sleep. At this moment the lower human consciousness is floating free from the body, but switched off. Thus it can be extracted, powered-up, and giving the user a chance to operate it in the equivalent of a dream state. Then delete any memory data, and return the lower consciousness back to its waiting position beside its associated physical form.

A user needs to study the automated responses it will be subjected to, and how to modify them. In respect to human subjects outside the initial around 1,000 group, this is very easy. A subject participating in an experiment will believe itself to be acting of its own free will. Once it thinks it has made a decision of its own volition it will not only act upon it but self-justify acting upon it. Thus an unaware subject will resist the prospect that it had just been enrolled into an experiment.

Within the around 1000 group, more care needs to be taken. If the subject perceives it has done anything out of character, it usually blocks further interventions for a while. Only after a long debate with it, will it cooperate again. Such is the effect of human consciousness exercising higher awareness and actually noticing what drives them.

Within the around 100 group, the situation is altogether easier. These human subjects will be aware interventions are occurring, but have incorporated this into their self-image. They will operate as a two way channel and generally be aware of a user's presence, though initially not a user's precise identity. It is unhelpful to seek to stimulate self-justification in this group as this will render them suspicious and relegate them to the 1000 group until the mistrust is cleared; i.e. putting them out of action for most other users as well.

In terms of subjects that are fully interactive, to the extent that this is achievable in the early 21st century, at the point these words were first typed, they number less than 10. With typically only 1 or 2 of them being fully online at any time.

Ironically, reading this encyclopaedia and works stimulated by it, will contribute to many human beings needing psychiatric treatment for perceived attacks by alien operators. So for the record, alien operators (the users, and users' trainers) wish to clarify that they would never do that to any of their subjects. So if someone is "losing it", do not blame them.

Visiting The Training Centres

No human consciousness can reach these centres unaided. It could reach an illusory mock-up, but unless severely deluded, it will nevertheless question if it actually reached its target. If a human consciousness is invited in, it will know it for sure and there will be little scope for uncertainty.

Visits are normally initiated by resident advanced alien consciousnesses (the users and users trainers), and an early 21st century human mind has no free will in this matter.

Many Training Centres

Upon inspection, a visiting human consciousness will realise that the extent of these operations significantly exceed what is achievable through a mere (around) 100 human beings. Great cooperation and advances lie ahead for humankind as a result of the increasing numbers of human subjects.

For completeness, it is helpful to observe that the Moon is not the only location where alien training centres with respect to entering the human world, are located. Similarly there are a multitude of other projects, often including other groups of subjects. Advanced alien races look forward to the time when human consciousnesses can participate in equivalent experiments.

Users

For completeness "users" are defined as extensions of souls, which generally inhabit advanced alien bodies as opposed to earthly ones.

A5 Large Greys Domes

INTRODUCTION

Whilst researching the Large Greys 1's home planet, they were keen to show off their visitor domes. These are large structures whose outer composition is similar to a thick layer of blue tinted Perspex, with an external profile which is more like a flat ellipse as opposed to spherical, should you find yourself examining it from the outside.

Inside the domes are representative evolved species from all over the universe living in harmony. So if you want to research a cross-section of physical life across the universe you are experiencing, this is a fantastic place to visit.

Visiting these domes is a stark reminder that this encyclopaedia barely scratches the surface of describing all the life forms in the universe. An analogy would be attempting to study all of European culture and heritage in a weekend trip, or trying to catalogue all the animal species in the Amazon rainforest in just one afternoon. In this brief investigation just a few of many domes and their species are examined.

Re-engineered Species

Researching one subject for this encyclopaedia unsurprisingly tends to reveal other topics of interest. In this case, the practicalities of physically travelling using the black hole technology, mentioned in the chapter on how the universe operates becomes pertinent. A considerable obstacle to such travel is that if organic beings are moved to even a mildly different dimension in another part of the current universe, they may be unsuited to it and die. So in order to populate their domes, the Large Greys 1 needed to deal with the fact that collecting living examples of other species would often be impractical.

To solve this difficulty, in the Large Greys 1's domes almost all the species in them appear to have been initially grown from samples. For example, in the case of representative human beings, they were developed from DNA samples originally contained within human sperm and eggs. The DNA in these samples was then mapped in order to translate it into a mathematical code. It was then possible to copy the original DNA using locally adapted organic material, and thus grow specially adapted human beings who would flourish in the dome's environment.

From a spiritual or soul perspective, when using this approach, you still end up with a human being. All physical life forms need to be energised and brought to life by higher beings. In fact it is better to describe, for example, a human body as just a vehicle that allows manifestation in a lower dimension. So the higher beings which manifest as human beings on places such as Earth, have been able to manifest in bodies (or vehicles) that have been re-engineered to be compatible with other dimensions.

DOME 1

This is not the first dome to have been constructed to house collections of representative species, instead it is simply where an astral traveller from Earth is likely to be initially taken.

Characteristics

Whilst the sky is relatively dark outside the dome, inside it is more like Earth in good weather. The dome appears to be around 30 km (20 miles) in diameter and around 8 km (5 miles) high. The air pressure inside appears to be higher than outside so as to help keep this structure inflated.

Lakes, shorelines, rolling countryside, and plenty of vegetation all make it a relatively green habitat for a wide variety of species. The atmosphere is sufficiently similar to Earth that it is breathable for a modified human being.

The biblical prophecy of the lion lying down with the lamb applies to this environment as there is quite an array of species that live in excellent harmony. A visitor might on first impression think that they had found human heaven, but this would be incorrect for three reasons: F*irstly*; human heaven is not a physical place. S*econdly*; human heaven is not packed with different species and races from other planets. T*hirdly*; you are unlikely to find your deceased physical relatives here.

Diet

There is a sufficient supply of food provided so that, metaphorically speaking, 'the lion would have no need to eat the lamb'. Most of the food required to feed the diverse population is created in an integral factory farm where proteins and vegetable fibres are grown. The final products are not immediately appetising to the traditional human eye, but locals profess that this is a far superior diet. A limited amount of naturally grown fruit and vegetables are also cultivated within small agricultural areas.

Birth

As described, the original population were all engineered and adapted from samples. Once a species is introduced it is then normally continued through its traditional reproductive means. Spirit beings who come to occupy the resulting bodies consider themselves to be akin to ambassadors.

Death

Traditionally for human beings, death mostly results from the human vehicle getting old and breaking down. Inside the dome species can, to a large extent, adjust the aging process and to a considerable extent reverse it; e.g. An adult can have children, and then regress back to being a child.

Eventually though, it becomes appropriate to die, and typically the species here all adopt the same technique. They lie down on what looks like a bed of thick greyish grass, fall asleep and leave their bodies permanently; i.e. Die. Friends and relatives wave off the departing spirit. So the whole process has a lot in common with an airport departure point. The bed the body is lying upon then consumes this spent vehicle and decomposes it.

On occasion, the deceased might choose to soon after reincarnate into the body of a newborn baby. Feedback given was that getting born is generally traumatic compared to the preceding and very comfortable death.

Time Distortions

When visiting Dome 1, it is worth attempting to observe the time distortions which occur because of the dimensional differences between where you projected from compared to where you have reached. Furthermore, upon reflection, you may begin to wonder if time in another dimension can function independently of nearby dimensions.

For example, when visiting Dome 1, you will probably sense its time zone to be parallel to Earth's, albeit occurring at a different speed. Then when observing the dome's examples of 'Future Human Beings' you will sense you are meeting something from Earth's future, but apparently alive in the present.

Traditional logic would suggest that Large Greys 1 had simply obtained copies of Future Human's DNA and grown some fully functional bodies from them. So this logic dictates that Large Greys 1 must have accessed human beings' future. However, from the Large Greys 1's perspective, they got their samples in their present.

DOME 1: SPECIES EXAMPLES

There appear to be over 1000 major species living side by side in excellent harmony. On top of that there are 1000s of minor, less advanced species there too, in a way that produces a both balanced and diverse mini-eco system.

Species are categorised here as either Major or Minor. Major species have created their own civilisations, whereas Minor ones have not particularly done so at the point in time we are examining them. Major species would similarly have developed the ability to intentionally modify the world around them, for example by farming.

Major: Human Beings

Adapted Human Beings number approximately 1000, with the population split across roughly 10 sub-species types. So for example, there are Neanderthals. However, inter sub-species breeding is not encouraged so that, for example, said Neanderthals remain relatively pure. Intriguingly, there are genetic interventions during otherwise natural reproduction in order to maintain a healthy diversity within all the sub-species.

All Human Beings have modified brains in order to assist with telepathic skills. Even a modified Neanderthal would possess far superior telepathy when compared to that of a typical early 21st century reader of this encyclopaedia. This upgrade is essential as telepathy is the universal communication language.

When looking at the human population as a whole, it seems that a progressive development in intelligence is one of the key factors being represented. So at the other end of the spectrum from the Neanderthals are what you could call Future Humans, who have already been dealt with more thoroughly earlier in this encyclopaedia.

Human Beings living under Dome 1 are often naked, but might adopt some clothes if the social conventions of a visitor's preferences so dictates. Though wearing shoes of any sort is uncommon, nor does it appear generally necessary. Most ground surfaces being so clean and smooth that a foot injury would be unlikely. Intriguingly most floor and pathways are made from soft materials, which are pleasant to walk on.

When you arrive at Dome 1 you will tend to be greeted by Future Human Beings, who often show up in family units. The kindness and warmth is wonderful to behold.

Minor: Large Flies

On some planets, flies grow relatively large when compared to Earth. In Dome 1 there is a representative cross-section of large fly species. In appearance they look very much like flies that have simply grown much bigger, at 30 to 60 cm long (1 to 2 ft).

In terms of intellectual advancement, Large Flies are similar to a human child in the early 21st century. They do not appear to make much use of technology. On the other hand these species have learnt to live in large and organised social groups, with individual members often adopting specialised skills.

This might tend to make a human being think Large Flies are just large but otherwise primitive creatures. Whilst the Large Flies for their part take the view that human beings are generally primitive creatures. This species look down upon human inability to fly. They consider the human race to have spent too much of its development fantasising and thinking without being productive.

These flies are particularly quick thinking. They take a great deal of care over the development of their young. They live in what could loosely be described as communes. They are not very inclined to imagine things. They love meeting new people. But are not that interested in technological advancement.

Major: Advanced Birds

Birds in general are intelligent social animals, which make them suitable candidates for advancement. Flying animals exist on most advanced planets, and birdlike creatures are very common. On researching the variety of birds present in Dome 1 it is apparent that Earth birds have two evolutionary failings: F*irstly*; it would have helped if they retained hands of some sort (as do bats), and *Secondly*; they have to show some interest in what created them (more self-awareness).

The birds you meet in Dome 1 are all fascinated by what created them, and have very well-developed brains. Some have feathers as on Earth. Some do not use feathers and have a lot in common with earthly bats.

In terms of what they look like, they mostly have a great deal in common with earthly birds. The most interesting difference which stands out is that developing larger brains depends on either becoming flightless (due to weight issues), or finding more nutritious food.

Birds that have taken the flightless route tend to maintain or redevelop hands, thus ending up similar to human beings with beaks. Some birds have further taken the mammalian approach and dispensed with laying eggs, gestating their offspring instead.

However, retaining both wings and hands is of great evolutionary advantage to birds. Most flying bird hands observable in Dome 1 are relatively small and fold into their wings for aerodynamic advantage. Retaining hands makes it possible to work with tools, and very importantly to make fire. Fire makes it possible to cook food and increase its nutritional value, which in turn makes it possible to feed a larger brain whilst shrinking the intestines.

Having hands at the leading edge of flight wings does not aid flight, and conversely can be a considerable impediment. As any aeronautical engineer will confirm, a smooth leading edge to a wing is of the utmost importance. The representative advanced birds in Dome 1 have a number of solutions to this issue: *Option* 1; is to extend the fingers forward in a cone shape, *Option* 2; is to hide them under feathers and fold them into the wing, and *Option* 3; includes placing a flap of skin over them as well as having the folding arrangement.

Birds with hands have become technologically advanced, but have (as of Earth year 2015) rarely sought to visit Earth. In fact, according to them, staying away was guidance given to them. The reason for such avoidance is apparently that human beings have yet to pay sufficient attention to what creates humankind and similarly develop greater respect towards other species.

Advanced birds stand out from many other alien species, because like human beings they have advanced speech. In fact probably around half of advanced birds have the ability to speak a primitive human dialect if trained. They also joked that they could make sounds human pet dogs would respond to but beyond the range of human ears.

These birds are classed as a major species because in their own right they have become sufficiently advanced to create their own civilisations. In the case of the vaguely humanoid flightless ones, they got to grips with space travel in a relatively similar timescale to humankind. This suggests that bird species in general have a great deal in common with human beings.

Minor: Ground Cleaning Carpet

When observing how human beings in this dome rarely had need of footwear, it was apparent that the ground and pathways were exceptionally clean. It was then observed that a sort of Ground Cleaning Carpet (or slime) would sweep across it in irregular shapes of up to around 2 m (6 ft) across.

This creature is actually a group of animals, so if you divided the slime carpet in half, the individuals would continue as two halves.

This living carpet does not in practice appear that slimy, and the top side is what can best be described as ‘furry’, whilst the bottom side does not leave residues. On closer examination it looks like a group of vertical worm like creatures all bunched together. The slime carpet appears able to move faster than you might walk.

The slime carpet does not like being stepped on, and can sense where anyone is walking. A general lack of wheeled vehicles makes it reasonably safe for this slime carpet. The slime thus appears to feed off and polish pathways with wonderful ease. You could even let it clean your feet if you wanted to.

Major: Ape

These have a lot in common with Neanderthal Man. They are about the size of large chimpanzees with scaly furry skin, but they lay eggs. Unlike earthly apes, they started paying attention to what had created them at a much earlier stage, and were rewarded with increased intelligence. At the stage of their evolution we find them, they are a predominantly jungle or forest species who behave similarly to humankind of around 6000BC.

In a similar way to how the Neanderthals got phased out in favour of modern human, a similar evolution is scheduled for this species. Something akin to a modern human will ultimately replace them. Nevertheless, in the meantime they represent part of an important evolutionary development for their species.

An unusual feature of their development is that the eggs they lay have soft, leathery shells, which enable them to expand after laying. From an evolutionary perspective this seems to throw up an interesting limitation; no means of supplying additional nutrients to a developing foetus. A side effect of which is that the brain in a newborn baby occupies approximately 40% of the cranial cavity, with the rest being filled with water until after hatching out, when a better nutrition supply becomes available.

Females, and to a lesser extent males, can lactate (produce milk) to feed their young. Though the milk is more akin to a liquid lard (very fatty). This is because the young need less water than a human baby.

They are also highly telepathic in a way that would shame humankind of the early 21st century, and very aware of their environment.

Minor: Physical Nymphs

Animal species (such as humans) with a fertile imagination, who have sex for pleasure, are invariably stimulated by nymph spirits; i.e. Spirits that encourage this activity and make it pleasurable. Spirit nymphs are notable for their ability to stimulate human thoughts and encourage fantasies. Sex would be very dull without their assistance.

Whilst human beings will often see nymphs as human-like, and more often female in appearance, this is not their default manifestation. These spirit beings simply adapt themselves to resemble their host's possible perception of what constitutes attractive. Similarly, when stimulating other species, nymphs tailor their appearance to suit.

The Creators occasionally experiment with giving spirits such as nymphs physical bodies. This is an interesting experiment highlighting the limitations of enabling a substantially single activity spirit to become an otherwise complete physical being. Having a conversation with a nymph demonstrates that its interests are very narrow and specific to sexual activity. Nevertheless such physical forms need to be augmented with some other lower spirit forms to make them functional. Otherwise they would, for example, not eat or generally look after themselves properly.

There are a number of ways of giving life to any such spirit form, the easiest of which is to create physical vehicles from an advanced form of coalescing single-celled organisms similar to large bacteria. This technology can produce animals or host vehicles of almost any conceivable appearance.

If for example, a human being took a Physical Nymph as a companion, it would progressively convert itself into a sexually opposite replica of that human being (with a homosexual alternative if required). The resulting physical form is something that will endeavour to be pleasing to its host, but of little practical use beyond sexual pleasures.

Spirit nymphs feed on human emotions, much in the same way that human spirit forms can feed on nature's or heavenly emotions. Physical Nymphs are only a little more complex in that they require physical food as well. Note that; whilst both spirit and Physical Nymphs can operate in teams, they do not readily feed off each other.

In the Large Greys 1's Dome 1 you can find small clusters of both male and female appearing nymphs living and in groups of typically around a dozen. They do not do much and generally await a humanoid to come past and offer to play with one or more of them.

Nymphs are not much use for anything apart from sexual entertainment, and need to be fed and generally looked after. On the other hand, they strive to please and stimulate the human mind. Not only are they very telepathic, but they can project fantasies into a human mind. Reading this section and energetically connecting to it will enable them to probe the mind of the reader.

Physical Nymphs offer the companionable qualities of a dog combined with the stay-home tendencies of a cat. Loyalty is dependent upon a loose allegiance to who best feeds them. They can be territorial with respect to relationships with host humanoids. They can also discourage other humanoids they disapprove of from forming relationships with their host.

Nymphs would easily give a 2015 human being the impression that the said nymph was doing everything possible to please a human being. But most 2015 human beings would not recognise that such a nymph could easily project a fantasy of what a nymph wants into a human brain.

This arrangement has many parallels with having a pleasurable relationship with a parasite. On the other hand, sometimes this is potentially a better alternative to, for example, a human paedophile's desires being expressed on small children. Though as species such as human beings evolve, paedophile behaviour becomes phased out, and the usefulness of nymphs entertaining such desires, eliminated.

In the Earth's future, human beings will have access to advanced space travel and hence this highly engineered species. If, for example, a solitary human male explorer wanted a companion that only wanted to sexually pleasure him, but was hopeless at cooking and cleaning, this is an interesting option. It would be the ultimate sexy 'air head'. By comparison, for women who want to devote themselves to business, there would be a passionate male waiting for them at home. Again, the observation must be made that; it's a bit like having a stay-at-home dog, which can infiltrate your mind.

With respect to breeding, Physical Nymphs are fundamentally asexual and designed not to physically breed with each other. Instead they can live for a very long time, and energetically have qualities similar to amusing fictional vampires, minus the blood drinking. However, if one forms a strong attachment to a human being, when that human dies, this can cause the nymph to want to leave its physical form, and hence also die.

Physical Nymphs normally occupy artificially engineered bodies specially created for them. Since such bodies can shape-shift and replicate many different forms, they can potentially replicate reproductive organs as well. So in principle a human being can breed with one. This produces a family of fast growing babies which soon mature into adults and generally leave. This would all be very simple and convenient, only for the fact that after a few generations of interspecies breeding the nymphs really do become a lot more like their host species, and then family life does get complicated.

For completeness, the Creators add that this particular companionship experiment worked out far better than the many attempts at creating sexual androids (robots). In addition, in some variations of the physical nymph experiment they reproduce by dividing their bodies like an amoeba, which has made them free to replicate and thus be properly classified as a true species in their own right.

Minor: Human Nymphs Hybrids

The following observation is difficult to morally classify as depending on your mind-set it is either an amazing experiment or a Frankensteinian aberration.

In humankind's future, some human beings get envious of Physical Nymphs allure. This particularly applies to human females. The issue is that Physical Nymphs are expert at being very attractive and companionable. So for example, in some ways they can outperform human females' ability to attract a mate. On the other hand since they are not much use at everything else, in physical form they have considerable limitations. Furthermore, any offspring that result are arguably classifiable as mutants.

Human beings are already heavily affected by spirit nymph activity, and rely upon spirit nymphs for their sexual fantasies. Human reproduction has thus always been assisted by non-physical nymphs who encourage copulation for pleasure. Thus it is pragmatic to regard nymphs as a necessary part of the human emotional anatomy. This fact is quite obvious from the vantage point of the Astral World should a reader wish to verify the facts.

The issue that arose was that Physical Nymphs, particularly the female variant, could be particularly alluring and thus become partners with a human male. But this had the effect of excluding human females from relationships with that male. Such males would often be reluctant to end happy relationships with a Physical Nymph, and this interfered with the normal bonding process with human females.

The obvious solution was for a physically manifesting nymph to once again become an etheric spirit entity, so as not to obstruct physical bonding between human males and females. In their original form nymph spirits could quite naturally bond with human minds, and conveniently be accommodated, both usefully and pleasurably. However, the new challenge was that physically incarnate nymphs were reluctant to die, even when there was an opportunity to immediately reconnect with a human being in the traditional way.

The hybrid solution was for a physical nymph to somehow become absorbed into a human being, so that some part of the original nymph could physically be alive in a new host body. The resulting composite, mostly human form, would then have a foreign life form living within it. The practical result was a human being displaying a generally good composite personality, and a blend of the two originally separate physical attributes.

The many permutations of what can result exceeds what can be written down at this time. So observing this from the perspective of species native to the Large Greys 1's domes, you can observe hybrid human beings who have a far higher nymph spirit content. The interesting, or Frankensteinian result, depending upon the reader's perspective, is that; some hybrids never really die, they just blend into a younger host and continue within a new youthful body.

DOME 2

Taking these domes in order of possible relevance to a human visitor, Dome 2 could be described as the Big Alien Dome. A normal human being would probably choke on the atmospheric gas inside, suggesting a carbon dioxide level of around 10%.

DOME 2: SPECIES EXAMPLES

There appear to be over 500 major species and it immediately becomes obvious that increased size does not necessarily produce a more intelligent being. Whilst you can telepathically communicate with all the species inside, the conversation is mostly not that dissimilar from one you would have with earthly dogs, cats or horses.

The large species assembled in Dome 2 appear to have had their birthing systems adapted in order to be able to breathe a common atmosphere containing around 40% Oxygen.

Half of the species look dinosaur-like, whilst the rest look as if they have evolved from insects. On closer inspection only around 5% of the dinosaur-like species look like something that would have existed on Earth, and apparently less than 1% were originally from Earth. The Large Greys 1 were of the view that most of the dinosaurs-like species were created from a DNA library they were given by another alien race.

The Earth dinosaurs also appeared to be predominantly plant eaters, as apparently it was not possible to dissuade most carnivorous predators to accept the alternative diet on offer.

Species Group: Non-Earth Dinosaurs

Animals up to 3 or 4 times the size of the largest creatures ever seen on Earth are present here. Some appear reptilian, and others more mammalian. The striking feature is that most do not appear to be particularly intelligent. The animals here have mostly not created notable cultures, or made any particularly striking technological advances.

Taking them as a group, if you simply accumulated a collection of mostly very large reptile and mammal-like creatures, and put them into a domed wildlife park, this is what you would end up with.

The Large Greys 1 explained that there were other very large highly intelligent mammal or reptile-like species, but mostly not in Dome 2. Furthermore, large bodies tended to place such a strain on their brains that intellectual functions were sacrificed to accommodate crucial motor functions.

Species Group: Large Insects

Insects on the other hand are better at creating secondary brain tissue when compared to mammal or reptile-like creatures. This has resulted in some large insects with brain tissue throughout their bodies. This adaptation opened the evolutionary door to very large intelligent insect beings.

Insects' evolutionary challenge seems to be getting enough oxygen in order to grow large. With the simple improvement of better and multiple lungs, they can thus grow very large.

Another notable feature is that despite growing very large, many of them can move very fast. A first estimate being up to around 100 km/h (60 mph) in notable cases. With the lungs issue solved, exoskeleton animals have inherently stronger bodies and use a greater variety of skeletal materials. Intriguingly, the Creators have engineered animals that digest metal ores, and secrete it into their skeletal tissue. The result is similar to reinforced concrete or even metal cladding.

In summary; large insects appear to be generally better at supporting higher intelligence compared to large reptilian or mammalian animals.

Species Group: Splitters

A group of animals only known to Earth science in very small and relatively primitive forms are present here. They reproduce themselves in a similar way to bacteria; i.e. Sexual reproduction is not necessary. These beings simply give birth to smaller but otherwise fully-formed versions of themselves. In terms of their appearance they look similar to reptiles, whilst giving birth like mammals. Child care appears next to non-existent as the young normally have to fend for themselves.

Splitters 1

This is an animal that would make an ideal candidate for some sort of science fiction horror film, were it not for the fact that this is a herbivore variant. Its appearance is humanoid with an ape-like head. Large ones are around 6 m (20 ft) tall. Its lungs are in cauliflower-like clusters on its back. It has a grey, brownish slimy appearance. Reptilian claws for hands and feet. No genitals, but gives birth at the base of where a pelvis appears to be.

It moves in an apelike manner and is generally upright when stationary. Speaks in a grunting way, which is done by belching. No ear lobes, just small holes in the side of its head.

It would be a truly terrifying creature, except for the fact that it had short blunt teeth adapted for chewing foliage.

Splitters 1 reproduce themselves if there is abundant food available, and continue until their numbers render food a little scarce. Young emerge from the womb as small but otherwise fully-formed versions of their parent, literally dropping out. They immediately start fending for themselves.

Thus this is not intrinsically a social animal and is very comfortable living a relatively solitary life.

Splitters 2

Not present in Dome 2 is the carnivore variant, which is largely similar except for a few appropriate variations. The Large Greys 1 projected an impression of what this animal is like for scientific completeness.

Teeth are almost needle like at the front of the jaw, and saw like at the back. Altogether a more athletic body. One of its favourite foods is Splitters 1.

The evolutionary point at which this species is being examined is where it is learning rudimentary social skills, such as hunting in packs. Similarly, it is learning how to pass on useful technical information such as starting fires, which in turn leads to cooking its prey.

DOME 3

This is a smaller species dome. The arrangement being that the needs of advanced but small alien races should be catered for. This is not to suggest that different sizes of beings could not live together, but their physical needs are different. To use a very simplistic example, a chair for a mouse would be on a different scale to that in a human being world.

DOME 3: SPECIES EXAMPLES

There appear to be over 1000 different species residing here, with a preference for more intelligent ones. With respect to humanoids (species with similarities to human beings), there are over 100 of them. The challenge is therefore to choose helpful representative species, not otherwise covered elsewhere in this encyclopaedia.

Small Species Group Intelligence

One of the discoveries emerging from researching this encyclopaedia was that advanced physical beings placed a great deal of reliance on their non-physical minds. The discovery emerged as a result of exploring how some species with no obvious brain could exhibit intelligence as if they had equivalent physical brains. Hence the non-physical mind was observed.

Small species suffer the obvious handicap of having limited scope to develop large brains. So as they advance they compensate for any physical limitation by making greater use of their non-physical minds. Because non-physical minds can overlap, they can similarly interconnect the processing ability of many neighbouring minds. The result is that some small species are able to combine the intellectual ability of their physical minds so as to achieve an intelligence level that would otherwise be the preserve of larger species' brains.

By combining the intellectual capacity of physical minds using their overlapping non-physical minds, a physically small species can easily outperform a larger species that makes less use of its non-physical minds.

Species: Small Humanoids 1

If human beings only grew to around 30 cm (1 ft) tall, what would they be like ? Here is a good example of the result. Small Humanoids 1 originate from a small planet where most things occur on a smaller scale. So in general they live like human beings would, except everything is on a smaller scale. With respect to life in a dome, this does have the implicit difficulty of dealing with stronger gravitational pulls.

The first obvious difference between earthly humans and these small humanoids seems to be that they are part reptilian. So they have no body hair, though wear clothes to keep warm. They gestate their young like mammals, and both males and females can lactate fluids to feed their young. Females appear better at rearing the young, and proud of it.

In appearance, they have similarities to the human concept of an elf, so for example pointy ears. Faces have lizard-like similarities. Hands and feet are relatively larger than human beings and well adapted to grasping. A good analogy would be birds' claws or feet, for hands and feet. Hence shoes are not normally worn unless specifically required for protection.

The interesting anatomical point is how Small Humanoids 1 are adapted to be intelligent despite having much smaller brains. Indeed their intellectual processing power is less than an earthly human, but they have compensated for this by using their brains altogether more efficiently. In particular they don't daydream very much.

Due to increased mental efficiency they talk very fast. They are also even more inclined to specialisation than human beings; i.e. Individuals are very specialised in what they can do, or not, as the case may be. They are also very telepathic, so can be aware of what a fellow Small Humanoid 1 would think and know. By this means, as a group they are relatively more capable than current early 21st century human beings.

It is also entertaining to have their view on current 21st century human beings. To conduct this research the author had to link with them, thus a two-way portal was subsequently open. Comments ran as follows (translated into English):

- Earthly humans appear very ponderous and mostly asleep (by daydreaming or contemplating most of the day).

- Very poor connection with your young, especially by parents.

- Try not to blow yourselves up through incompetence or social unrest.

- Surprised that the Earth had no asteroid defence, the resources having instead been devoted to internal feuding.

- Earth appears to be a mechanised society full of cars, which looks great fun (by comparison they use less technology and walk a lot more).

- A lot of books and television, which seem to be more about entertainment than education (they have these potential pleasures but use them far less and mostly for education).

Species: Small Humanoids 2

This is a more apelike small humanoid, which shares an almost identical anatomy with earthly human beings. Typically between 30 cm (12 in) to 40 cm (16 in) high and looks just like a small human being.

It is worth noting that there are many variations of humanoid species that look vaguely like earthly humans, and this general design of species seems to be very common throughout the universe. Earthly humans of the early 21st century can be classified as advancing, but still exhibiting primitive warlike tendencies and only rudimentary self-awareness. By comparison, the Small Humanoid 2 now being examined is derived from a sample point when they were more advanced than early 21st century humans, but not quite as much as the Small Humanoids 1 group.

Small Humanoids 2 are very wary about visiting the Earth as they consider it to be on the list of hostile locations. They were of the view that if they did visit and got captured, they would be tortured until they revealed all their technological secrets. Given the advanced alien consensus that human beings should be largely confined to where they are for the time being, any earthly visits are only to be undertaken whilst exercising extreme caution.

The Large Greys 1 re-engineered version of Small Humanoids 2 exists at a higher dimension to Earth, and would quickly die if they tried to live on Earth. However, the original species are mostly to be found at a very similar dimension and could survive on Earth. Hence the risk inherent to any visits they might contemplate.

Culturally, the Small Humanoids 2 being observed here are very similar to human beings of approximately 2700AD to 2900AD, with whom they would be friends. Both Small Humanoids 1 and Small Humanoids 2 originate from what in human terms would be a dwarf planet. Such planets, have similarities to Earth, but typically little or no volcanic activity, and less gravity.

Species: Smart (ish) Bees 1

Whilst in Dome 1 there were relatively large flies with considerably higher intelligence than their earthly counterparts, in Dome 3 there are (what human beings might consider to be normal-size) flying insect some of which have become highly intelligent.

The main condition that encourages improved intelligence amongst insects appears to be the forming of social groups, as opposed to just groups. In general, insects similar to termites and ants will enjoy favourable conditions for this to occur. The next triggering factor is the Creators, deciding in that instance, to make a particular species more intelligent.

Smart Bees 1 lived in colonies much in the same way that earthly ones, who live a life of collecting nectar. Smart Bees 1 do not have the colouring of earthly bees and in many ways could be loosely described as similar to brown flying grasshoppers without stings. Neither are they confined to the one-queen-per-colony arrangement. The evolutionary leap was being able to live in groups with multiple queens. This social innovation is more complex and required a far more intelligent species to manage such an arrangement.

A further innovation that took this species forward was learning how to cultivating nectar-rich crops. This development advanced the use of tools to assist agricultural activity. Tools made it easier to purge the environment of anything threatening or likely to consume nectar harvest. The similarities between how mankind overran the Earth and what Smart Bees 1 accomplished are remarkable.

The main difference between Smart Bees 1 and early 21st century humankind is that they established a cooperative social system far sooner, whereas by comparison, mankind is much more warlike. This cooperation allowed advanced alien races to commence educational interaction with them at a much earlier stage and completely revolutionised everything in their society.

The specimens you can meet in Dome 3 are best described as 'laid back', and disinclined to excessively work. Somewhat disappointingly, whilst this species displays a higher self-awareness than early 21st century humankind, it does not keep up with the far higher standard displayed by some other advanced alien species.

In conclusion, the intelligence displayed falls within an intermediate category when compared to other species. For better or worse, interacting with Smart Bees 1 connects the observer to an interesting reluctance to do anything he or she might consider tedious. "Busy as a bee" is not an expression easily attached to the version of this species observed here.

Species: Land Jelly 1

The best way to introduce this species is to consider what a cross between an Earthly sea sponge and a jellyfish would be like; a translucent blob with retractable tentacles. This species comes in many shapes and sizes, with the one being examined here typically having a diameter of around 7 cm (3 in), and tentacles of around ten times that length.

This species is extraordinary in that it is devoid of any obvious internal anatomy. For example, most species have some sort of stomach, but Land Jelly 1 merely has bits of food floating inside of its jelly interior. Similarly, there is neither an obvious brain nor muscle visible.

Communication with this species is easy, albeit difficult to avoid. It is very telepathic and able to read primitive minds with ease (early 21st century humans would be categorised as easy). The effect is that it easily strikes up a conversation in your head in your own language. If it wants to influence you, it can make you want to serve it by giving you the feeling that this is what you desire. Only species who exhibit a reasonable degree of Free Will can cope well with this sort of invasive telepathic interaction.

This species is in many ways what could be described as a joke experiment (advanced aliens having a laugh). The experiment being; to introduce high intelligence into a very primitive ocean-dwelling animal. The almost instant result was a very intelligent species that instantly dominated its environment. The equivalent of the fish it shared the ocean with were either turned into its servants, or if threatening, wiped out. With the ocean conquered, it was then encouraged to come out of the water and colonise the land, again subjugating the native species.

Fortunately, this is a relatively lazy species and not very technologically advanced. So left to its own devices, Land Jelly 1 would not have got off its home planet.

Species: Rodents 1

Humankind has been evolved from something akin to a rodent, and earthly rodents are known to exhibit reasonable intelligence. It follows that in some evolutionary permutations, rodent-like creatures should exhibit higher intelligence and succeed in becoming advanced beings.

Rodents 1 can reasonably be described as humanoids derived from a mouse. The forearms have become adapted to work with tools, whilst the legs have elongated to permit exclusively upright walking. There are the remnants of a tail which is now very stubby. The lungs are relatively large and a consequence of having been evolved in a relatively thin atmosphere. The otherwise pointed head has shortened so as to better enclose the mouth and enable more refined speech. However the nose is on the equivalent of a very short elephants trunk, which enables enhanced directional smell sensing. Fur is thin and depending on the individual there can be extensive baldness.

Rodents 1's brain is surprisingly small, which makes it a fascinating evolutionary example to examine. It has better intellectual functions than most early 21st century human beings.

The brain is only around 5% the size of a human brain, but contains a more advanced neural network. A crude analogy is to say that most earthly animals including humankind have, in electronic terms, 'old valve radio' brains, whereas Rodents 1 has 'advanced microprocessor' brains. So Rodents 1's brain, has more connections, hence more processing power, and because it is smaller it calculates much faster.

An interesting side effect of having such a compact and complex brain is that it is more fragile than the earthly equivalent. So Rodents 1's skull has to accommodate a shock absorber layer of half-fatty, half-muscle material, which protects its brain from vibration or impacts. By comparison, a human brain fills most of the cranial cavity in the skull and does not need to be protected by a special shock absorber.

A human astral explorer's experience of interacting with a typical Rodents 1 can best be described as, meeting someone who thinks you are part of a relatively stupid race. Be alert to the possibility of a condescending attitude.

DOME 4

Dome 4 is devoted to microscopic life that has achieved a higher awareness. Many of these species are under 1 mm (0.03 in), so would be barely visible to the human naked eye. Nevertheless they are represented because of the considerable advances they have achieved.

Humankind's main experience of micro-worlds mostly comes from studying life in the ocean. Water is one of the most favourable environments for micro-organisms, however, it presents enormous impediments to technological advancement. Neither does the life on land offer a complete solution for micro-organisms, because basic technologies such as fire are difficult to harness at a microscopic level.

Alternative Means Of Advancement

Investigation reveals that whilst it is nevertheless possible for micro-organisms to become advanced, their scale tends to produce a different developmental path. Most large species, of earthly mouse proportions upwards, can achieve substantial technological development early on because the world around them is easy to manipulate. Whereas for small species, things a reader may take for granted such as fire, are initially unmanageable at a microscopic scale. Furthermore, fire is not normally available to anything that lives in water.

As described in the chapter on how the universe works, matter only exists because of energetic templates. For microscopic organisms, physically manipulating matter is challenging due to the scales of processes. So their main avenue for advancement becomes learning how to manipulate the non-physical templates that determine the existence of matter.

Fleeting glimpses of manipulating physical matter at a non-physical level can be gained if, for example, you see someone who has switched on an immunity to the effects of fire, or can genuinely produce objects out of apparently nothing.

In summary, many advanced micro-organisms can physically manipulate matter to make and build things, but their small scale produces many challenges. This significant advancement depends upon them learning to manipulate matter using their consciousnesses.

Warlike Aliens

There are plenty of aliens with sufficiently ingrained warlike tendencies that they would happily invade Earth given the chance. It should be noted that human beings themselves fall within this group, and would similarly be liable to invade other planets given the opportunity. Fortunately, since most habitable (with respect to life forms with a similar physiology to humankind) planets are some distance apart, the vast distances of space prevent invasions of other species on other planets.

When technologically advancing aliens do get access to an understanding of how to transport themselves across the vast distances, this step forward is normally preceded by a new understanding of what they really are. Hence advanced aliens are reluctant to be destructive.

However, micro-organisms can make staggering advances before necessarily developing a cautionary attitude towards the destruction of other habitats. Similarly they can and do learn to transcend space-time before acquiring the cultural maturity to use such technology wisely. So if Earth were to be invaded by aliens, they would be more likely to fall from the sky in drops of rain, as opposed to raining down with massive hostile spacecraft.

Dome 4 Arrangement

Unlike the larger species examples of Domes 1 to 3 where aliens happily mingle, in Dome 4 considerable quarantining is often required. Habitats have to be populated in such a way that the occupants are not inclined to attack each other.

Groups of micro-organisms are kept in a variety of segregated ponds, lakes, or enclosed strips of land. The simple objective is to keep competing micro-organisms apart. Airtight segregation is often employed with sterile buffer zones between the different holding areas.

Whilst this might make Dome 4 appear like a prison, that is not the case. All species contained within, exist there voluntarily. This is crucial as the more advanced species have the ability to, in effect, reconstitute themselves at new locations in space-time. So total confinement is not ultimately possible, thus segregation is largely a voluntary and pragmatic way of avoiding accidents.

DOME 4: SPECIES EXAMPLES

Micro Shrimps 1

This is a water-dwelling species that can reach up to 2 mm (0.1 in) long, but is typically around 0.5 mm (0.05 in) long. In many ways it is similar to a tiny earthly shrimp, hence the categorisation. It preferably lives in warm, very salty or acidic water that would not support most similar life forms on Earth.

If you visit this species you will immediately be struck by the speed at which they acknowledge your presence, and gather in groups to examine you. Their heads are the largest part of what can be described as conical white tapering bodies, equipped with large black eyes.

Micro Shrimps 1 have a non-physical spirit group leader (sub-god) who is responsible for the entire sub-species. Sometimes, the shrimps develop a new evolutionary permutation, and a new non-physical spirit takes responsibility for the new sub-species. Individual shrimps have an infinitesimally small amount of individuality, but conversely a very high self-awareness of what controls and created them. In many ways, you are dealing with one being, whose individual parts have excellent communication.

Micro Shrimps 1 had a very typical developmental path with respect to this category of advanced micro-species. They developed as an ocean-dwelling species, eating smaller life forms, and themselves being eaten by larger ones. The Creators, via advanced aliens, ran a successful experiment to encourage good communication between them, and they became highly telepathic. The telepathy advance is crucial to achieve for any advanced species, and in particular for micro-species as without it they would be restricted to operating with very limited, small brains. With the telepathic advance, Micro Shrimps 1 had access to their interconnected non-physical minds, so they were able to utilise their combined brain power and outperform larger species.

This telepathic advance in turn allowed more sophisticated spirit forms to take control of whole sub-species. By comparison, without this advance, similar spirit forms would otherwise mostly only control single large animals such as a future human being. Whereas with it, a whole group, large or small, can be usefully directed.

Using their telepathy, Micro Shrimps 1 developed the ability to dissuade anything else from eating them. Accordingly everything else of similar or larger size to Micro Shrimps 1 got eaten. When there was nothing left for the predators to eat except Micro Shrimps 1, the interruption in the food chain caused the larger predators to die of starvation.

If a new and larger sub-species of Micro Shrimps 1 evolved, the dominant by numbers main sub-species would attack and kill it. This left the one main sub-species of Micro Shrimps 1 in control of their own ocean, feeding off smaller life forms.

Technologically Micro Shrimps 1 advanced in a similar way to any land species by, for example, constructing housing and protected breeding facilities for its populace.

The next breakthrough came when they acquired access to advanced alien species using astral projection. Having found it impractical to operate out of water, forging metals was consequently impossible. However, using insights gained from astrally interacting with advanced species they learnt how to manipulate matter using the energy templates. Micro Shrimps 1 were thus able to manufacture almost anything they desired. Similarly, this led to the discovery of how to transport themselves through space and time.

Early 21st century human beings spend most of their day focused in their bodies. By comparison, Micro Shrimps 1 spend much of their day part focusing their consciousness in the Astral World. Thus they experience their lives in the form of a duality.

Because they retain physical form, this gives them abilities which would otherwise be unavailable to equivalent spirit forms.

Micro Shrimps 1 have the capability to invade other planets and as far as possible create a replica species. In this instance it is not directly done by physical invasion, but instead by creating a virtual copy of themselves using the nearest available species. In practice this approach tends to produce a different sub-species, so the new host planet is left with a new species, which will endeavour to thoroughly dominate it given the chance. However, this ability has only been occasionally used as it can destroy existing habitats in new worlds.

Small Ants 1

On many planets, ant and termite species, which are insects of some variety, have often grown larger and hence developed as intelligent individuals, albeit often operating with a very strong sense of community. Conversely, remaining very small tends, as again in this example, to restrict individual development.

Small Ants 1 at first look similar to perhaps a cartoon version of a small earthly ant, particularly as they can stand upright in a biped posture. From a distance the anatomy appears very similar to an ant, with a body of typically less than 2 mm (0.1 in). Closer inspection reveals a face that has much in common with mammals; a teddy bear face is a reasonable analogy. It also becomes apparent that they have an internal skeleton as a result of growing additional skin and muscle over an insect skeleton. Their bodies are divided into sections like a typical insect, and they possess antennae.

In common with Micro Shrimps 1, they achieved higher intelligence through excellent telepathic communication. This seems to have occurred before advancing beyond warlike tendencies, and for the equivalent of a millennium, Small Ants 1 have been a fearsome predator due to their coordinated attack capability. Similarly, because scouts can operate at long range, they possess an excellent reconnaissance capacity with respect to whatever threats or prey were near its home territory.

Unlike typical earthly ants, all members of the population evolved to breed, much in the same way that earthly aphids would. The effect of this permutation is that Small Ants 1 have a high level of individuality, and this is combined with no one dominant spirit controller (near the low astral level). The cultural effect of this permutation was an increase in rivalry between individuals, with a corresponding decrease in a sense of oneness.

One of the reasons for picking out this species for inclusion in the encyclopaedia is how they developed industrial technologies such as fire, but reconfigured to a small scale. Fire is, in general, very difficult for any small species to master. So Small Ants 1 learnt to create extreme heat by telepathically creating a hot plasma. The effect gives the impression that they create balls of white fire near their hands and place it wherever required.

Telepathically creating plasma is a technology that ultimately bridges the gap between space travel with primitive rockets, and recreating black holes to collapse and then reform matter elsewhere in space-time. Primitive spaceships propulsion relies on the amount of fuel that can be transported, whereas telepathically created plasma is by comparison a relatively abundant source of propulsion. Hence this is a very interesting species to meet and learn from.

DOME 5

Not really a dome, but instead is a large laboratory building where intelligent bacteria and other single-celled organisms have been collected.

On Earth, single-celled organisms largely operate independently of each other, apart from their natural tendency to form clusters. Crucially, such organisms mostly show little higher intelligence. By comparison, the species collected by the Large Greys 1 include a multitude of examples of species where far more intelligent species have emerged.

DOME 5: SPECIES EXAMPLES

In Dome 5 there appear to be over 1,000,000 examples of interesting bacteria and single-celled organisms, and in particular, examples of life forms not found on Earth.

On Earth there are fundamentally three categories of life forms:

- S*ingle-celled* life forms; where the cells operate independently of each other.
- M*ulti-celled* life forms; where specialised cells conjoin to form an animal.
- V*iruses*; which rely on implanting themselves into other cells in order to reproduce.

Not ordinarily seen on Earth is what happens when single cells combine to create larger, complex organisms, but still remain essentially independent of each other.

Blob 1

This is an example of a species where the cells, whilst more or less similar and choosing to stay together, remain independent. The result is to create a large blob of irregular shape, which is made up from many individuals. An earthly analogy is a school of fish all swimming together in the ocean.

Most blob species live in water and are fundamentally porous, allowing prey or food particles in the water to pass into the central body where they are progressively consumed. If they live on land they have difficulty maintaining an upright shape, so instead often look like some sort of moving carpet.

Blob species are an excellent example of beings that exhibit intelligence without any obvious brain, which is something that has not otherwise been seen on the early 21st century Earth. Though if you looked at it from an astral perspective you would see a mechanism which enables modest computations and management of combined bodies.

Blob 1 is one of the waterborne variants and exhibits a green colour on account of its constituent cells being capable of photosynthesis. It was not possible to determine a precise typical size for the Blob 1 species, as it coalesces in too many variations.

Another reason for studying this species is that by comparison, human beings make relatively little use of their non-physical minds, instead overly relying on their physical brains. This is not to suggest that human beings do not utilise their available non-physical minds, but at the time these observations were first made almost all such usage was sub-consciousness. The particular insight the Blob 1 therefore imparts is that effective use of a non-physical mind enables a physical being with no physical brain to function as if it had one. By comparison, all the advanced species make far better use of non-physical cognitive functions.

Researching Blob 1 therefore stands out as the point at which a new discovery, which is progressively being transposed into the human thinking process, was first made.

Blob 2

This example of the species differs from Blob 1 by allowing its cells to modify and perform specialist functions such as digestion (internally) or defence (externally). The difference between this and a multi-cellular animal is that the cells are not fixed in position and can commute around its adopted shape. A useful analogy is the way in which blood cells in a mammal or reptile can move around the body within the vascular system.

This arrangement of specialised cells is an evolutionary advance that existed briefly on Earth approximately half a billion years ago. Similarly, it occurs on most planets where life forms are being evolved from basic single-celled species.

Like Blob 1, Blob 2 utilises a non-physical mind as its primary control system for day-to–day body management. However, by comparison, the development of such a non-physical brain did not sufficiently occur on Earth, and otherwise similar species had to develop physical brains or become extinct. Thus Blob 2 was able to evolve without fixing its cells to particular locations in its body.

Shape Shifters 1

Whilst it is possible for most categories of species to alter their shape and appearance to some extent, a fundamental constraint is altering the structure and shape of their brains. Accordingly, species which principally rely upon non-physical minds are spared such constraints.

Shape Shifters 1, like most similar species is fundamentally not particularly intelligent, however it is an excellent mimic and due to its high degree of telepathy, able to copy and adapt other species' capabilities. You could summarise that it is as intelligent as whatever other species it is interacting with. Because non-physical minds overlap, this species can therefore be as intelligent as the company it keeps.

This particular species is relatively naturally occurring, taking into account that all species are to some extent engineered. It is related to Blob 2 in that it has specialised cells, which retain both independence and individuality. So for example, you could cut it into two, and end up with two with physical forms without causing any particular harm.

Given the fundamental adaptability of species like Shape Shifters 1, many variants have been subjected to considerable genetic enhancement as they, for example, make excellent probes. If an advanced alien wanted to survey another world, but for whatever reason its own physical form was too unsuitable, it could develop an alternative life form such as Shape Shifters 1. Such an alternative life form could then venture around the world being explored, but substantially be controlled by an advanced alien from a remote location.

DOME 6

Not really a dome, but instead again a large laboratory building where intelligent viruses in particular are studied. Since all viruses are living organisms, they are equipped with various forms of group consciousness. If a group's consciousness takes more of a commanding role, the viruses become very responsive to its direction and commands. If you have a working relationship with the higher spirit being who controls that virus's consciousness, it is possible to direct how the physical virus will behave.

Early 21st century traditional human science has only so far observed the activities of physical viruses, and not observed the beings which control the intelligent ones.

This section overlaps with the chapter on Engineered Viruses, so you can skip it if you desire. Nevertheless, since virus technology is fundamental to the development of intelligent species, potential repetition or a reminder, is of value.

Hostile Viruses

These are the viruses which cause apparent damage to organic life forms. Though in practice any hostile behaviour they exhibit is done with the ultimate consent of the recipient.

Because hostile viruses can only act with consent, if you interact with them at a higher level, you can agree for them to cease an attack. At this point the host organism is normally instructed upon how to cleanse them from its system, whilst at the same time the virus acts less aggressively, possibly even benignly.

Benign Viruses

Most living organisms are inhabited by a variety of viruses that are not significantly damaging that organism, hence a strong immune response is not triggered. The vast majority of viruses fall into this category.

Intelligent Viruses

These are viruses with whom you can have a specific working relationship. Furthermore, they have the potential to operate in targeted ways. Intelligent viruses are controlled through non-physical group minds. The result being that each strain of virus is operated by an advanced being with whom you can collaborate on specific projects.

Viruses As Genetic Modification Tools

Physical beings normally modify themselves over time by the mechanism of random genetic mutations, some of which are successful, some not. Hence the successful modifications will make the species self-evolve. Viruses can similarly introduce modifications, and should those modifications be arranged by a higher being controlling a virus, then a species' evolution can be steered by altering the DNA.

Physical forms or species are all vehicles for spirit beings of one sort or another to experience. Spirit beings are of course extensions of the ultimate Creator or super-consciousness, through which can they experience a variety of insightful perceptions. Hence physical forms are designed to perform various observational and experiential functions. Engineered viruses are a tool that enables organic physical forms to be modified so as to perform specific functions. An obvious example would be improving intelligence so that better self-awareness observations can be made.

Up till the 19th century humankind was substantially of the opinion that all life on Earth had been created by God. Then scientific discovery spearheaded by Charles Darwin pointed out that an evolutionary process was at work. The pendulum of scientific understanding then swung in favour of a belief that all life self-evolves. This latest research indicates there are numerous alien beings who are of the firm opinion that they have been involved in modifying species on many worlds including Earth. In particular that humankind's evolution has been steered, in this instance, through the use of intelligent virus technology.

Species Updating

Intelligent viruses make it possible to alter a species' DNA mid generation. Normally, random genetic variations occur upon the birth of each new generation. Viruses have the capacity to alter a host's DNA whilst it is alive. For example, an intelligent virus can be created so as to alter a human being's hair colour, or skin shade. Many possibilities exist.

Virus Creation And Control

Viruses are one of the simplest life forms a genetic engineer can assemble. You need do little more than manufacture the desired DNA strands, insert them into an appropriate organic casing, and it will spring to life. Though obviously you require a detailed understanding of genetics in order to code your virus so that it functions in the desired way.

Controlling an intelligent virus requires a significant additional ability, because this is achieved by having a working relationship with the higher being which controls it. An uneducated human mind will readily jump to the conclusion that this involves making some sort of higher connection, which would be half correct. The reality of the matter is that everything depends upon whether the higher being controlling that human wishes to direct the virus. If the higher being controlling the human is disposed to do so, it will make the necessary arrangements with the being controlling the virus. If the human being has developed the necessary ability, it can be part of the decision making process.

DOME 6: SPECIES EXAMPLES

Intelligent Viruses Classifications

Most intelligent viruses fall within the following classifications:

- H*ealth.* Viruses which keep a species alive and healthy. For example; keeping cancer at bay, or improving immune system responses.

- I*ntelligence.* Increasing the intellectual capacity of a species. For example; increasing skull size so as to allow for a bigger brain, or improving the efficiency of a brain.

- S*exuality.* There are occasions when it would be helpful to encourage a species to reproduce more. The desire to reproduce is driven by a connection with nymph spirits, and viruses can influence this connection by making brain cells more responsive.

- P*hysical Modifications.* When developing a species, there are occasions when nudging the evolution process in a particular direction is helpful. For example, adding a vertebra (extra bone) to the spine of a species.

- I*ntuitive Modification.* If you want to increase or decrease an individual's or even a whole species' intuitive ability, for a specific period or on an on-going basis, a suitable intelligent virus can be created. For example, there might be a good reason to put a race through some sort of dark age.

- *Vehicle Control.* All species are vehicles for higher beings of one sort or another to experience. Species have to become quite advanced before an advance being can exercise easy in-the-moment control of it, whilst focused within it. A combination of all the aforementioned viruses are required to rapidly achieve significant improvements.

- *Behavioural Modification.* It is possible to influence the behaviour of a species or individuals within it. For example, it is possible to make a group within a species more subservient and compliant.

- *War.* Inevitably, once a civilisation gets competent at engineering viruses the potential to use them for the purposes of harm arises. Any primitive species who uses viruses for offensive purpose will not have higher control over them, so such viruses are unleashed without any (lower level) control. Thereafter the out-of-control virus can infect and mutate as it pleases. The aliens assisting the researching of this subject indicated that viruses released by primitives had devastated the ecosystems of many planets.

A6 Summary

SUMMARY

The first edition of this encyclopaedia is undeniably a work in progress. It is inevitable that many of the new observations and discoveries need further research to improve their accuracy. Similarly, there are many more alien species who could potentially be included in future editions.

In the interim, a wide range of observations and discoveries have occurred that need to be publicised. So in no particular order, here is a summary of some key points:

1. Importance of Personal Verification

Everything in this encyclopaedia is open to further validation and where necessary, correction. It is the responsibility of every reader to, where possible, validate information for themselves.

2. Astral Projection Advancement

Human beings have always enjoyed the possibility of using astral projection to explore the many universes, but until very recently, have only made significant progress in the direction of their personal heavens. With respect to exploring neighbouring alien worlds, significant exploration has hitherto been difficult because human minds have been influenced in a way that distracted or dissuaded them from doing so. But now the blanket of energies, which have largely compelled human consciousnesses to stay put, is progressively being lifted.

3. Invitation

The human race is being cautiously invited to join (as a junior member) the "club" of more advanced species. Accordingly, the human race's relative isolation from advanced alien species is now being gradually reduced. The human race is now being given limited, but increasingly reliable, astral access to a wide range of advanced alien species.

4. Species Similarities

Astrally visiting alien worlds reveals that the evolution of species is steered in order to meet common design objectives. For example, the vast majority of close encounters with visiting alien species indicate that they are bipeds (stand on two legs).

5. Common DNA Structures

The DNA structures observable on Earth are repeated throughout its universe, and were first developed in another universe altogether. Earth was seeded with primitive micro-organisms that have also been replicated millions of times elsewhere. Whilst there are other forms of DNA, they still perform similar functions.

6. Assisted Evolution

Physical beings are simply vehicles for higher consciousnesses or Soul-Beings to experience physical form. Species such as human beings cannot simply evolve into highly advanced beings all on their own. Researching this encyclopaedia led to encounters with many examples of different alien species who are contributing to the evolution of humankind.

7. Alien Heritage

Every soul giving life to a human form on Earth also experiences living in alien bodies on other worlds. This does not make a reader an alien. The consciousness that energises you, the reader, is neither human nor alien. It just experiences many different physical forms. So all readers have family ties to other worlds.

8. Insects and Reptiles

Most of the Grey alien species are fundamentally insects. Whilst many other alien species lay eggs as opposed to gestating their young. So whilst more mammalian alien life forms are still common, there are plenty of other life forms from other groups.

9. Telepathy

Telepathy is the universal communication language. Whereas early 21st century human beings are for the most part barely telepathically literate. Much in the same way that English is becoming the common language on Earth, interacting with the rest of the universe requires telepathy.

10. Other Dimensions

Most of the aliens who visit Earth are not designed to reside in this dimension, so they need to keep any physical visits short. It similarly follows that most early 21st century human beings are not suited to living in other dimensions. This fact emphasises the importance of improving astral projection skills as a means of exploring the many universes.

11. Pairing

Aliens from other worlds are very interested in working with human beings. Any reader interested in working with advanced aliens has the opportunity to do so.

12. Non-Physical Mind

All advanced species make considerable use of their non-physical minds. This advance came to light examining micro-organisms that had tiny brains, which they linked together with their overlapping non-physical minds in order to facilitate higher intelligence. Using your non-physical mind immediately improves your astral vision and telepathic communication skills with advanced beings.

13. Sub-Gods

Whilst there is only one super-consciousness to be found in the Creator's World, all societies at least have a small seed of a sub-god that can guide their day-to-day existence. However, many societies have failed to energise their allocated sub-god, and as a result there is considerable conflict. In more advanced societies, all the population contribute to lovingly energising their sub-god, which provides them with loving guidance upon how to govern themselves. You could understand a sub-god to be a group consciousness desiring to have a well-run, peaceful society.

14. Mutual Assistance

Researching this encyclopaedia made it very apparent that advanced species endeavour to assist the development of other species. So much so that there is a whole system of looped development.

15. Apathy Blanket

Until now, humans beings on Earth have been subjected to a blanket of energies that make them apathetic about actually exploring alien worlds. The effect is that a human mind will happily fantasise about visiting alien worlds, or put huge effort into ineffective exploration approaches. However, bit by bit this blanket of apathy-inducing energies is lifting like a sunrise spreading across a dark landscape. The earthly early 21st century is akin to a pre-dawn situation where the new sunlight is visible, but yet to properly arrive.

16. Aliens Engineering New Worlds

Whilst the universe the reader experiences can operate somewhat automatically, there are many alien species at work determining what worlds come into existence.

17. Many Similar Worlds

There are many other worlds with similarities to Earth. Humankind now has the opportunity to start astrally identifying and exploring them.

18. DNA Libraries

All of the important species in the universe humans experience have had their DNA catalogued in the form of mathematical specifications.

19. Parallel Dimensions

Many of the alien visitors to Earth not only come from other dimensions, but parallel dimensions. Humankind is in the process of discovering an enormous interlinked collection of universes which affect each other.

20. Individual Contribution

Your adopted human body is reading this book in order to encourage it to actively take part in further research and exploration. Its mind already contains latent memories of other worlds on which you have manifested.

TRAINING

Training & Exploration

TRAINING

Everything you are experiencing on Earth is an engineered illusion. With specialist training it becomes possible to move your consciousness beyond the earthly illusion and into worlds where aliens and other beings are manifested. Developing this ability in your current human body will have a life-changing effect upon it.

Earth is only one of the worlds you have chosen to experience. You have soul friends and family living in other worlds. Reading this book is part of the "wake-up" mechanism you have placed before your current human form. Your soul friends and family want to assist you.

Train your human consciousness how to regain access to the Astral World and the many universes. This is a fundamental skill your consciousness would already demonstrate if your physical body was living in a more advanced environment.

Re-igniting this ability is a crucial step, which enables your higher-self and soul friends to give you life-changing support.

Training Materials

The www.GreatSimulator.com website provides a range of practical tools, which enable you to step beyond the engineered illusion of the Earht Plane.

If you have not already done so, access the range of downloadable books and training videos from the website today.

1 - 2 - 1 Training

Relearning to astrally project and reform your consciousness elsewhere in the Astral World and the many universes is easy with proper training. Astral projection is a natural ability and proper training converts it into a conscious exploration activity.

In many ways, learning fully-conscious astral projection can be compared to learning to fly an aircraft. The fastest way to learn to fly is by practicing in the company of a trained instructor; i.e. Instructor and student practicing side by side in the same aircraft at the same time.

When learning with a trained instructor, you both go simultaneously on the same journeys, exploring the same places. This approach provides instant feedback and students normally progress very rapidly.

The 1 - 2 - 1 training approach resolves all the basic mistakes which might otherwise take lifetimes to overcome.

EXPLORATION

The universe human beings principally experience has barely been explored by them. This is your opportunity to become part of the growing team of pioneers who are making amazing discoveries.

Work With Us

Living on Earth is a compelling engineered illusion you choose to experience. But this does not mean that you have to be locked into the illusion all the time.

If you want to take part in the exploration of the Astral World and the many universes, then contact us today. Send us an email to:

info@GreatSimulator.com

www.GreatSimulator.com

Notes

Typos:

If you should find a typo, then please send us an email to info@GreatSimulator.com with "Typo(s)" quoted in the heading. Note that "Earht Plane" is not a typo. Please identify the location of any lingering typos by:
Page, Paragraph, Line, ERROR
Eg: 107, 3, 7, where = were

Thank you for your assistance.

Notes

www.ingramcontent.com/pod-product-compliance
Lightning Source LLC
Chambersburg PA
CBHW060512230426
43665CB00013B/1493
* 9 7 8 0 9 5 5 7 1 3 8 1 1 *